Development

to a different drummer

Development

to a different drummer

Anabaptist/Mennonite Experiences and Perspectives

Richard A. Yoder,
Calvin W. Redekop,
& Vernon E. Jantzi

Good Books

Intercourse, PA 17534
800/762-7171
www.goodbks.com

Front cover photograph: MCC/Matthew Lester
Back cover photographs: (left) MCC/Matthew Lester;
(center) MCC/Mark Beach; (right) MCC/Matthew Lester

Design by Dawn J. Ranck

Development to a Different Drummer:
Anabaptist/Mennonite Experiences and Perspectives

Copyright © 2004 by Good Books, Intercourse, PA 17534
International Standard Book Number: 1-56148-453-9
Library of Congress Catalog Card Number: 2004020666

Library of Congress Cataloging-in-Publication Data
Yoder, Richard A.
  Development to a different drummer : Anabaptist/Mennonite experiences
and perspectives / Richard A. Yoder, Calvin W. Redekop & Vernon E. Jantzi.
     p. cm.
  Includes bibliographical references.
  ISBN 1-56148-453-9 (pbk. : alk. paper) 1. Economic development--Reli-
gious aspects--Mennonites. I. Redekop, Calvin Wall, 1925- II. Jantzi, Vernon
Eugene, 1941- III. Title.
  BX8128.E36Y63 2004
  261.8'5'0882897--dc22

                                                                    2004020666

Table of Contents

Part II:
A Variety of International Development Experiences

Part III:
The Analysis

Acknowledgments

Numerous people made significant contributions to this book's shape and content. First, there are the many people in various parts of the world with whom we have worked and drunk tea. From them we have learned much. Our lives have been made better as a result.

More specifically, we thank those persons who critiqued early drafts of this book. Some of them didn't have a choice, such as the students in Richard Yoder's *Economic Development* class at Eastern Mennonite University who had to write a five-page critique as a course requirement. Their comments were enormously helpful, particularly since one of the intended audiences for this book is students with interests in some area of development. Others did have a choice, such as the five individuals with expertise in one or more areas of the book's content who kindly agreed to give their critiques: John Driver, Ray Gingerich, Melvin Loewen, Ray Martin, and Harold Miller. Their thoughtful responses compelled us to reexamine much of what had been written.

We also thank the 24 scholars and practitioners who presented papers at the conference "Anabaptist/Mennonite Experiences in International Development," held October 1-4, 1998, at Eastern Mennonite University: Priscilla Benner, Frank Baer, Susan Classen, Octavio Cortez, David Cressman, Russell Freed, Jim Gingerich, Ken Graber, Ann Hershberger, Vernon Jantzi, Jan Jenner, Luann Martin, Pat Martin, Raymond Martin, Ron Mathies, Wayne Nafziger, William Reimer, Allan Sauder, Gerald Schlabach, Linda Shelly, David Shenk, Larry Smucker, Linda Witmer, and Richard Yoder. We recognize those among that group whose papers could not be included here because of limited space. However, all conference papers were used as data in our analyses, and we thank their writers for allowing us to benefit in that way from their information.

Sincere thanks to our editor, Phyllis Pellman Good, who provided invaluable guidance and support in the process of preparing and completing the manuscript. Her contributions in making the finished product more readable and challenging are greatly appreciated—particularly her challenge to be more bold in articulating perspectives generated from our experiences. We as authors take responsibility for weaknesses that remain.

Patty Eckard, Office Coordinator for the Department of Business and Economics at Eastern Mennonite University, carried out with grace and efficiency many administrative and logistical tasks necessary to produce the manuscript. Thank you.

Preface

As a young man, I wanted to help eliminate world poverty and to that end spent thirty years of my life as a development worker in Africa, Latin America and Asia. By the early 1990s, many of the cities I had experienced as dingy and remote sported luxurious modern airports, super highways crowded with late model cars, five-star hotels, gated residential communities, and air conditioned mega-shopping malls stocked with state-of-the-art electronics and elegant designer clothing from all over the world.

With that, David Korten begins his book, *When Corporations Rule the World.* But he continues:

To those who look no further it seems that development has been a stunning success. Yet look a little deeper, and it is like visiting an elaborate movie set and finding there is nothing behind the carefully constructed facade. Behind the facade, billions face an ever more desperate struggle for survival. By the hundreds of millions they are becoming displaced from the lands on which they once made a modest living, to make way for dams, agricultural estates, forestry plantations, resorts, golf courses and myriad other development projects.

The general optimism about the efforts of Western democracy and technology to lead the world into a brighter tomorrow seems not to have been born out. Rather than the world moving toward a globally improved quality of life, Korten believes that "manifestations of institutional systems failure constitute a threefold global crisis of deepening poverty, social disintegration, and environmental destruction."(page 31) Even some of the contemporary high priests of the cyberspace revolution question whether technology can really help. Bill Joy, a founder of Sun Microsystems, (one of the world's most profitable companies) says:

> We are dealing now with technologies that are so transformatively powerful that they threaten our species. Against such optimism [that technology will solve most problems] lies the weight of homo sapiens history. So many technologies, from chariots to flying machines, become killing tools in our hands. We tend to underrate our scientific ability, and our capacity for mayhem. (*The Washington Post*, April 16, 2001)

If the quality of life for the majority of humanity is not improving very much, and if technology and the science behind it are not providing much hope, what is the prognosis for improving the human quality of life during this current time? Was Korten following a futile dream as he spent 30 years trying to help improve the life of people in various nations and societies? Were his efforts, which he calls development, a failure?

Should the fact that progress has been slow, if there has been any, detain us from being concerned about the plight of the world's poor and dispossessed? How do the conditions of humanity and the idea of development relate? If we believe in a common humanity and want to share learnings and experiences with each other, how might we effectively and sensitively go about doing that?

We believe that there are various ways of doing development, some better than others.

In this work we propose that members of the Anabaptist/Mennonite tradition[1]—of which we are a part—have a peculiar perspective and ethic regarding how the common good can be promoted and that this will result in a particular approach to development. We do not claim that it is the best approach, or that our tradition—and what flows from it—has a corner on development theory and practice. But we believe that it has integrity and staying power and is worth offering as part of the larger development conversation.

We invite you to join us as we travel to "the field" and observe how some of our fellow dreamers have gone about the task which Korten felt was almost overwhelming and of dubious success. If you have interest in knowing a bit about development from a theoretical perspective, that is, what development is and how it is measured, read Chapter 2. If you are interested in understanding something of Anabaptist/Mennonite institutional involvement in development, Chapter 3 gives a quick overview. On the other hand, if you want to read what some development workers do, and about some of their experiences, Chapters 4, 5, and 6 are first-person accounts by Anabaptist/Mennonites doing development at the grassroots/village level, at the large-scale public policy level, and in between. If you want to consider some of the theological and ethical aspects of doing development, Chapter 8 gives an overview. Chapter 9 deals with some of the more controversial aspects of development, such as the tensions and dilemmas encountered, and how these are dealt with. Whatever your interest, we hope you will find this book useful.

Part I

Overview and Background

1.
Introduction

Purpose

Thirty years ago, Denis Goulet wrote, "For developed and underdeveloped societies alike, basic questions are neither economic, political, nor technological, but moral."[2] What he was referring to were largely "ends" questions, such as, what is the good life and what is the good society? Do more material goods, more leisure, and more choices, stronger relationships and communities, and greater justice and peace constitute the good life? Or is it something else?

But the moment we begin to think about ends—in our case, what is the *end* of development?—we are confronted with *means* questions—how do we get there? Are more material goods and services a means to development, or are they ends in themselves? Are healthy communities an end or are they a means to something larger? Is justice a means to peace, or is justice an end in itself? What *ought* to be the ends and the means of development?

What do we mean by "development?" Human development? Economic development? Social development? International development? The word is broad, with many different names and meanings.

Once we know what it is, how do we go about carrying it out?

Why do people do development? For some, development is a calling, a vocation, in fact, a sacred vocation. For others, it is one more profit-maximizing line of business. David Korten and others have written about "people-centered development," in contrast to the historical emphasis of large development organizations, such as the World Bank, on promoting *economic* growth. The claim, and often the practice, of many nongovernmental organizations (NGOs) is that their goals and methods are more people-oriented, while large development organizations tend to build infrastructure and promote economic growth. Are there different values implicit in these two orientations? If so, is that significant? Are the major donors, as well as the staffs, of large development agencies ever drawn to the values of people-based development? Or do the politics and national or strategic interests of those organizations, which are focused primarily on economic growth, make this nearly impossible?

Anabaptists/Mennonites, along with many other people and institutions, have been part of the development enterprise for many years. They have been involved internationally with humanitarian assistance of one form or another since 1920, when Mennonite Central Committee (MCC) was begun. The shape that this assistance has taken has varied over time—from relief and development at the grass-roots level to structural and institutional change at the public policy level. Further, Anabaptists have worked with nongovernmental organizations, both church-based (such as MCC) and non-church-based (such as CARE), as well as multilateral and bilateral organizations (such as the World Bank and U.S. Agency for International Development). Throughout this time, millions of people have been affected by these efforts, for good or ill, and millions more will still be affected. Anabaptists have brought their voices and values to the full spectrum of development organizations.

Unlike earlier decades, when answers to the "What is development" and "How do we get there" questions seemed to be clearer, the discipline today has few blueprints and no easy answers. Modernization theories of development in the 1960s, along with dependency and Marxist theories of the 1970s and the more recent market liberalization theories, provided their own perspectives. Each of these theories, their variants, and associated values, had their own strengths and limitations.

Do Anabaptists have something to contribute to these debates and issues? How have they been doing development, and what are the values and assumptions implicit in their "doing?" Do Anabaptists/Mennonites who are involved in development respond in distinctive ways to these questions, regardless of the organizations with which they work? Could those behaviors and attitudes be identified as an Anabaptist development ethic?

The primary purpose of this book is to hear and reflect on the stories and experiences of Anabaptists who have done international development work in organizations ranging from those with a grassroots orientation, such as the Mennonite Central Committee, to large development organizations with a public policy focus, such as the World Bank or the U.S. Agency for International Development. Out of these stories and experiences we will: (a) examine the themes and patterns of Anabaptists doing development work to see if there is a common set of values guiding what they think and do, regardless of their organizational affiliation; (b) explore and articulate an Anabaptist ethic of development, and compare it with classical Anabaptist ethics and theology; and (c) explore some of the tensions, dilemmas, and opportunities experienced by Anabaptists doing development work.

Methods

This book is the outcome of an extended and ongoing period of reflection and action by development practitioners and scholars, that is, those who "do" development work and those who intentionally reflect on and write about development. One of these periods dedicated to reflection and writing was a conference on international development held October 1-4, 1998, at Eastern Mennonite University (Harrisonburg, Virginia). At this conference, attended by some 150 people, 24 Anabaptist/Mennonite scholars and practitioners presented papers on their experiences in international development. The papers were a mix of storytelling and critical reflection. Each paper was shaped around six questions:

- Why have you chosen this occupational path?
- What has been your experience?
- Have you made a difference?
- What would you have done differently, given the opportunity?
- What have been the growing edges for you?
- What does the future hold for you; what are the major issues or themes?

These questions, and the thoughtful responses presented at the conference, brought us much insight to these presenters' personal experiences. In addition, they allowed us to identify inductively common values, themes, and patterns of these development practitioners. In that way they became a primary source in our efforts to determine the extent to which there is an Anabaptist/Mennonite ethic of development, regardless of where, or with what organization, a person works.

The men and women who presented papers came from a wide variety of development organizations (including public, private, NGO, grassroots, and public policy). They worked in a mix of sectors (including agriculture, health, education, environment, microfinance, and peacebuilding). We have too few voices from the so-called Third World; only representatives from nearby Central America were able to participate. As a consequence, some important perspectives are not adequately represented.

In addition to the conference papers, other sources of data for the book include ongoing conversations with practitioners, articles and books written by Anabaptist/Mennonites, and our participation in a variety of national and international conferences on different dimensions of development.

Note that we used an inductive approach to examine the practitioners' values and development ethic. Those who presented papers at the Eastern Mennonite University (EMU) conference were not asked to articulate their own values or development ethic. In fact, none of them mentioned either directly. Rather, it was by analyzing their responses to the six questions, what social scientists call "content analysis" and "unobtrusive measurement," that we are able to identify any such development ethic.

Although we give more attention to the terms "Mennonite" and "Anabaptist" in Chapter 8 and in the Appendix, a brief comment about the use of those words in this book seems appropriate now. We note that the terms have different meanings for different people—and are the subject of ongoing discussion.[3] Generally, "Anabaptist" is seen as a more encompassing term that includes a variety of church denominations, among them Mennonite, Brethren in Christ, Meserete Kristos Church in Ethiopia, etc. Historians say that "Anabaptist" refers to "particular groups and movements in a specific historical period (early- to mid-16th century), and that what comes after that may be Anabaptist-related but is not Anabaptist." For others, "'Anabaptist' identifies an attractive, liberating story whereas 'Mennonite' represents a more oppressive Anglo/Germanic-dominated story in which they do not feel at home" (10), particularly those coming from communities of color within North America or the global South where the majority of Anabaptist-related persons now live. Given the lack of clear consensus on this issue, and perhaps to the chagrin of theologians and historians, we use the terms "Mennonite" and "Anabaptist" in combination and somewhat interchangeably throughout the book.

Overview

The book is organized into three major parts. Part I provides an "Overview and Background" and includes, in Chapter 2, an overview of mainstream perspectives on the "What is development" and "How do we get there" questions. Chapter 3 is a brief historical account of Anabaptist/Mennonite involvement in missions, relief, and development, highlighting the role of MCC and Mennonite Economic Development Associates (MEDA), thus providing a historical context for understanding current development efforts.

Part II, "A Variety of International Development Experiences," consists of selected papers from the EMU conference. We have arranged the papers into three categories. The three in Chapter 4 are by development specialists who work at the grassroots level. They are involved primarily in villages or in specific rural or urban areas within relatively limited geographic boundaries, having minimal interaction with central government officials. In many cases they are providers of agriculture, health, or related services rather than being "advisors."

"Middle ground" experiences fall between grassroots and public policy work and characterize the three papers of Chapter 5. These practitioners interact with government officials, often in the form of advocacy for private sector or village-based programs, but system-wide change typically is not part of their mandate.

Chapter 6 consists of three papers prepared by people whose work has been largely at the public policy level on large-scale projects. Work at this level typically is with senior government officials at national and global levels where decisions affect large numbers of people. Large-scale "systems change" is typically the objective. Generally, persons working here have minimal interaction with people in villages except for occasional "field visits."

Part III, "The Analysis," examines the data presented in the previous chapters and within the broader development dialogue in an effort to make sense of it all, while drawing some observations and conclusions. Chapter 7 examines the assumptions, themes, and patterns of development practitioners. What are these and do they vary according to the practitioner's level of experience? Or are there no differences? After offering a brief definition of ethics, Chapter 8 attempts to answer the question, "Is there an Anabaptist/Mennonite ethic of development?" This is followed by a summary of Anabaptist theology and ethics, after which comparisons are made between those ethics generally accepted by the majority of Anabaptists, and those of Anabaptist development practitioners. Some comparisons are also made between mainstream development efforts, as presented in Chapter 2, and Anabaptist perspectives on development. Building on the practitioners' stories and experiences, Chapter 9 summarizes the kind of world we currently live in, and concludes with an analysis of several specific tensions, dilemmas, and opportunities experienced by Anabaptists doing development.

2.
Mainstream Development: Competing Perspectives

What Is Development?

Development, as the term is most commonly understood, is a fairly recent phenomenon, beginning, perhaps, when the United Nations identified the 1960s as the "first development decade." During this time, a variety of definitions, explanations, and understandings (models) emerged, each reflecting different approaches, assumptions, and values.[4] Traditionally, development has been defined primarily in economic terms, particularly increases in a country's Gross National Product (GNP), which is a measure similar to a country's income. Dividing a country's income by its population shows income per person or, as it is more often termed, income per capita.

The success of the 1950s and 1960s in increasing the GNP of low-income countries, however, was not matched by noticeable improvements in the living standards of the broad masses of people. In what is now a classic study of some 64 developing countries by Adelman and Morris,[5] it was demonstrated that among countries with the highest rates of growth of GNP, not only had the gap between rich and poor increased (relative poverty), but income levels of the lower 40 percent of households had decreased (absolute poverty). In other words, the poor had gotten poorer in absolute terms, not just relative to the upper income groups. This study, and similar ones, had a significant effect on dethroning GNP and per capita income as the primary measures of development, as well as "trickle down" theories of development, and led to a broadening of the definition of development to include income distribution and other measures of distribution. A country's economic growth was still important, but how that growth was distributed among the population became equally important. "Growth with equity" became the dominant theory of the 1970s, along with a focus on basic needs and direct attacks on poverty, unemployment, and inequality.

Dudley Seers, for example, argued that if poverty, unemployment, and inequality have decreased in a country, then that country has experienced development.[6] During this same period, Denis Goulet defined development in terms of three core values or goals common to all societies. These included, but went beyond, the material needs of people and included sustenance, self-esteem, and freedom from servitude.[7] Sustenance includes having the basic needs of physical survival—food, health, housing, and security. Self-esteem refers to a sense of self-worth, dignity, respect, honor, and that "others are not using him (sic) as a tool to attain their own purposes without regard for his (sic) own purposes." (page 89) Freedom here "is to be understood in the sense of emancipation from alienating material conditions of life and from social servitude to nature, ignorance, other people, misery, institutions, and dogmatic beliefs, especially that one's poverty is one's predestination."[8]

How Is Development Measured?

Although most current definitions of development are variations of what has just been described, measuring development is sometimes more complex, as illustrated by the difficulties in measuring freedom from servitude or self-esteem. Indicators of basic needs, on the other hand, are more easily measured. For example, health can be measured by life expectancy or infant mortality in a country; education can be measured by literacy rates or the percentage of school-age children finishing primary school. Economic growth, as shown earlier, is relatively easy to assess by measuring changes in the GNP.

It is clear, however, that any single measure of development has its shortcomings. Because of these inadequacies, several indexes of development have been formulated. In 1979, the Overseas Development Council (ODC) designed the "physical quality of life" (PQLI) index. It is a weighted index comprising three variables: life expectancy at age one, infant mortality, and literacy rate. In 1990, the United Nations Development Programme (UNDP) introduced the "human development index" (HDI) which combines measures of life expectancy at birth, educational attainment (combining average years of schooling and adult literacy), and GNP per capita (but only up to the world average of approximately $6,000 in 1997). In spite of a variety of alternative and more comprehensive measures, a popular textbook on economic development argues, " . . . income per capita remains the most useful single indicator of development . . . ." [9, 10]

How Do We Get There?

Although we have a variety of definitions for development, as well as ways to measure it, the greatest divide is over the question, "How do we get there?" Development theory, as in other disciplines, seeks to explain and predict, that is, it seeks to explain why some countries are "developed" and others are "underdeveloped." If one can explain this with some degree of accuracy, then it becomes possible for development planning to be done more systematically and with an increased predictability of outcomes.

Over the last 50 years, a variety of development theories have been articulated, with the literature being dominated by four or five major strands of thought, some of which are overlapping: modernization theories, growth with equity theories, dependency theories, Marxist theories, and neo-classical theories. Perhaps one of the more clear and helpful descriptions of these theories is that articulated by Vernon Jantzi,[11] adapted and summarized in Exhibit 1, where he evaluates four major development models in terms of how they provide answers to four questions:

- What is the problem that impedes development?
- Where is the source of the problem located—internally or externally?
- What is the general solution to the problem?
- Where is the source of the solution located?

Exhibit 1:
Mainstream Theories of Development

Modernization for Economic Growth: 1950s and 1960s

Modernization and Basic Questions about Underdevelopment

1. **What is the problem?** Traditionalism impedes the generation and investment of capital needed for economic growth.
2. **Where is the source of the problem located?** The problem is within the value system and practices of the developing country.
3. **What is the general solution to the problem?** Modernization for economic growth achieved through the adoption of modern attitudes, values, and practices leading to savings and entrepreneurial activity; highly dependent on external assistance for cultural and economic inputs.
4. **Where is the source of the solution located?** Found in the value system, practices, and economic resources of developed countries; transfer of cultural and economic resources needed.

Modernization: Types of Organizations and Programs at Various Levels

- **International level:** International transfer agents, such as World Bank, USAID, Peace Corps, World Vision, Church World Service, Mennonite Central Committee, etc.
- **National level:** Infrastructure-type organizations and programs, such as agriculture extension services, road systems, education systems, energy systems, mass communication systems.
- **Regional level:** Infrastructure supplied largely by churches in areas, such as agricultural demonstration farms and rural centers, hospitals, schools, etc.
- **Local level:** Individual-oriented programs in which foreign personnel play key implementing roles in areas such as literacy, modern agricultural technology and practices, youth work, skill development for industry, basic health and social services delivery.

Growth with Equity: 1970s

Growth with Equity and Basic Questions about Underdevelopment

1. **What is the problem?** Structured marginality of large segments of the population, denying them access to development's benefits.
2. **Where is the source of the problem located?** Found within the value system and structures of the developing country.

3. **What is the general solution to the problem?** Growth with equity achieved through modernization, but benefits of economic growth made available to all through regionalization, decentralization, use of appropriate technology, and popular participation in planning and program implementation.
4. **Where is the source of the solution located?** In value system and structures of developed countries that emphasize equitable distribution; transfer of organizational technology needed.

Growth with Equity: Types of Organizations and Programs

- **International level:** Transfer structures, such as World Bank and USAID continue to be important; consulting firms become increasingly important.
- **National level:** National planning ministries key to providing access through designing systems for regionalization and decentralization.
- **Regional level:** Creation of market towns; construction of road grid; regionalization of major public services; government often assumes basic services formerly provided by churches.
- **Local level:** Appropriate technology; paraprofessional programs in health, agriculture, etc.; creation of local planning structures to enhance popular participation.

Liberation from Dependency: 1980s

Liberation from Dependency
and Basic Questions
about Underdevelopment

1. **What is the problem?** Dependency on developed countries leading to distortion of national policies and value systems to the detriment of the national population.
2. **Where is the source of the problem located?** Found in international economic and political structures and in elite enclave structures of developing countries that subordinate national economy to developed countries and class interests.
3. **What is the general solution to the problem?** Liberation from exploitative international and national structures through: revaluation of national culture, development of critical consciousness of people of all levels, popular/grassroots organizations to break power of elite enclaves, creation of a New International Economic Order.
4. **Where is the source of the solution located?** In developing country as people organize to restructure society and call for new international structures; solidarity with the North desired.

Liberation from Dependency:
Types of Organizations and Programs

- **International:** Creation of New International Economic Order focusing on more solidarity with poor countries and less on transfer functions.

- **National level:** Government programs fostering regionalization and decentralization.
- **Regional level:** Creation of market towns; construction of road grid; formation of regional mass organizations.
- **Local level:** Work at creation of social consciousness; formation of locally based mass organizations.

Globalization and Liberalization: 1990s and beyond

Globalization and Basic Questions about Underdevelopment

1. **What is the problem?** The lack of understanding at the national and international levels of the limitations of the state in achieving development goals; too much government, not enough free markets.
2. **Where is the source of the problem located?** Primarily at the national level where governments, often undemocratic, maintain too much control over economic activity and do not free up prices and markets.
3. **What is the general solution to the problem?** A new set of ground rules that free up international economic and political relations, such that countries function on the basis of democratic governance, free markets, and comparative advantage, recognizing distinctive contributions of each country.

4. **Where is the source of the solution located?**
Principally at the international level with secondary importance at the national level. Existing
organizations such as the World Trade Organization must be strengthened and new multilateral
organizations developed to emphasize interdependence in trade and finance. Nations will need
to submit to these organizations.

Globalization:
Types of Organizations and Programs

- **International:** International regulatory or coor-
dinating agencies such as WTO; strengthened
U.N., World Bank, IMF; creation of multilateral
agencies in the church and professional communities; bilateral organizations like USAID and
CIDA placing emphasis on trade and privatization of economic activities.
- **National**: New ministries or departments dealing with promotion of privatization, trade, and finance, as well as negative effects of globalization
and debt burden.
- **Regional**: Organizations to promote specializa-
tion in economic activity.
- **Local**: Grassroots mobilization to mitigate negative affects of globalization and debt repayment.

At the risk of substantial oversimplification, the four
models can be summarized as follows. *Modernization theories* hold that poor countries are poor because of traditional values within those countries that impede economic development; that the way to become "unpoor" is
to replace those traditional values with modern values, at-

titudes and practices; and that these are like those found in North America and Europe. To become modern means to become like the Western world; for example, adopting a scientific worldview; assuming a future time orientation; promoting mastery over nature; exercising deferred gratification that leads to the practice of saving in order to accumulate capital; taking calculated risks; valuing efficiency; and being committed to an individualistic orientation in human relations.

Growth with equity theories are a variation of modernization theories and do not disagree with the analysis provided by modernization theories. They do differ in their argument that the benefits of economic growth and modernization should be more widely and equitably distributed among the population. In other words, modernization and all that it entails must be tempered by the value of equity, and technology must be appropriate for the contexts where it is applied.

Liberation from dependency theories represent a substantial departure from the values and assumptions of modernization theories. They argue that poor countries are poor primarily because of external reasons, not internal ones. The values and practices of rich countries keep poor countries poor and keep them dependent upon rich capitalist countries. Further, this dependency occurs not only between rich and poor countries, it also happens between rich and poor *within* countries. Thus, the solution to underdevelopment is to get rid of the yoke of dependency formed during the period of colonialism and create a new international economic order.

In many respects, liberation theories are class-based, which is why they call for a restructuring of societies both inter-nationally and intra-nationally, thus leading to revolutionary movements around the world.

Dependency theory is also an outgrowth of Marxism, where many of the ideas of dependency find their original expression. However, and contrary to conventional wisdom, Marx had little to say about what the structure of society should look like, including communist society. His strength was in his analysis of capitalism, its historical development, and the class conflicts inherent in capitalism; that is, his analysis was descriptive, not prescriptive.

The liberation-from-dependency perspective values political and economic structures that put local persons and groups in control, especially in relation to the most influential sectors of the economic and political systems. It values a communitarian and collective orientation rather than individualism, which finds its ultimate expression in liberal capitalism. The intended outcomes of this view of the development process are political and economic structures which are based on justice and social solidarity.

The *globalization (liberalization and privatization)* model of the 1990s and beyond is characterized by a resurgence of the free market and a reexamination of the role of the state. What's the problem? Big government. What's the solution? Get government off our backs and let the free market do the work of deciding: (a) What goods and services to produce (Answer: What people "demand" with their dollars); (b) How to produce them (Answer: At the lowest possible cost and highest quality); and (c) How to distribute them (Answer: Whoever has the money to buy the goods and services produced). In low-income countries, these reforms typically include measures such as reducing the size of the public sector through a reduction in wages or in the number of civil servants; freeing prices; reducing or eliminating the minimum wage; reducing subsidies for food, fuel, transportation, and social services; devaluing local currency; providing a more favorable climate for trade and foreign investment; and charging user fees for health, education, and other social services.

As can be observed, and unlike the first three models described earlier, all the above measures involve a reduction in the role of government and an increase in the role of the private sector. While the International Monetary Fund (IMF) and the World Bank led the way with their economic reform remedies—dubbed the "Washington consensus"—they have been closely followed in the bilateral foreign aid programs of nearly all the rich countries. For example, one of the editors of this book recalls that while working on a USAID-financed health project in Swaziland in the early 1980s, he was asked by a USAID official to prepare a report on "what areas of the health sector in Swaziland can be privatized." On the instructions of the United States President at that time, Ronald Reagan, through the USAID Administrator in Washington, every USAID mission around the world was preparing reports identifying what areas of low income countries' economies could be privatized.

The mandate of the World Trade Organization (WTO) is essentially to set the rules for international trade among countries (primarily reducing trade barriers), further reflecting a reduction in the role of national governments. The values inherent in this model are those that foster greater global interdependence. The nation state is an obstacle, politically and economically. Its survival conflicts with the principles of maximizing comparative advantage[12] and environmental sustainability, both of which require global-oriented thinking that is not limited by the interests of the nation state. Some of the implicit values at the core of the globalization model are interdependence at the global systems level, social tolerance, free markets, entrepreneurship, global networking, and global citizenship.

Needless to say, this so-called "Washington consensus," or globalization model, is not without its detractors. In fact, there is an increasingly noticeable shift among policy-makers and -observers away from some of the more harsh aspects of its structural adjustments and economic reforms. Beginning perhaps with the "Asian crisis" of the late 1990s, the shift gathered momentum with the continued failure of economic reforms in the former Soviet republics, Russia in particular. During this time, substantial differences in views emerged among the architects of economic reform within and between the World Bank and the IMF. Joseph Stiglitz, chief economist of the World Bank, broke diplomatic convention by critiquing the economic advice of the IMF in the Asian crisis, as well as the IMF's record in transition economies. The relative success of some nongovernmental organizations in drawing attention to the debilitating effects of Third World debt, particularly the Jubilee 2000 campaign, contributed further to the momentum.

While the story is still being written, history may show that the shift culminated with the failure of the World Trade Organization to agree on an agenda for trade talks in Seattle in December of 1999 and intensified with the anti-globalization protests which have occurred since then, most recently, the failure of the WTO meeting in Cancun, Mexico, in 2003. What this shift will lead to is not at all clear. But it does seem that global systems will need to be more responsive to "stakeholder" interests—the environment, preservation of community, low-income country interests, people as the bottom line—as well as increasing economic growth in low-income countries. Some observers looking for a third way suggest that the choice need no longer be between a "hard-headed capitalism, in which workers are sacrificed at the altar of lower prices, efficiency, and higher profits, or a soft-headed capitalism that sacrifices jobs and growth for economic security." The challenge is to combine sustainable growth and social cohesion. It is the quality of government, not the size of government, which is believed to account for the large variations in living standards among countries with otherwise similar endowments.[13]

In contrast to the four models summarized above, some development specialists argue that there are really only two models of development—the capitalist model and the socialist or communist model—and that other models are simply variations of these two.[14] Under the capitalist model would fall modernization, growth with equity, and globalization (liberalization/privatization). Under the socialist model would fall dependency theories, as well as Marxists theories. With the collapse of the Soviet model and the adoption of more free-market policies among formerly socialist-oriented countries, some analysts argue that globalization and liberalization reflect the triumph of the capitalist model over the socialist model, notwithstanding the questions being raised about the globalization/liberalization model.

A third framework by which to understand the variety of models for "getting to development" is that articulated by David Korten.[15] While Korten's framework focuses on strategies used by NGOs, it also can be used to describe the work of multilateral and bilateral aid organizations. It is useful also in that there are literally thousands of NGOs, both national and international, doing some form of development work. Kenya, for example, has over 800 national NGOs, not to mention the large number of international NGOs based there. Much of the work of Anabaptists/Mennonites has been with NGOs.

Korten argues that it is possible to identify four distinctive strategies or generations of NGO work: relief and welfare, technical training or capacity building (small-scale, self-reliant, local development), facilitation (sustainable systems development), and transnational networks or social movements. Borrowing liberally from the summary of Korten by Terrence Jantzi,[16] these are summarized below.

First Generation: Relief and Welfare. Since the problem is defined as a shortage of goods and services, this first generation approach focuses on providing specific goods or services like food, clothes, or medical supplies, often to individuals or families, in order to meet an immediate need. In the fish analogy, this strategy involves giving a person a fish so he or she might eat. Values related to this model are transfer of goods and services. It is task focused. Thus, the task—producing more goods and services—is what is important.

Second Generation: Training/Capacity Building, Small-scale, Self-Reliant, Local Development. With local inertia being defined as the problem, the second-generation strategy emphasizes self-help initiatives that are community- or village-based, such as improved farming practices, preventive health measures, and local road-building to get the community's goods to market. With sustainability being a problem in the first-generation strategy, the intent in the second generation is that the benefits be sustained beyond the period of NGO assistance. Using the fish analogy, the strategy is to teach the person to fish so he or she can continue to eat when the NGO leaves. This model espouses popular participation and the "small is beautiful" philosophy typically associated with an appropriate technology orientation. The important concern here is "who" does the task and "how"—capacity building concerns.

Third Generation: Facilitation or Sustainable Systems Development. The first two generations are primarily assistance strategies that are largely externally driven and relatively prescriptive, that is, "from our perspective, this is what is needed." The Third Generation evolved in response to these shortcomings. The emphasis turns toward encouraging reflection and allowing initiatives to be internally directed and flexible. Values undergirding this strategy include "valuing local knowledge," "being grassroots driven," and "participatory." The reflection process and non-prescriptive approach urges people to think differently about issues and encourages solutions to come from within rather than without— "the capacity for change and development lies within you rather than coming from outsiders." NGOs give up some control of the final outcome through emphasizing devolution of power and control of the process to that of the local communities and groups. The fish analogy involves helping persons to reflect on and define what would be the most appropriate way to fish, given his or her context and resources, and encouraging people to develop their own way of fishing. This model is concerned with autonomy and self-determination. Who defines what tasks are needed is the most important concern.

Fourth Generation: Transnational Networks or Social Movements. The Third Generation seeks to devolve power to the grassroots, facilitating reflection and valuing local knowledge. Fourth-generation strategies build on this by attempting to promote grassroots networks and mobilizing across national and international boundaries to gain political voice or access. The fish analogy for this generation is the person and his or her neighbors have banded together to confront the powers-that-be over why they must make do with just fish while there is a surplus of food elsewhere. The most important concern at this stage is the ability to think and act globally in the interests of the grass roots. The concern is not so much what the task is, who carries it out and how, or even who defines it, but rather what the barriers are that keep the other three concerns from being realized adequately.

Korten notes that the four generations are more appropriately applied to individual programs within an NGO rather than to an NGO as a whole. A given NGO typically has numerous programs, each of which could fit the characteristics of several different generations. Although Korten argues that NGOs have a long history of influence on changing public policy and institutions, and provides examples such as The Pathfinder Fund, the Bangladesh Rural Advancement Committee, Helen Keller International and others, it is the exceptional NGO who does so. The vast majority, at least in terms of numbers of NGOs, do not. Only rarely do NGOs evolve into the Fourth Generation, although the movement toward globalization of both development initiatives and protests against them suggest otherwise.

Who Is Responsible and Who Has Control?

Two fundamental issues in all of the models of development are: 1.) who or what is responsible for poverty, and 2.) who or what has control over reducing poverty. Are poor people and poor countries to blame for their condition, or are they victims of forces beyond their control. Derald Sue and David Augsburger[17] provide a way of looking at these questions that both belies simplistic answers and shows very different worldviews of "health" (development) and "illness" (underdevelopment). Sue's model is based on what he calls two psychological orientations: (a) locus of responsibility, that is, who is responsible for my condition of poverty (or wealth); is it internal or external, and (b) locus of control, that is, who has control over changing my condition; is it internal or external. Placing these two orientations on a continuum at right angles produces four different orientations toward life as shown in Exhibit 2.

Exhibit 2:
Four Different Orientations Toward Life

Who has *control* over changing my condition?

Internal Control

	Internal Responsibility	*External Responsibility*
Who is responsible for my condition?	**1** (I'm responsible; I can change it.)	**2** (I'm not responsible, but I can change it.)
	3 (I'm responsible, but I can't change it.)	**4** (I'm not responsible, and I can't change it.)

External Control

Two observations about this framework: first, by placing these internal-external dyads on a continuum, it disallows a simplistic choice of either-or. Second, by placing the continua at right angles to each other, it shows a range of at least four worldviews, or an infinite number of choices when the continua are not viewed at their extremes.

Individual responsibility and an achievement orientation characterize individuals in Quadrant 1, according to Sue and Augsburger. Western cultures place a premium on these kinds of characteristics. Collective action and social concern characterize individuals in Quadrant 2. This approach is illustrated by people active in the anti-Vietnam War and Civil Rights movements in the U.S., the dismantling of apartheid in South Africa, or the anti-globalization protests in Seattle in 2000. Persons in Quadrant 3 see themselves as defined by others and are unable to change an undesired situation. This view unites powerlessness and self-blame, a combination, Augsburger argues, that is rarely sustained except when imposed by dominant others. Cultural racism is an example of this. The "white man knows best" attitude is an example from the foreign aid and development context. Persons in Quadrant 4 are characterized by an ability to compromise and adapt to life's conditions. They have no options and their place is pretty well set no matter what they do. The caste system among Hindus or the perceived fatalism of some Muslims (enshalla—if God wills) illustrates this orientation.

What is of particular interest in these four orientations to life is what different cultures view as health (development) and unhealth (underdevelopment). For example, the individual responsibility and achievement orientation of Quadrant 1 is viewed by Western cultures as the apogee of a healthy individual and society: high self-reliance with self-control, assertive, self-sufficient, and responsible for self. On the other hand, these same characteristics are viewed by "Eastern tribal" or traditional societies as sociopathic, an isolated individual with no community or group identity.

By contrast, what is valued and seen as healthy in traditional culture is one who is able to compromise and accept his or her position and conditions of life. Masamba Ma Mpolo captures this in the following quote.

> Traditional culture defines the individual's identity in the following ontological formula: *Cognatus ergo sum: I belong, therefore I am.* To belong is to participate in and contribute to the life and welfare of the family. This is in opposition to the individualistic dictum of Descartes: *Cogito ergo sum: I think, therefore I am.* It is not the individual's capacity to think which is the prime source of his or her identity formation, but rather the reality and the ability of belonging, participating, and sharing. The sharing of one's life with another's leads to wholeness and guarantees health.[18]

In response to this, Western society tends to say, "And this is why you in traditional societies remain in poverty."

Terrence Jantzi highlights this conflict about what constitutes true development by drawing on Robert Putnam's concepts related to the types of capital present in all communities.[19] Jantzi identifies four types of capital which development addresses—economic, political, social, and environmental. Most development organizations claim to have strategies that span several or all of these types of capital formation. However, typically only one of these categories is used to determine if development has ultimately occurred. In an interdisciplinary effort, everyone would likely agree that development needs to include political reform, economic growth, and ecosystem maintenance. Yet each member of an interdisciplinary development team would likely use his/her discipline's criteria for measuring whether or not development had really happened. For example, for the economist, development has not taken place if there is no economic growth, even though political reform may have occurred. The political scientist would argue that development had not occurred if there was no political reform, even if there was economic growth.

So who is right? Or is that the wrong question? Is rightness relative to what a culture values?

In summary, there are many ways of describing the problem of "development and how to get there." In fact, there are so many variations that to characterize a common set of definitions and approaches as "a model" is to risk oversimplification and misrepresentation. We have provided a general sense of the variety of perspectives and some of the major characteristics of each. What does seem to be clear is that there is no blueprint.

Values are inherent in both defining and doing development. Which values or whose values is the question, since there is no such thing as "value free" development. The currently dominant liberalization or privatization model may or may not be the preeminent model 20 or 30 years from now. Do Anabaptists/Mennonites have distinctive values to bring to the discussion that can help shape the content, process, and direction of development? We address this question in some detail in Chapter 8.

3.
Historical Overview of Mennonite Work in Development

Introduction

Mennonites, as all other groups, affect and are affected by the larger social and cultural milieu in which they live. Therefore, their activity in development reflects, at least in part, the conditions present in the larger context. Henry Rempel suggests that the availability of government funds for nongovernmental organizations in both Canada and the United States encouraged Mennonite organizations to move into development.[20] Mennonites already had their hands in development when they began missions and relief work, although they didn't call it or think of it as "development."

To better understand the history of Mennonites in development, we will briefly review Mennonite mission work beginning around the turn of the 19th century, and then the emergence and growth of the Mennonite Central Committee and Mennonite Economic Development Associates. These two organizations played a powerful socializing role as members of Mennonite and Brethren in Christ (BIC) congregations served the needy through them—physically, economically, and spiritually. Through these programs, Mennonites and BICs intensified their commitment to service. They also developed a more globally-sensitive and justice-oriented worldview with a clear bias for the marginalized and introduced large numbers of young men and women to human need in many countries throughout the world. They also brought a level of cross-cultural international awareness into North American Mennonite and Brethren in Christ churches that indelibly imprinted the needs of the world on their collective consciousness.

Mennonite Missions: Pioneering in Development Work

North American Mennonites established their first foreign missions in India in 1899. The three oldest missions there were major efforts, "each with a staff of 30 to 40 missionaries at their height."[21] A substantial Mennonite church subsequently emerged, composed of three major conferences totaling around 80,000 members in 2003.

These early mission initiatives generally consisted of establishing the traditional mission compound, peopled by expatriates who spent most of their time preaching and teaching.[22] However, their work also "included direct evangelism, educational, medical and industrial missions, and also leprosy work."[23] In his writings on early Mennonite work in India, John A. Lapp noted, "The American

Mennonite Mission considered itself to be a servant of God to the whole man."[24] This expressed itself first in charity. Thus, ". . . it was not a mere accident that it was a famine in 1897 which aroused the concerns of the Mennonite Church for missionary activity."[25] Edmund G. Kaufman, in his extensive study of Mennonite missions, detailed the gamut of schools, hospitals, clinics, orphanages, women's and men's homes, and "industrial education" established under Mennonite auspices.[26]

The missionaries launched educational work soon after they arrived in India. While their first efforts focused mainly on training their own children, and then local converts to teach and preach, their educational program did not stop there. A normal school soon emerged that "prepared teachers primarily for rural village schools, for rural life and leadership."[27] It is easy to understand why education would be part of a missionary strategy, since knowing how to read is a prerequisite to knowing how to teach and preach, and all three skills were necessary if the emerging church was to become self-sufficient. Establishing schools in all fields where Mennonites worked was one of their major accomplishments. In fact, a primary contribution made by many missions around the world has been raising the level of education through mission schools. However, this should not be construed as an intentional effort on the part of the missions to improve the social and economic standards of the indigenous peoples in the interests of their greater social well being. Rather, the missions' first and foremost intention was to bring new members into the church.[28]

Relief work was also part of the missionary task. Kaufman, referring to mission work in India, stated, "From the very beginning of the Mission, relief has played an important part. Famine funds were utilized to provide permanent improvements such as buildings, roads etc., by giving the starving people a chance to work for their food."[29]

Because the mission wanted to address both physical and social needs, it became involved in medical assistance early on. Lapp maintained, "Since the establishment of the American Mennonite Mission in 1899, medicine has been an integral mission activity."[30] This included the establishment of hospitals and dispensaries and supplying them with doctors and nurses. While this may be seen as basically short-term charity and relief, principles of good health practices, hygiene, and diet were disseminated throughout the communities. As we have noted, the Mennonites may not have considered this kind of activity legitimate for its own sake, but it was, nevertheless, development.

Early missions also carried out activities more directly related to economic development. Lapp entitled his chapter 13 "The Mission and Economic Uplift," and there he reviewed initiatives in industrial work and economic welfare activities.[31] Among these were carpentry schools, trade schools, and gardening, dairy, and poultry schools. These efforts were motivated, according to A.C. Brunk, by the belief "that no amount of missionary effort would be successful until the entire society was reorganized on a more productive basis. He felt only a major industrial transformation would overcome the poverty of the masses."[32]

Similar efforts were undertaken by several Mennonite conferences; this sketch illustrates the emergence of development work alongside the compassionate expressions of mission work. The reverse also took place, in which emergency relief work contributed to the establishment of mission programs, best illustrated by the many missions that were opened as a result of Mennonite Central Committee's relief work.

So far in this section we have focused on how mission work often nudged the beginning of development. But mission programs were not the only places where physical and economic assistance was offered. Immediately after World War I, Mennonites set up a variety of relief and service agencies to provide emergency aid, as well as longer-range assistance, much of which could be defined as development work. The American Friends Service Committee (AFSC) organized a construction unit under the general direction of the American Red Cross to do reconstruction work in areas devastated by World War I. In January 1919, the recently-formed Mennonite Relief Committee sent 54 Mennonite men to assist this effort. The builder's unit constructed or repaired over 500 homes and ended its work on April 1, 1920. The Mennonite Relief Committee continued similar work in Belgium after World War II, operating from 1947 to 1950, when a missionary effort was established. That resulted in the emergence of several Mennonite churches.[33]

The evidence indicates that Mennonite mission and relief activity led to some work which could be considered elements of development programs. Nevertheless, there is little documentation or evidence that these grew out of a self-conscious vision for changing the life conditions of individuals or communities as a legitimate activity for its own sake.[34] Clearly, proclaiming the Gospel and winning converts to the Christian faith was paramount. Anything that contributed to this goal, especially education, was seen as a means toward that end. Historian James Juhnke suggests, "In its motivations and strategies Mennonite missionary renewal was more Protestant than Anabaptist. The differences between Mennonites and Protestants seemed less significant than the cultural gulf between pagan traditionalism and modern Western Christianity."[35]

Nevertheless, as we will aim to show in our last chapter, the ethic out of which Anabaptist/Mennonite missionary and development efforts have sprung is inclined to care for people's bodies as well as their souls, individually and collectively, in North America and around the world.

Mennonite Central Committee and Development

The Mennonite Central Committee (MCC) is a relief, development, and service arm of Mennonite and Brethren in Christ churches of the United States and Canada. It serves as the channel through which 15 different groups within these churches respond to human need around the world. When MCC emerged in the 1920s, it was the latest in a long line of efforts by Mennonite and BIC congregations in North America to respond to natural disasters, famines, and flights from persecution experienced by their Anabaptist brothers and sisters in other parts of the world. Mennonites in Canada and the United States organized relief committees as early as the 1870s to aid 18,000 Russian Mennonite immigrants arriving in the prairie provinces and states.[36]

From its beginning, MCC has tried to practice the faith described by Menno Simons, the sixteenth-century Anabaptist leader after whom the Mennonite Church is named, who wrote: "True faith cannot lie sleeping, it clothes the naked, it comforts the sorrowful, it feeds the hungry, it shelters the destitute, it cares for the sick, it becomes all things to all people."[37]

MCC has an annual budget of $70 million (US) with over 1,400 workers in 57 different countries. Four program priorities and two overarching foci—gender justice and environmental integrity—orient the organization's activity:

1. *Relief:* MCC assists communities recovering from natural disasters and human conflicts.
2. *Capacity building:* MCC works to develop locally rooted sustainable capacities in food security, health, education, community services, and income generation.
3. *Peace:* MCC works with community groups and national and international organizations in building bridges of understanding and developing peace-building skills.
4. *Connecting:* MCC facilitates interchange and mutual learning between its supporting constituency and those with whom the organization works around the world, so that all may give and receive.

During the 30-year period 1920-50, MCC offered assistance to Russian Mennonites in the 1920s and relief and reconstruction efforts in Europe following World War II. From that activity, MCC developed an identity within North American Mennonite and Brethren in Christ churches that made its name nearly synonymous with relief, reconstruction, and refugee resettlement work. The agency took major responsibility for resettling Russian and German refugees and displaced persons in Canada and Paraguay from the latter 1920s through the 1940s.[38]

Relief and reconstruction were major MCC activities during the World War I to World War II decades, from 1920-1950. However, peace- and nonresistance-related efforts also occupied considerable institutional energy. The agency spearheaded the search for and implementation of alternative service to military duty for conscientious objectors. The MCC Peace Section, created in 1942, took primary responsibility for this agenda and other peace and justice issues through the 1980s, after which it merged into other program areas of the organization. MCC assumed the administration of the Civilian Public Service (CPS) program in 1940, through which conscientious objectors could perform alternative service by doing humanitarian work of one sort or another—from building national park infrastructures, to working in mental hospitals, to serving as human guinea pigs for medical research. CPS participation peaked in 1945 with a total of 4,228 men in MCC-administered camps.

Probably the earliest agricultural rehabilitation, as well as the earliest development work, sponsored by MCC took place in Greece beginning in 1952. As a continuation of the CPS alternative to military service, MCC initiated Pax Service in 1951, a program in which young men could perform an alternative to military service outside of the United States. Pax participants in the initial years primarily built houses for refugees in Germany and Austria. The first unit of 20 men arrived in Germany in April 1951 to construct houses for homeless refugees. These German refugees came mainly from central and Eastern Europe, displaced by the advance of the Russian army.

The nature, variety, extent, and significance of Pax work in development is not widely known, nor carefully documented, and awaits more scholarly attention. Nevertheless, current evidence suggests that beyond aiding the needy, no explicit theoretical or practical frameworks guided Pax-initiated development work. The Pax program responded to vigorous appeals from recipient countries who hoped to obtain aid from an organization that had proven itself to be trustworthy, innovative, committed, and dedicated to responding to human need "in the Name of Christ." The lack of explicit theoretical criteria did not seem to hinder Pax men from giving the development challenges their innovative best.

By the mid-1950s the Pax program had expanded to include road construction and agricultural development, including resettlement work in Bolivia and vocational training projects in a number of low-income countries in Latin America and Africa.[39] Some 1,150 young men had served in Pax when the program ended in 1976.[40]

MCC and MEDA (Mennonite Economic Development Associates) development work followed chronologically the lead established by Pax men of the early 1950s. Inspired by the Pax program, MCC launched a new service effort in 1962. It, too, had a reconstruction focus, although it was in education rather than physical rebuilding. After an exploratory visit to Africa by Robert Kreider, MCC decided to establish a project to send teachers to Africa, known as the Teachers Abroad Program (TAP). TAP was a response to the importance placed on education by newly emerging African nations. It also coincided with development thinking in that era which emphasized modernization, especially through education (see Chapter 1). MCC placed primarily American and Canadian teachers in secondary schools and teacher-training institutions in a number of African countries. Early on in their classrooms in African schools, MCC volunteer teachers began to question the cultural appropriateness of the prevailing formal education systems in Africa and whether the schools were as helpful as they should have been in meeting local development needs. In 1974 MCC began phasing out its TAP program and instead started providing assistance to non-formal education programs in low-income countries.[41]

With this shift, development work as a specific activity distinct from "reconstruction" began to occupy Mennonite practitioners. Some of the pioneer thinking on the subject appeared in *Beyond Good Intentions* authored by Edgar Stoesz, MCC's Latin America director in the early 1970s. In this book and his later *Thoughts on Development*, Stoesz (1972) proposed that development demands a conceptual advance beyond mere charity and relief work, mainstays of MCC work from its earliest days. He articulated a major shift toward development and away from humanitarian assistance. The impulse had been building within MCC circles. His writing provided a significant impetus to think more explicitly about local empowerment in contrast to the earlier relief mode. Stoesz maintained that development aimed for more than making people rich. It was a process rather than a specific outcome, although it might include positive consequences such as improved health, nutrition, and agricultural production. Stoesz's claim that development was for and by people lay at the core of the institutional reorientation he promoted.[42] It challenged the assumption that typically supported earlier relief work, namely, that help for poor or disadvantaged people needed to come from outside sources in the form of goods or services. The reorientation also highlighted the need for programs and technology to be culturally appropriate by placing the focus on people in the local context as the "engines" for development.

The early '70s brought another change in MCC programming as TAP phased out and agricultural development moved to the fore in a renewed form. Agriculture had always been an MCC concern, notably its agricultural work in Greece in the '50s and other countries throughout the '60s. However, only with the adoption of the Hillsboro Resolution at the 1974 Annual Meeting in Hillsboro, Kansas, did agricultural development become the central focus of MCC activity. The Resolution called for MCC to significantly strengthen rural development and family-planning programs in developing countries and in North America, to encourage less consumer-oriented lifestyles in North America, to call for greater financial and material resources for development, and to attempt to influence United States and Canadian public policy regarding food security for poor countries.[43] It also called for MCC to do development education in North America so MCC constituents could clearly see the impact of their lifestyles on poor people in developing countries.

During the relief era, MCC work focused on reconstruction and resettlement outcomes, but through its people-to-people emphasis showed that fostering relationships was of equal or even greater importance than output. However, as MCC took on a development focus, particularly agricultural development, it tilted toward planned change as its primary goal. Relationships served as important instruments in helping MCC be more effective in achieving that goal. Despite that, villagers in Bolivia still recall with great satisfaction the relationships MCC volunteers developed with them, even though they cannot always remember specific development outcomes achieved by or with the volunteers.

So how does one measure MCC's impact or effectiveness in these situations? Some would say that the relationship aspects are important and nice, but unless the institution can identify how villagers are better off in areas such as nutrition, health, education, income, or political capacity, its work has not been effective. Others would claim that its work has had an impact, but the organization must be more efficient by achieving greater development output from human and economic resources invested in the endeavor. This debate has continued within MCC, its supporting North American constituency, and partners in places where it has a programmatic presence. The discussion will repeatedly resurface in different forms throughout this book.

During MCC's history, relief and reconstruction, education, and agricultural development have each had their turns as dominant program themes. Peace has also been a long-term MCC concern that has received more or less emphasis, depending on the needs at particular times. For example, along with its relief and reconstruction emphasis, from 1940-70, MCC's peace work focused on issues related to conscientious objection. Beginning in the latter '70s, but particularly in the '80s, MCC's peace activity turned to conflict in regions outside North America.

Currently MCC's peacebuilding efforts take different forms from country to country, but clearly the agency's priority is to become more proactive about peace.[44] This comes in response to rising levels of conflict and violence throughout the world, along with the search by the Christian church for a way to address the conflicts that are commonplace in many countries. This change in program emphasis also coincides with the growing consensus among MCC workers that development cannot take place, flourish, or be sustained where there is conflict, violence, and oppression.

Today MCC has satellite offices in Ottawa and Washington, D.C., as well as near the U.N. in New York, where it maintains a presence committed to the Anabaptist understanding of nonviolence and advocates for political and economic policies that promote justice and peace. MCC also offers conflict transformation training and practice with its local counterparts in countries where it funds programming.

The emphasis on development moved MCC to focus increasingly on measurable outcomes as its primary standard for success. Relationships remained important but tended to be viewed more and more in instrumental terms. They were important, but only to the extent that they helped achieve development objectives. MCC's shift to a justice focus, though seen as merely a token move by some, redefined its measure of success from social change that promoted development outcomes to political and structural change oriented toward creating a more just society. Relationships were increasingly redefined in terms of solidarity with justice-based groups. This required a new look at power in all its manifestations, including where MCC itself fit into the power equation. Justice concerns called for a rethinking of how MCC viewed armed insurgent groups across the world and what peacemaking implied in relation to insurgency and injustice.

Some MCC personnel and constituents would claim that the organization is too oriented toward peace through conflict transformation processes and not enough toward justice. Critics who take this position call for MCC to align itself clearly with the oppressed and to work to create a more just world through denouncing evil and advocating vigorously for the poor, recognizing that change ultimately occurs only through struggle.[45] This call arises more frequently in relation to areas where conflict has raged for many years, such as Central America, the Middle East, and the Philippines. However, it does raise the important question of what criteria one should use to measure the "success" of MCC's work over the years. Depending on the standards used, MCC work is seen, on one hand, as highly successful in helping to make life more humane for hundreds of thousands of people throughout the world. On the other, it can be judged at best as an unwitting instrument for perpetuating injustice globally as well as locally through promoting palliative social change, rather than engaging in the hard struggle for justice that will ultimately be counter to the interests of MCC and its North American constituency.

MCC work has indeed undergone significant changes in the course of the past 80-plus years, whether for good or ill. In all of the change, is it possible to discover an MCC development model? Robert Kreider notes that MCC's work displays certain features that are distinctive, though not necessarily unique, in relationship to people, scale, style, and the political arena.[46] Recent research in the MCC Africa Listening Process corroborates Kreider's points, even though debate continues on whether or not his analysis is still valid.[47] The following summarizes four of the areas he used to describe MCC's work.

1. People:
   - Personal relationship is paramount;
   - Accent on friendship building;
   - Emphasis on establishing and preserving a network of trustful relationships;
   - Professionals and untrained individuals work together.

2. Scale:
   - Preference for the small, the village, the neighborhood;
   - A bias for the grassroots;
   - An understanding of the macro in order to focus on the micro.

3. Style:
   - Understatement of purpose and achievements;
   - Priority given to telling the story in reports, articles, photos, videos, etc.;
   - Practical rather than ideological;
   - Minimal need for immediate, measurable results;

- Staying with the job until it is done;
- Seeking to be at home in the host culture.

4. Political:
   - Often out of step with conventional political passions (Vietnam, Central America, Gulf War, Somalia, Afghanistan, Iraq, Native American affairs, criminal justice);
   - Reluctance to be partisan or factional;
   - Prepared to work with varied agencies, governments, situations, political systems;
   - Maintaining a bit of distance from U.S. agencies abroad and wary of U.S. funding;
   - Encountering injustice in fields of service, then cautiously speaking truth to authorities.

MCC has been involved with human need from its origins in the early 1900s. However, Kreider has outlined an approach that, according to Ron Mathies, MCC's current executive director, derives from its understanding of service as learning. Mathies summarizes the claims made by Tim Lind that "for centuries western Christianity underscored the helping aspects of service when what should have been emphasized was servanthood. The latter does not come with the answers or solutions to the needs of others, but rather with one's self and puts this at the service of the context it encounters."[48] Thus, MCC's development work must be seen as an expression of servanthood by its constituency churches. This gives MCC development efforts a distinctive quality, often referred to in development circles as the "MCC style of development."

Personal and practitioner experience suggests that MCC, as much or possibly more than any other institution, has shaped how the broad Mennonite community thinks about development, international relations, and peace. Even the smallest congregations have members who served with MCC in some capacity at one time or another and who connect the congregation to a world beyond the local community. In addition, events like MCC Relief Sales, newsletters, and the itineration of former volunteers and guests from around the world help reinforce a cosmopolitan and people-centered understanding of relief, development, peacebuilding, and justice advocacy.

As noted above, questions remain about the adequacy of MCC's framework and style, but few would deny the powerful socializing force MCC exerts in the Mennonite constituency and beyond.

Does the distinctive Mennonite approach to development, peace, and justice affect the work of Mennonites who work with development institutions *beyond* the Mennonite world? This will be explored in more detail in the remaining chapters of this book.

Mennonite Economic Development Associates and Development

As described in the previous section, MCC was organized in 1920 to provide material aid and relief from the famine experienced by Mennonite refugees in the Russian Ukraine in the early 1920s. But another crisis soon followed the famine, for in the mid- to late 1920s, the Bolshevik collectivization caused a large segment of Mennonites to leave Russia seeking religious, political, and economic freedom elsewhere. One of the few countries that would take the Mennonite refugees was Paraguay. But Paraguay at that point was one of the most economically backward countries in South America and could not help the refugees resettle since their needs were so massive. MCC bought a substantial tract of land for the settlements and helped settle the refugees beginning on April 12 in 1932, with a major movement to Paraguay of some 6,267 persons between 1930 and 1947.[49] J. Winfield Fretz reported that the MCC action "helped the colonies only to set up housekeeping and provided a means for temporary survival. [But] what was needed in addition was capital for economic development."[50]

It became clear that MCC was not structured to address the ongoing needs of the Mennonite refugees as they struggled to become established in Paraguay. The problem soon became very urgent. Mennonites continued emigrating from Russia after World War II, with another major migration of displaced Mennonites arriving in Paraguay in 1947, composed of 2,305 persons. Thus, early in 1952, "a group of six men decided to fly to Paraguay at their own expense to study economic conditions there."[51]

The group took several other "flying missions," and then selected a number of projects in the Chaco to support. The first was a dairy project and the second a tannery project, both in the Fernheim Colony. A need was being filled. On December 10, 1953, Mennonite Economic Development Associates was officially launched. All eight of the original founding members of MEDA, including Orie O. Miller, executive secretary of MCC, were staunch supporters and members of MCC, but all felt they had gifts for which MCC had no program.[52]

"These men were not ordinary businessmen looking for profitable investments. Their willingness to risk loss was offset by their desire to help others get a new start."[53] They developed a set of guidelines for MEDA, the first of which states: "To help people to help themselves by entering into partnership agreements, either as individuals or groups who are related to Mennonite churches or missions." Point 5 affirms, "Projects undertaken should have a high potential as an economically viable business venture including the repayment of the debt and a modest return on capital."[54] The modest return on capital was designed to increase the capital base for revolving loan funds to more needy people.

MEDA's assistance program in Paraguay was very successful. Because MEDA provided loans and counsel, numerous projects, including dairy operations, cattle-feeding, a tannery, a shoe factory, a foundry, and rice plantations, were quickly created. All of them became self-supporting and fully independently owned. MEDA's work in Paraguay expanded as it began to take over the Indian resettlement program which had been initiated by MCC. The vast amount of land for future expansion of the Mennonite colonies, which MCC had purchased, was never needed, so MEDA established an extensive program of offering small business loans to the Indians. These were to assist them so that they could buy some of this land and become independent farmers/landowners and occasionally small businessmen.[55]

This venture is still in operation today and is a most unusual example of cooperation between a relief/service/development agency (MCC), an economic assistance and development agency (MEDA), and the local Mennonites, who themselves had been settled only a few years earlier.[56] Fretz proposed a rationale for MEDA's role as follows:

> MEDA has come to serve the larger interests of the MCC by providing financial credit and other forms of economic aid on a business basis. MEDA organized long-term partnerships, made financial loans, and charged interest, as well as collecting repayments which neither mission boards nor the MCC were pre-

pared to do. MEDA thus came to perform a needed service within the Mennonite church that no other church agency had been created to perform.[57]

MEDA has gone through a number of changes since its founding. These have come about in part because of its broad membership which now includes smaller business entrepreneurs, operators and laborers, women, and members with a wide range of ages. The program has also expanded in response to the needs of its local chapters, who not only support the international projects, but also want help to have their faith and ethics shape their businesses and commerce. MEDA now sponsors chapter meetings and local projects such as micro-enterprise related activities, similar to the ones they oversee internationally.

By 1978, MEDA projects were operating in 25 countries, mostly in Latin America, Africa, and Indonesia. Even though the projects are varied, the largest emphasis in recent years has been in micro-enterprise development in which MEDA provides loans for small entrepreneurs to start or expand small businesses. These entrepreneurs repay their loans at reasonable rates of interest so that the fund is constantly replenished, allowing for a growing number of future clients. Credit unions, organized on a local basis, are a major part of this program.

MEDA has accepted development funds from Canadian International Development Agency (CIDA) and United States Agency for International Development (USAID), as well as from private sources. In 2003, MEDA received grants totaling $3,663,478.* In the same year, MEDA had a budget of $5,859,637. Contributions were $1,364,414. MEDA has 179 full-time field workers and 17 staff officers.[58] *The Marketplace* is its bi-monthly publica-

* All amounts are in U.S. dollars.

tion, which presents an Anabaptist/Mennonite perspective on economic life and Christian ethics.

The MEDA approach to development is largely implicit, consistent with the historical Anabaptist/Mennonite tradition. That is, Anabaptist/Mennonite theology and ethics are less creedally and doctrinally determined than they are an implicit way of life expressed by discipleship. J. Lawrence Burkholder articulates the idea in this way: "Anabaptism had little to say about the great questions of faith in relation to divine acceptance. The question of the Anabaptists was, 'What does it mean to follow Christ as a disciple?'"[59]

MEDA's development philosophy and role is periodically examined. Mel Loewen, World Bank retiree, wrote an evaluative article entitled, "Seven things countries need."[60] Neil Janzen analyzed its activity in his article, "A Journey in Development: Parting thoughts from MEDA's former president." He explores several basic issues in development: partnership, integrity, balance, responsibility, and intervention.[61]

In a short but comprehensive history of development, veteran development practitioner Henry Rempel provides an excellent overview and briefly analyzes the nature of Mennonite development. Rempel maintains that one of the shortcomings of NGOs is that "they do not spend much time defining what constitutes development work. Development requires change: in political, economic, and social institutions; in ways of life, beliefs, and attitudes. Without a theological basis for an understanding of changes required, development work has not been able to realize its full potential."[62]

Some observers believe that Mennonites lacked a clear and unified vision and passion for development. The reasons may include "the wide diversity of theological/mis-

siological understanding and emphases, [hence] considerable effort is expended in interpreting program to the various parts of the Anabaptist family."[63] A MEDA agency
staff person stated, "Progress is constrained by lack of vision and passion on the part of organizational leaders for
joint thinking, planning and implementation."[64] Another
agency representative proposed a more economic dynamic: "Central to the difficulty [of achieving mutuality
and cooperation] is the matter of control and decision
making on use of resources. [For example] I think [the
agency] is too little aware of the immense power it wields
in terms of its resources base and the appeal of many of
its programs."[65]

There may be a lack of public discussion and published material on the philosophy undergirding MEDA's
work, but MEDA staff continue to try to refine and establish it. Wally Kroeker, editor of MEDA's bi-monthly
magazine, *The Marketplace,* for 15 years, states that, "It
might be useful to [note] that MEDA's understanding of
its task was fine-tuned over the years. Clearly, we made
some mistakes. In fact, we have sometimes said that
MEDA had to go through the missiological learning curve
in a couple of decades, something that took the larger
mission enterprise centuries. What we learned (or
thought we learned) from our mistakes led to some shifts
in self-understanding."[66]

In the mid-1970s, he suggests, "some hard-nosed evaluation took place, leading to a period of Direct Service
Delivery. The MEDA mandate evolved to offer credit and
training in tandem, to provide management support services as part of in-country integrated development, and to
concentrate on developing human resources." Finally,
Kroeker maintains, "in the 1980s another kind of shift occurred. We consciously began to work at understanding

our work from a theological perspective. Thus, if you look closely at the articles [in *The Marketplace*] describing MEDA's overseas work you will find an emphasis on 'seeking justice,' and many references to our work being based on a biblical understanding of *shalom* (rooted in texts like Isaiah)."[67]

The *Corporate Statement: Mennonite Economic Development Associates,* published in 1986, describes the following as one of its goals: "to accept and work with dedication at the challenge of economic development in undeveloped countries or regions where counsel, assistance in marketing, and other business practices, as well as investment, can help to correct inequities and establish justice."[68] Though relatively little has been said by MEDA regarding the term *development* and its meaning, MEDA membership and its staff workers have done considerable "development work."[69] This is in rather stark contrast to Mennonite mission strategy, which has produced a substantial history of theological and ethical discussion and research.[70]

MEDA has had two basic objectives—to assist people both abroad and at home to become economically independent, and to assist MEDA membership in understanding the relationships between their economic life and the ethical implications of being Mennonite Christians. The issues of why Mennonites should be in development domestically and abroad, what in fact the concept means and how it should be done, remain relatively unexamined.

A MEDA member, associated for many years with several leading Mennonite organizations, reflects: "I have long observed that MEDA is an organization of owners, not professionals or managers. While I concur that MEDA has a program of ethical and spiritual edification,

I wish there were more space for reflection on the inherent weaknesses of the business system. Would it be a fair observation that the church at large is more prepared for self-criticism than are business people, and that the church listens more intently to the critique of the business community than vice versa?"[71] It seems that *development*, perhaps because it is a rather abstract concept, and because it is often so closely associated with helping, has not yet been fully and critically explored by Anabaptists/Mennonites.

MEDA has frequently been criticized for being too concerned about improving the material circumstances of people and having too little interest in exploring larger social, ethical, and religious issues, or linking with organizations that are working at those factors. One specific area of concern has been MEDA's lack of cooperation with MCC and with Mennonite mission efforts in the localities where MEDA operates.

MEDA has usually located its foreign assistance in areas where MCC is already working. As MCC has moved beyond its original emergency relief and service program to become a development agency as well, there has occasionally been confusion and even tension between MCC and MEDA personnel and supporters. Are two organizations necessary? How are their spheres different and should each be maintained? Ironically, in recent years MCC launched development projects that have far outstripped MEDA development work in terms of personnel and cost.[72]

In the MEDA-sponsored official history, *The MEDA Experiment*, Fretz maintains, "One of the objectives of MEDA is to help people to help themselves in order that they may increase support for the local church. Whether or not this happens remains a matter of conjecture. So far as this writer is concerned, the evidence that it does happen is limited."[73] Fretz states that he "was told in Tanzania by veteran missionaries that a successful MEDA project partner, instead of supporting the church more generously, acquired an additional wife with his increased earnings. His successful business venture actually resulted in less interest in the church."[74]

This lack of coordination or interaction between Mennonite mission programs and MEDA personnel reflects some hesitation or structural factors on both sides which seem to hinder confronting the issues involved. Mission programs have focused on spiritual and religious activities, even while giving lip service to the importance of dealing with material and economic needs. Similarly, MEDA personnel have emphasized the importance of economic and material issues when improving people's lives. The mission statement in the *1999 MEDA Annual Report* makes no reference to linking efforts with Mennonite churches, stating simply, [MEDA is] "An association of Christians in business and the professions, committed to applying biblical teachings in the marketplace. MEDA members share their faith, abilities and resources to address human needs through economic development."[75]

In light of the limited cooperation between MEDA, MCC, and other church organizations noted above, could there be philosophical and structural reasons why MEDA has found it difficult to reach out actively to MCC and Mennonite agencies, especially when they are working in the same areas? One reason may be that MEDA members tend to subscribe to a business model in which tangible and measurable results are the criteria for administering a program, whereas MCC and Mennonite mission agencies are driven more by ethical concerns. Another factor may be that MEDA is a Mennonite lay organization, whose members may not be overly attracted to "churchly" assumptions and operating procedures. For example, Mennonite organizational policy tends to promote flat structures and decision-making by consensus, and that tends to exasperate business persons in Mennonite congregations.[76]

We conclude this chapter with several generalizations. First, Mennonites have been self-consciously active in development work for at least five decades, but development had been part of Mennonite mission activity since the beginning of the twentieth century. Ron Yoder states, "Prior to the emergence of MCC and MEDA, international Mennonite mission organizations that were established at the end of the nineteenth and beginning of the twentieth centuries adopted a 'holistic development' philosophy and practice as defined and demonstrated in the New Testament."[77]

Second, and based on extensive evidence, we propose that even though there has not been much theoretical discussion and analysis of the nature and purpose of development, this fact has not hindered MCC, MEDA, and other Mennonite agencies from applying tremendous amounts of effort and resources to the benefit of other people in North America and around the world.

Third, we observe that Mennonite involvement in development is related to the very core of Anabaptist faith, namely, that one is constrained to "do good to one's neighbor," but that this has not consistently been articulated verbally. This observation leads naturally into the summary analysis Rempel makes about Mennonite development work. He proposes that the form development took was to a considerable extent a response to global conditions, the availability of resources, such as the Canadian Food Bank, and the "place of the recipients in the development process." He believes that "the struggle by many societies for independence from their respective colonial masters" has been a dominant force in determining the shape of development work.[78]

Clearly, a variety of forces has shaped the development enterprise for Anabaptists/Mennonites. One veteran Mennonite agency staff person reflects a pluralistic, philosophical approach: "I no longer believe there is or should be one mission of the church. There should be mutual respect and, whenever appropriate, coordination. But the church has been endowed with a number of gifts, and each can usefully enhance the work of the Lord." He continues, "Who defines Christian mission or Mennonite priorities? Are mission agencies and programs a more authentic witness than MCC or MEDA? I doubt it."[79]

Indeed, the Anabaptist/Mennonite understanding of development and its implementation is a collection of visions and one form of witness to faith among many. Thus, rather than trying to determine which Mennonite expression of faith is the most appropriate, or the right one, it is more reasonable to accept Anabaptist/Mennonite development efforts as one of its peculiar gifts to an amazingly pluralistic world. We will return again to this topic in the final chapter.

Part II

A Variety of International Development Experiences

4.
Grassroots
Perspectives

Introduction

We begin with papers from practitioners who work at
the grassroots. It will soon become apparent that there is
a strong grassroots, or a "from the ground up," approach
among the practitioners represented in this collection, no
matter their current level of work. This perspective, although variously expressed, tends to focus on the central
importance of creating close, reciprocal, and lasting relationships with people in the communities in which de-
velopers work. This emphasis is strongly supported in the
papers by Susan Classen, Ann Hershberger, and Jan Jenner.

One senses quickly in Susan Classen's presentation
her intimate and egalitarian identification with the people
she is trying to help. "She is not in a hurry," and she is
ready to spend a lifetime at the effort, despite not being
able to predict exactly what will eventually happen. "I
like to think that I can predict what the fruits will be," she
says. "But the fact is, I am not in control. I want to be

open to embrace tomatoes that grow when I think I'm planting flower seeds." Classen recognizes the interconnection of forces. She is focused on "taking small steps toward lasting changes, to contributing my grain of sand." Her orientation can be described as an "organic" one in which her self, her spirit, and those of the persons she works with are linked together in a dynamic fashion, each affecting the other.

Ann Hershberger reflects the "liberation theology" motif to some extent by using "God's preferential option for the poor" as a major point of orientation. Hershberger's approach to development hinges on developing relationships with the people being helped. These relationships are not ephemeral nor pragmatic nor contingent on the presence of the development worker on the field, but they are to continue throughout life. She candidly explores and reveals the tension between a development worker's commitment to the ones being "helped" and his/her own personal career ambitions and objectives. She believes that personal lifestyles cannot be detached from the expectations and conditions of one's development activities. Her idea of making a difference is contingent on "mentoring and encouraging individuals in their work." She unmistakably infers that development demands a commitment with the other "for life."

Jan Jenner proposes that stories of human experiences and struggle are a very effective means for both discovering the problems in human communities and for deciding what needs to be done to achieve some desirable outcome. She maintains that these stories point to the brokenness of human relationships in human communities and that "without [achieving] peace, development, in whatever sense, cannot occur." The existence of violence and injustice, whether organized, spontaneous, or ethnic,

will defeat development if it is not addressed and resolved. The consequences and causes of violence and injustice must be addressed and dealt with before development in any form can be sustained.

Development as Connectedness

Susan Classen

Susan Classen worked with MCC for 21 years in Bolivia, El Salvador, and Nicaragua. She initially was involved in training local health workers, but in later years she focused more on providing pastoral support for MCC workers, as well as leading retreats and workshops for Central Americans involved in peacemaking.

Susan is currently the assistant director of a small retreat center sponsored by the Sisters of Loretto in eastern Kentucky. Beside the retreat center work, she is also involved in issues related to environmental sustainability.

Why did I choose this particular path?

I could easily say that this path chose me. For years, I thought I joined MCC primarily because of the influence of my parents who worked for 10 years with MCC. But I recently learned of a significant influence that I wasn't conscious of previously. My grandmother died before I was born. She felt called to overseas missions, but, since she couldn't go, she prayed that her offspring would be interested in service overseas. Two of her children and many of her grandchildren, including myself, are answers to her prayer.

Maybe it would be helpful for me to think about why I *continue* to choose this path. My understanding of "development" has broadened to include anything that involves nurturing life. Pastors, teachers, administrators, nurses, and social workers all participate in calling forth life. Whether I'm in Central America or in the U.S., my vocation is to nurture life in some way.

After about 13 years with MCC, primarily in El Salvador, I decided to return to the U.S. I thought it was important to make sure I wasn't staying in Central America because I could no longer see a place for myself in the North. After about a year, I felt comfortable enough here to feel the freedom to go back to Central America. I like the challenge of there and here. I like the work. I feel a sense of life. I'm healthy and like the food! Which country I live in no longer seems as important as in the past. My sense of call gives priority to using my gifts for the good of the poor. Where and how I do that is open to change.

Have I made a difference?

I've struggled over the years with this question. Have I made a difference? How is "making a difference" defined? How much "difference" does it take for me to feel successful or worthwhile? Why do I need to see a measurable difference? What's the relationship between being faithful and being successful?

I've spent most of my years with MCC in health-related work. I find a certain gratification in knowing that some people are alive today because of my work. There's Ernesto who was a seven-month-old dying of malnutrition. He is now a small but healthy 14-year-old. Or I could point to the many people who received treatment for tuberculosis because of the program that I helped coordinate. I could name people injured in the war who would have died without the immediate first aid that the health promoters and I provided.

Because of MCC's work in the parish of San Francisco Gotera, El Salvador, there is now a small, self-sustaining health program run by three Salvadoran health workers. Later, I helped start a health program in a newly formed Catholic diocese during the height of the civil war. It quickly became one of the most respected programs in the country and included over 200 health promoters in about 60 villages isolated by the fighting. I also helped start a micro-enterprise, which, after six years, continues to provide steady employment to five women.

I learned a lesson about "making a difference" when I left El Salvador. During the many good-bye celebrations little mention was made of the programs I started, the health manuals I wrote, the courses I taught. But story after story was shared about the time I spent visiting families, eating together, working on the road that needed to be fixed in order for the trucks of returning refugees to pass. "You got blisters with us. You shared our food. You suffered with us during the war." Those were the experiences that made a difference to my Salvadoran friends.

I now live in a small Nicaraguan village where I fixed up an abandoned mud house along the river. My home is a small retreat center where individuals can come for rest and prayer. Several friends who were my first visitors brought up the question of a retreat center in such a poor area. "What difference will it make in this village to have a place of beauty and prayer here?"

The youth began organizing themselves last year. First they met only for church services. But now several are involved in a small micro-enterprise. A number of youth learned to make friendship bracelets and a young woman is excited about learning to weave. A project making Catholic school uniforms is in the first stage of becoming a reality, and dreams of fishponds, wells, and improved tiles are floating around the community.

Children come weekly to my home to color and read. The first time five-year-old Marlin came, she grabbed a handful of crayons and refused to share. By the next week, Marlin had already learned that when all the children take just one crayon there are enough to go around. She realized that she didn't need to take a handful. Such a minor, insignificant example. But how different the world would be if we all learned by age five not to hoard more than our share of the resources.

Change is slow and the seeds are tiny. But I'm not in a hurry. I'm trying to live the lessons I learned in the past.

What would I have done differently?

Perhaps it would be better to ask what I'm trying to do differently. I'm trying to put into practice some lessons that sound simple but are a challenge to live.

1. Be open to surprises.

The dirt in front of my house is hard, worthless clay. One afternoon I chipped a hole out of the clay and filled it with good compost dirt for a flowerbed. I carefully planted the seeds and watched anxiously for the first sprouts. Finally I saw a green head poking through. I watered it tenderly and watched it grow, wondering why the other seeds didn't sprout. My question sharpened as the green shoot took form. It didn't look like the flowers I planted. I kept watching. It didn't look like a flower at all. It was a tomato plant! Evidently a tomato seed survived from the kitchen scraps I threw in the compost pile.

I wasn't at all pleased with the tomato plant. I'm organized and I like things where they belong, and that tomato plant definitely did not belong in my flowerbed. I was tempted to yank it out. Finally I had to stand back and smile. The flowers never did sprout, but I carefully tended the growing tomato plant, grateful for the reminder that I'm not in control.

I like to think that I know what seeds I'm planting as I work in the pastoral area of community development. I like to think that I can predict what the fruits will be. But the fact is, I'm not in control. I want to be open to embrace the tomatoes that grow when I think I'm planting flower seeds.

Many of the "health promoter" seeds I planted turned out to be "teacher" seeds. I was tempted to feel resentful because of the energy it took to train promoters in order to see a "teacher" sprout. But I tried to celebrate that somehow the health courses helped put the young people I was training in touch with their true vocations.

2. Live in connections.

One August I learned a lesson about connections: The steering wheel is connected to the front wheels of a vehicle. I learned that when I cut a corner too sharply and hit a curb with the front tire of the jeep I was driving. The steering wheel suddenly spun so hard that it broke my thumb.

Connections. I often take them for granted. Of course the steering wheel is connected to the car wheels. But I never gave it a thought until pain jolted me out of my oblivion.

The steering wheel spun so hard that it pulled my arm in. I thought at first that my wrist was broken because it looked deformed from the impact of the steering wheel. My thumb didn't hurt significantly until hours later. The place where we first experience pain isn't necessarily

where the real problem lies. It's important to keep following the threads of connection back until we get to the root.

I sometimes find myself frustrated and angry when
people come to my door wanting things. When I ask myself why I react so intensely and then follow the threads
of my emotions back to their root, I realize my reaction is
connected to my struggle with feeling powerless. People
knocking on my door remind me that I'm powerless to
solve the root causes of their poverty.

As I learn to be present to my frustration about not
knowing how to respond to the global issues that affect
my neighbors, I'm able to be a more gentle and compassionate presence in their lives. I'm able to take
small steps toward participating in efforts to make lasting changes, to contribute my grain of sand without
berating myself for not being able to do more. It's
humbling to recognize how intertwined my own needs
are with the life of service I've chosen. We all have
personal needs that motivate us—the need to be needed, to see results, to make a difference, to appease our
guilt. I'm thankful that I don't have to reach altruistic,
selfless perfection. But it is necessary for me to be conscious of the ways my own needs affect how I respond
to others.

3. How is God present?

The lectionary reading one morning was from Psalm
33. "The earth is full of the steadfast love of the Lord." It
seemed an appropriate verse for a morning spent working with my plants. As I worked the earth, I wondered
how the love of God could be present in such worthless
soil. The response came quickly. "God's love is present in
the agony of land, once fertile and fruitful, now ex-
ploited and destroyed."

How is the Spirit present in a given time and place? Is the Spirit groaning in agony? Celebrating? Giving fruitful growth? Patiently waiting?

Once again my plants taught me a gentle lesson. A fungus was ruining one of my hanging plants so I trimmed it back, not paying attention to the stems that fell to the ground. As I watered the pot during the following weeks, I didn't realize that the water was dripping through the holes onto the stems below. One afternoon I noticed that they were growing. As a matter of fact, they were much healthier than the ones I had left in the pot. The plant in the hanging pot eventually died, but underneath I have beautiful, healthy flowers.

"Okay," I said smiling as I shrugged my shoulders. "You didn't want to grow in the pot. You wanted to grow in the ground. So be it." I hope I bring that sensitivity to my life and ministry. It involves not trying to force people into my way of doing things but discerning the Spirit's movement and celebrating when ideas take root, even it it's not what I had in mind.

4. Work with, not against.

It's a challenge to discern the flow of the Spirit and to work with it, but nature reminds me to keep trying. As I washed clothes in the river behind my house one morning, I was reminded of Fritz Perl's advice: "Don't push the river. . . it flows by itself." As I watched the coursing rain wash away the remnants of topsoil still left in my yard, I reminded myself, "Work with, not against." The year before I tried to stem the flow and succeeded only in creating pools of stagnant water. Ministry consists of learning to channel and structure the energy of the Spirit's movement.

Bits of truth come in scattered fragments. "Listen. Pay attention. Dream dreams. I plant and water but

God gives growth. It's not my work. It's God's work.
Give myself wholeheartedly but take neither the credit nor the blame. I'm invited to participate in the Spirit's movement but the flow doesn't depend on me."

5. Trust in the God of life.

"Don't ask yourself what the world needs," Howard
Thurman wrote. "Ask yourself what makes you come
alive and go do that, because what the world needs is
people who have come alive."[80]

Life flows from our willingness to live open to risk,
to live listening intently to the way the Spirit is present, to live humbly, taking neither credit nor blame as
we participate in the movement of the Spirit in a giv-
en time and place. Life flows with a spirit of appreciation and celebration because we're not trying to es-
cape the reality of a world gone wrong but seeking to
live the reality of the Reign of God coming to birth
among us.

6. Caress the earth.

Petrona, a good friend, agreed to teach me how to
make clay pots like those her grandmother used to
make. She patted the clay around a pot we were using
for a mold. Then she took a burned corncob and
combed out the lumps. The last step was to sprinkle
water on her hands and smooth out the scratches left
by the corncob. As her hands gently stroked the clay
Petrona turned to me, her eyes twinkling with their
characteristic sparkle. "You have to caress the earth,"
she said enjoying the play on words.

Ultimately, development work is about being kind,
being gentle, and walking compassionately on this
earth that God has given us to share.

What are the key challenges and growing edges for me?

The concept of development as we've come to know it began with Harry Truman in 1949. In his inaugural address he identified the majority of the world as "underdeveloped areas." The world became defined as an economic arena using U.S. indicators as the measuring stick for "success." Wolfgang Sachs, a German economics professor, points out that development always looks at others in terms of what they lack.[81]

While development theory has changed considerably since 1949, I think we still tend to define development in economic terms and still tend to focus on what's lacking. I wonder what a Christian spirituality of development might look like.

During some recent studies, I had the opportunity to look at Anabaptist history from the perspective of power. I identified five areas of power that I find relevant for development work today.

1. The power of goodness

The Anabaptists had an optimistic view of human nature. They believed that the presence of God in creation enables humankind to distinguish between good and evil and to choose to turn toward good. Grace nurtures the essence of goodness within us and enables us to grow in the divine image.

Development—An Anabaptist development model would focus optimistically on how life is present in a particular situation or group rather than emphasizing what is lacking. Key questions for development workers would be:

- How is life present?

- What "time" is it? (based on the Hebrew under-standing of time as season, i.e., a time to plant and a time to harvest, a time to break down and a time to build up . . .)

2. The power of free choice

The power of free choice was the basis for the An-abaptists' belief in nonviolence, the separation of church and state, and adult baptism. Their understanding of non-violence went beyond the belief that Christians should not take up the sword. They also believed that it was wrong to force someone to accept a particular position through threat and coercion.

Development—Tapping into the power of free choice stretch-es my understanding of nonviolence. It means not forcing others to accept my ideas even when they are good ones. All development workers and funding agencies have to deal with issues of control, both personally and institutionally. The power of free choice challenges us to lead in a way that genuinely allows others to make their own choices.

Living the power of free choice in the communities where we work requires development workers to:
- Deal with personal issues such as the need to see im-mediate results and the need to be needed.
- Recognize the ways we are both powerful and power-less. I may feel powerless in the face of overwhelming odds, but my neighbors perceive me as powerful.
- Recognize that money isn't mine to control but ours to use for the common good.
- Understand that the heart of sharing resources is kindness and justice, not control or economic "solu-tions."

3. The power of the faith community

The Anabaptists believed that the church is the body of Christ and that the faith community lives out Jesus' Incarnation. The early Anabaptists weren't highly educated or powerful. A Dutch martyr described the community of believers as a "poor, simple, cast-off little flock . . ."

Development—The Anabaptist understanding of the power of the faith community brings two key elements to current development work: The church as the ongoing Incarnation, and God's love for the poor.

Believing that the Incarnation is ongoing means recognizing that Jesus is being crucified in those suffering from famine, war, injustice, abuse. It also means recognizing that Jesus is resurrected in our efforts to live out the Kingdom of God, which he came to inaugurate.

Jon Sobrino, a Latin American theologian, writes that it's time to take Third World people down from the cross. Taking those who are suffering off the cross is a bloody, messy task. Accompanying them demands that we risk confusion and powerlessness, trusting that somehow, in some way, the resurrected Lord will come to us.

Henri Nouwen points out that power doesn't allow room for intimacy, and that God wants to enter into intimate relationship with us.

As development workers, we can choose to protect ourselves or to allow others to see our vulnerability. The way of the Incarnation challenges us to let down our defenses and share our lives with our neighbors.

4. The power of suffering

The Anabaptists' belief in the separation of church and state, and their emphasis on transformed lives, resulted in alienating both church and civil authorities. Intense persecution forced the Anabaptists to come to terms with suffering. "The only true church is the suffering church," wrote Menno Simons.

Development—Living the Incarnation will inevitably result in suffering. If Jesus lives in us as the Body of Christ, then we are no longer outside observers of his passion, but participants.

As development workers who ask hard questions about why people are dying, why children don't have enough to eat, why resources aren't justly distributed, we will experience opposition. We will come to know the costly, purifying grace of sharing Christ's death and resurrection.

5. The power of surrender

The German word *gelassenheit* is still used today to express the Anabaptist understanding of surrender to God. I believe that *gelassenheit*, which means surrender, yieldedness, and detachment, is the foundation for all other sources of power.

Development—Gelassenheit does not mean passively surrendering to injustice, but surrendering to God whose love empowers us to stand against the forces of evil. The challenge of living our theology of service forces us to search for a spirituality to sustain us. We are invited to yield ourselves ever more deeply to:

- God who created us in love and goodness,
- God who enables us to choose life,
- God manifest in the ongoing Incarnation,
- God who brings life out of death and hope out of suffering.

Tapping into the power of surrendering to the God of love will put us on the cutting edge of socially relevant living. It will result in development work that both nourishes good and denounces evil. Do we have the courage to allow ourselves to be led by such a God?

Carrying Tortillas into the Ivory Tower and Theories into Mud Houses:
Connecting Competing Realities Along the Path of Service

Ann Graber Hershberger

*Ann Hershberger teaches nursing at Eastern Menno-
nite University. She has worked with MCC- and Rosedale
Missions-sponsored health programs in Nicaragua and El
Salvador. After an extended stay in Central America, she
completed her Ph.D. in nursing and returned to teaching.
She currently serves on the MCC East Coast, U.S. and
Bi-National boards and has chaired the East Coast
board. Ann has practiced, specialized in, and teaches international, community, and public health.*

Why have I chosen this occupational path?

While I would like to label myself a grassroots health
worker, I must admit that I have spent more time in academia than anywhere else. Even so, my closest connections
have been with the grassroots, and I've dabbled in policy.

My path has been winding, but it has essentially been
the same path for the last 20 years. I was formed in a

Mennonite farming community and taught that service to others is an expression of faith in Christ. If a farmer was ill or injured, his crops were planted or harvested by neighbors who acted out of their faith. Visiting missionaries, often nursing classmates of my mother, stimulated my interest in other cultures and independence from traditional female avenues of service. Coupled with these value-forming experiences was my deep sense that I was predestined for service. My parents, like Hannah, prayed for a child, and when one was finally available for adoption, they also gave thanks and dedicated me for God's service. I grew up surrounded by their thankfulness to God and their prayers.

After college graduation I shunned the tradition of spending several years in hospital nursing to gain experience and traveled instead to Nicaragua to work in rural, nurse-run clinics where there were no government health services. I was culturally and politically naive but determined to use my budding nursing skills to help others. I awoke to find myself in a country in the throes of a revolution, a revolt not only from a dictator but from the financial and political grip of the United States. Living in Nicaragua during the last years and days of the Somoza government and during five years of Sandinista leadership was formative in my developing a commitment to the grassroots, to understanding the lives of everyday people, and to believing in their capacity to direct and change their lives. By observing the Contra war in the 1980s, I formed a deep distrust of the United States government's involvement in other countries.

A second key influence from that time was the current of change in international health. The UNICEF/WHO conference at Alma Ata in 1978 set the stage for the concept of Primary Health Care (PHC), a philosophy of healthcare delivery which values local input. I had good access to the writings and discussions of PHC through Nicaraguan health professionals who were at the forefront of developing and implementing PHC in their country even before Alma Ata. I became involved in PHC programs, working with local health committees and training and supervising lay health workers as the concepts were being developed in international health policy circles. In my opinion, there was no trickle-down effect; I saw it as a trickle-up. My experience with country NGOs was more positive than my experience with governments.

A third stream of influence on me in those early years was liberation theology and its espousal of options for the poor. The theology contradicted some of my Anabaptist theology, including the problem of violence. However, my faith was deepened and strengthened from my interaction with persons who not only believed in God's preferential option for the poor, but who also gave their lives, sometimes literally, to serving with the poor. While some of those persons were in positions where they could influence policy issues, they all remained rooted and grounded in a base community to stay in touch with everyday life.

An additional incident shaped my view of development. After the El Salvador experience in 1983, my husband and I faced a crossroads. From contacts earlier in Nicaragua and through my masters program, my name reached a USAID-funded NGO called Project Hope. We were approached by the Project and asked to consider directing an enormous rural health project in all of northern El Salvador. The job offer was extremely lucrative. We interviewed and were horrified at the confidence in and resources available for an obviously doomed project, since much of the planned activity and infrastructure were in guerrilla-controlled territory. We were not sure whether this was a complete cover operation for U.S. military objectives or an absolute misunderstanding of the situation due to ignorance. Thus, our views of large NGOs with U.S.-government funding were shaped, and we became almost completely cynical about any group connected to USAID or other government-funded sources.

There are parallel paths of service and education, and I have walked on them alternately. After graduation from Eastern Mennonite College (now University) in 1976, I spent three years with Rosedale Mennonite Missions in Nicaragua. I met Jim Hershberger there, and after months of working and traveling together in a lay health-worker program in the context of community development, we decided we would much rather walk the path of service together.

I taught nursing at Eastern Mennonite University (EMU) and eventually completed a community health nursing masters program. While Jim worked on a masters degree in Latin American history, we volunteered for a six-month term with MCC in El Salvador in a displaced persons camp in the war zone.

We returned to the States and I went back to teaching. But within a few years, Jim began talking about doing a longer term of service with MCC. I was enjoying teaching and needed to be convinced. But I knew intuitively that I was not ready to face the power that accumulated easily in the academic setting; I needed to be re-informed about grassroots life and people with little power. We began a four-year term in Nicaragua in 1985 and extended for one more year.

Since 1990 I have been teaching again, until a sabbatical last year during which I returned to school to pursue a doctorate. Does this move seal my marriage with academia, or am I still free to follow other service dreams as well? I am also now part of the board structure of Mennonite Central Committee (MCC). There is plenty of power available in both settings. Am I ready to hold and exercise this power? The answers to these questions likely depend on the influences I have experienced along the way and on what I choose to do with those influences.

From the time I entered nursing I have been drawn to teaching. I have been a teacher of patients, expectant parents, experienced nurses, lay health workers, church social outreach workers, nursing students, cross-cultural students, and senior ethics students. The mentoring and the relationships I can enjoy in teaching give me life. Passing on my own experiences, helping birth the ideas and experiences of others, and then watching them grow and develop way beyond what I could offer, gives me joy and motivation to continue.

What has been my experience?

I've had both joys and frustrations during the last 20-plus years. My greatest joy comes from the relationships I've formed over the years.

Graciela Garcia was a teenager in the village where I first worked in 1977. She came looking for work in the newly formed clinic and was approved by the community committee. We trained her as a receptionist and then as a pharmacy aide. I enjoyed her wit, her eagerness to learn, and her wisdom. She taught us about culture, community power, and politics and shared her family with us. Graciela married and had two sons who are now in high school. She's worked for more than a decade at a government health center pharmacy. Several months ago I received these words in a letter from her, sent over 20 years after that first encounter. "I want to thank you again for teaching me how to work. My life and my family's life is different because of being with all of you in the clinic."

Marcos Orosco is another friend from that first clinic experience. As he related to us, he chose to become a Christian, and then a lay health worker, carrying the work of the clinic when we nurses were forced to leave at the height of the war in 1979. He later became president of the Mennonite Church in Nicaragua and represents Nicaragua at the Mennonite World Conference table.

Miguel Mendoza and Ignacio Gutierrez are pastors of small churches and are deeply involved in local and conference outreach. We worked closely with them under an MCC assignment 1985-1990, seeking ways together to affect change in communities and churches and studying the biblical basis of service to others. They became our personal standards of faithfulness as a family as we observed them sacrificing more lucrative jobs to serve the local church and community. Sometimes when we are contemplating whether we really need a potential family or household expenditure we ask ourselves what would Ignacio and Miguel think about this.

We have continuing relationships with professional colleagues as well. Hernaldo Lara lived with our family from 1987-1990 when he needed to move to Managua for medical school. During the time he lived with us, he, and then MCC, were part of creating a nongovernmental organization formed to respond to health care needs of the population on the east coast of Nicaragua. I have been moved to see dedicated professionals put their faith and convictions into practice in a way that benefited so many others. Over the years we have shared personally and professionally with Hernaldo and hope to collaborate on a research project in the next year.

Likewise, Lidya Zamora, director of a nursing school, provided a professional connection for me in nursing. We remained friends through her time of study in the U.S. in the early 1990s, and now her daughter lives with us as she begins her first year at Eastern Mennonite University.

In my 12 years at EMU I have developed another long list of relationships that were and are still very important. Teachers relate to students at vulnerable times in their lives, often when they are making major decisions. I consider myself to be walking on holy ground when I am able to accompany a student through such choices. Persons whom I taught have become my advisors and even supervisors. Former students remain friends of our children and will likely provide them with guidance in the future.

But I've also struggled with several issues that come with teaching. I'm tempted to believe that teaching and health-related work are inherently more faithful to the gospel than many occupations. With that comes the temptation to arrogance one experiences when comparing oneself to others. I want always to be cognizant of the tendency to be arrogant. I frequently remind myself of the Bible story of Elijah who complained to God that he was the only faithful prophet left in Israel. God instructed Elijah about what he should do next, and then added that Elijah should go looking for the more than 7000 other faithful souls in Israel who had never bowed down to Baal.

I stew sometimes about income, even as I am grateful not to be burdened with the decisions that accompany a larger salary. I am confident that my work is valuable to humanity and to the church's mission of sharing in the God-given ministry of reconciliation. Yet it is difficult to see Mennonites who choose to work at a policy or structural level make a lot more money than our family. I do not believe those positions are inherently more effective in serving the world. I believe that a simple lifestyle and concerns about money are necessary to remain in touch with those we serve, but it is difficult to struggle with having less than many of my colleagues. I get tired of calculating what effect buying a Coke will have on our family budget, when those around me seem to think nothing of eating out frequently. At the same time I have a quiet satisfaction when we are able to give our tithe so that others gain an education or when we realize that our choices of expenditures have not led us down a path that ties us to a certain level of income. Nevertheless, we feel as though we do teeter on an edge. In fact, some of our acquaintances tell us that we are not making good use of the talents God's given us, that we should seek to make more so that we can give more.

Related to my tendency to arrogance is what I call the "cancel-out effect." I know both good development principles and very bad development projects. I am much closer to the people affected by grand projects than to the shapers and funders of those projects. I have learned to predict when a project or parts of a project will not be a success, and so I find myself wanting to protect a community or group from yet another impossible good idea from someone not personally involved. In so doing, I, too, become paternalistic, even as I accuse others of being so in their project design. Then, because I insist that something must be done the "right" way, I end up neither doing nor supporting any projects at all. I've come to realize that too often my life gives credence to the ivory tower stereotype.

Have I made a difference?

The relationships I hastily listed in the previous section form the basis for any contribution or difference I have made in development. I am convinced I have made a difference in terms of mentoring and encouraging individuals in their own work. The villages of Puertas Viejas and San Jeronimo and others are healthier because of my work. The Mennonite churches of Nicaragua have a different view of service to others than they might have had otherwise. Some EMU nursing graduates and alumni of cross-cultural groups which Jim and I have led see the world differently and work differently than their colleagues. Former nursing students are working in positions where they have relationships with Ministers of Health, they can organize programs for regions of a country or large city, they are involved in large community research projects, and yet they remain in close touch with the grassroots.

There are few impressive empirical indicators of my success. I do believe I have been able to reach a myriad of people through those I have taught and mentored. And I believe there is a qualitative difference in the lives of many people as a result of my commitment and service.

What would I have done differently, given the opportunity?

I think more about what I would *not* do differently than of what I would change. I would not trade the abiding relationships I've been part of. What they gave—and continue to give—to me, and what I gave and give in return, is precious. I believe they keep me on a path God smiles on. I am basically content with my choices.

I would make changes in my undergraduate education. I wish I had been encouraged to take courses in political science and international economics. On the other hand, there was not much space to maneuver in a nursing curriculum, and I would not give up the few electives I had, like touring choir and ornithology, courses which have provided me with a sense of the holy in life, no matter where I have found myself.

I wish I had remained more closely in touch with development projects while I was teaching. That is easier said than done in a small Christian university where research and service are not well funded and during the time when we had small children at home. We have remained in touch with grassroots life here in Harrisonburg by including foster children in our family and by developing friendships with new immigrants. However, I would like to have been involved in development projects here. We have resolved this somewhat by Jim and me dividing our time commitments. Currently he is the one volunteering at the local level, working with a broad-based community development coalition. Our primary commitment is to our family, although that includes modeling a commitment to our community and world.

What are the growing edges?

I am in a terminal degree program and am planning to do a dissertation in international health policy. I have become part of the board structure of MCC. Given my background and the assertions I've made in this paper about the importance of grassroots connections and the dangers surrounding the use of power, those moves may seem inconsistent. Am I tired of the economic struggle and just want to make more money? Have I come to believe that the most important work is done at the policy level? Where will these actions lead me?

In my attraction to teaching I have come to understand that I have been given a love of learning, both experiential and academic. I enjoy considering ideas and theories. I cherish the gift of a sabbatical year in which I can study, an opportunity so few have. My passion for learning is a God-given gift, and I am responsible to use that gift wisely. To continue to be an effective teacher I need to reflect and learn.

I am less absolute than I was 20 years ago about what constitutes compromise. I have seen God work in many ways. I have also made enough friendships over the years with folks in the policy world to recognize that they are not all pawns of United States foreign policy. Of course they have their own issues and struggles, but many of the persons I have interacted with desire to serve God faithfully.

What does the future hold?

The combination of these influences past and present, and my personal characteristics, make me want to be a bridge, a connection between worlds that do not know or understand each other. Why do I now feel ready or able to encounter the policy world I once shunned?

As I look back I realize that I never kept myself as separate as I thought I was doing. Even in high school and college I engaged policy issues. When I went to Nicaragua as a neophyte nurse, my first request to my parents for materials was not for childbirth books but for my senior course materials on change theory. When I look through files I find documents I sent to mission administrators about why their focus needed to change to community-led primary healthcare as opposed to foreign-nurse-run clinics.

I still believe it is not possible to be maximally effective at a policy level without maintaining close and long-term relationships at the grassroots level. I will continue to advocate for that kind of involvement and facilitate those experiences as I can with those at a policy level. At the same time, I do not believe it is possible to be maximally effective at a grassroots level without an understanding of and access to the thought and currents at the bi- and multilateral levels of program and policy. The various parts need each other. The parts of the body, as the apostle Paul said in Corinthians, dare not say to each other, you are only an eye, or you are only a foot; we do not need you.

There are pitfalls and a potential for dangerous compromise along the way. At this point in my life I feel grounded and rooted enough in the grassroots to have a context for the ideas and concepts coming from the policy level. I know I need the knowledge and expertise of those at the policy level. But I will be quick to ask my questions about ethics and compromise as I encounter new ways of seeing the development world. But I want to ask those questions from within relationships.

As I encounter the almost sacred Jeffersonian spirit in the halls of the University of Virginia, I find I think very differently than most of my colleagues and the faculty. Graciela, Marcos, Ignacio, Miguel, Lidya, Hernaldo, Jeanette, Fred, and a host of others accompany me into class discussions about the definition and source of knowledge, into readings about statistics and grounded theory, into papers about health and the quality of life, and into class presentations about the politics of economic reform. I also take with me and reread frequently the New Testament Corinthian passages about true knowledge and wisdom, as well as the Old Testament's stories of Daniel's use of power in the court.

My goal is to comfortably carry theory into a mud house and tortillas into the ivory tower. My commitment is to carry out service wherever I am with individuals and with institutions from the base of a relationship with Jesus Christ.

Development and Peace: *You Can't Have One Without the Other*

Janice Jenner

Janice Jenner is the director of the Institute for Justice and Peacebuilding, the practice arm of the Conflict Transformation Program at Eastern Mennonite University. She served with Mennonite Central Committee from 1989-1996 as country co-representative in Kenya where she worked with community peacebuilding groups throughout the country, especially with women and religious organizations. She has authored or co-authored several publications and holds a masters degree in conflict transformation from Eastern Mennonite University.

Why have I chosen this occupational path?

Currently I work with the Conflict Transformation Program at Eastern Mennonite University as a Program Associate for Networking and Grants Coordination. Twenty years ago, or 10, or even five years ago, had I been told I would be doing this kind of work, I would have laughed. I'm not sure that I chose this career path. Rather, I think it occurred through a series of steps which now make sense, but which I certainly didn't plan beforehand. "How have I *flowed* into this occupation?" might be a better question for opening a discussion about my journey.

Perhaps my personal history will give some helpful background. I have Mennonite ancestry and genetic material, although I was raised in a non-Mennonite home in a heavily Mennonite area. During college days, I found my home in the Mennonite church. I continue to find the Mennonite church, with all its warts and foibles, the place where I fit spiritually and communally. (I sometimes wonder how much of the Mennonite ethos was passed down to me from generations past through two generations of non-Mennonites.)

Following college, I did a term of voluntary service (VS) with the Mennonite Board of Missions for 18 months, part of a youthful protest against the Vietnam War and the fact that as a woman I could not register as a conscientious objector. "Service" was the key word; "development" as it is used in this volume was not a part of my vocabulary. During VS and following, I worked in the field of vocational rehabilitation for several years. "Service" remained an important part of who I was and what I wanted to be.

After marrying, my husband, Hadley, and I moved to Anchorage, Alaska, where we lived for nine years and where our three children were born. During this time, in addition to the intense work of mothering three young children, I continued to work, both paid and volunteer, in a variety of social service positions. At some point, the urge toward more adventure and a desire to experience the world outside North America led Hadley and me to consider "service." Again, "development" was not a part of my vocabulary.

After a process of discernment and with a growing sense of excitement, Hadley and I and our three children, ages six, three, and almost two, set off to do "service" in Kenya as MCC Country Representatives. Somewhere in the process of applying to, being accepted for, being oriented by, and being sent to Kenya by MCC, the word "development" began to enter my consciousness, but from the clarity of hindsight, I think that I used it as a more fashionable synonym for "service." In my mind, I used both words chiefly to distinguish my work from "mission work," which at that time in my life was a phrase with which I was decidedly uncomfortable.

I landed in Kenya, inexperienced and naive, without a lot of relevant education or knowledge, with three very young children, and with the idealism that Hadley and I would somehow make a difference. I was there to "be of service and do development." I returned to the U.S. seven years later, much less naive, with a greatly enlarged worldview, probably a bit more cynical, able to talk the language of development, and with more questions than answers.

I also realized in a very internal, very deep part of my soul, that for my children and grandchildren to survive, the children and grandchildren of the people I came to know and cherish in Kenya were also going to have to survive. We no longer had the option of living separate lives on separate continents. My world, and the world of my Kenyan friends, is extremely different from the worlds of our grandmothers, and very different from the world in which our grandchildren will live. Either we will all learn to survive together, or we will all perish together.

During my time in Kenya, because I interacted with the world of "development," many of my deeply held ideas were challenged and reshaped. I became radicalized in many important ways, and I came to realize that for me the path to continued faithfulness lay in pursuing something called "peacebuilding."

Unlike my move to Kenya, to which I gave comparatively little thought, my move to the Conflict Transformation Program here at Eastern Mennonite University has been very deliberate. It was the step I needed to take in order to be faithful to fulfilling my part of the body of Christ, to work toward the vision of the New Jerusalem. Peace and development cannot be separated. Without peace, development, in whatever sense, cannot occur. And peace without development cannot be sustained. I believe that we Anabaptists can—and must—help to articulate this holistic understanding of the relationship between peace and development. I believe we must support those people around the world who are working to make their communities stable, sustainable, and peaceful.

What has been my experience?

While my husband and I were MCC co-representatives for Kenya from 1989-1996, I had the opportunity to work with many Kenyans in many parts of the country, both in fairly straight-line "development" projects, and, as time went on, in the overlap between peacebuilding and development activities. I am very grateful for MCC's emphasis on developing relationships as an integral part of its programming. The people with whom I worked became friends, not just professional colleagues.

One of the many things I learned in Kenya is the power of stories, of sharing personal experiences and understandings. So to explain my experiences I will tell a story about what happened during and following a series of violent conflicts in Kenya.

In 1991, when we'd been in Kenya a bit over two years, the push for democratization became intense. In late November the president, under strong internal and international pressure, announced that opposition political parties would be legalized and that multi-party elections would be held. Hadley and I happened to be in a small ethnic-Somali town in northeastern Kenya that night, and I will never forget the joy with which that announcement was greeted. Radios blared the news into the streets and people chattered, shouted, and sang through the evening. It became clear very soon that people's perceptions of this change were not only political; these changes also had many economic/development dimensions. The talk on the streets was of an end to corruption, of better health care, of improved schools, of more jobs.

However, within six weeks fighting between ethnic groups began in western Kenya, some linked by the government to opposition groups and others by the opposition groups to the government. Within 18 months, 2000 people had been killed in western and in northeastern Kenya, and at least 350,000 people were internally displaced. While these losses were dwarfed by some of the larger conflicts in countries surrounding Kenya, the loss for individual families and communities was just as intense. I've come to see that it's impossible to quantify suffering.

During the months following the fighting, I visited with Kenya Mennonite church leaders and others from several of the affected areas, and I saw for the first time the effects of large-scale violence. I saw burned fields and houses, destroyed schools, shops, churches, and clinics, and I visited many graves. I heard the stories of people who had lost everything—family members, material possessions, and their sense of personal safety and security. I saw years of development work destroyed almost overnight.

Over the next several years, MCC worked with the results of this violence in a number of ways. We provided relief supplies through Mennonite and other churches;

we sponsored informal schools for children in the displaced camps; we organized learning trips for Kenyans from unaffected areas to visit the areas of violence. I worked with a coalition of groups working for peace, justice, and human rights, made up of Kenyan and international nongovernmental organizations and religious groups. The coalition came to be known as the Kenya Peace and Development Network, or PeaceNet. (Note the link between peace and development.)

This link between peace and development became more and more clear to me as time went on and as I worked more closely with victims of organized violence, whether Kenyans or refugees from neighboring countries which were disintegrating. As I saw the aftermath of the violence, it became clear that, despite the relatively minor scale of Kenya's violence, it would take years for Kenya to recover. Some small examples:

A great many of the families who were displaced during the ethnic fighting were solid, middle-class Kenyan families, well able to support themselves and to send their children to primary and secondary schools, and even on to higher education. When we left Kenya in 1996, some of the children from these families had been out of school for four years with little hope of returning. A generation of educated citizens has been lost to Kenya, and these children and the wider society will pay the price for years. Development projects for these youth are now aimed at preventing HIV and prostitution and providing low-level job skills for employment markets that may or may not exist.

The number of street children, the level of prostitution, and the incidence of violent street crime has increased dramatically in Nairobi and other Kenyan cities. Though not all of this increase can be blamed directly on the ethnic violence, surveys by the Catholic church and others have indicated that many of these problems are caused by displaced, formerly middle-class, self-supporting farming families now living in terrible conditions in the slums of the cities, with few options for existence other than begging or crime.

The amount of resources expended by the Kenyan government, NGOs, religious organizations, and the international community to ameliorate the effects of this violence has been enormous. To paraphrase President Eisenhower's famous line, "Every dollar that MCC spent for relief food and blankets was a dollar that did not go into development of communities." Although Kenya's violent conflicts are small compared to the violence in other places in the world, the costs—physical, emotional, and spiritual—are, I believe, being borne by all communities of the world, not just those specifically affected ones.

What was the response—internationally, nationally, and locally—to Kenya's violence? Internationally, the United Nations Development Programme took the lead in rehabilitating areas affected by the violence. In the opinion of many Kenyans for whom I have great respect, it was an unmitigated disaster. In many ways it compounded already bad situations and re-victimized displaced people and others suffering from the effects of violence. The program was a model of stepping on local institutions, being co-opted by powerful people and institutions, and operating very much out of sight of the people it was purportedly serving. Many governments also provided assistance, either through the UN, through the Kenyan government, or increasingly through NGOs.

What did the NGOs and religious organizations provide? A lot of relief. NGOs and religious organizations are good at providing relief. They basically know how to do it, it involves a lot more "how" than "why" questions, and it fills very obvious human needs.

On the whole, they did it fairly well. Some dubious NGOs appeared, and some corruption in distribution was evident, but on a short-term basis, relief supplies were provided, displaced camps were set up, and water supplies were brought in. Did these efforts address the long-term issues, either development or peace? No.

Churches provided ongoing relief and assistance to people in the displaced camps, in the slums of the various cities, and to those who were able to return to their lands. They offered spiritual and emotional support to victimized and suffering people. Though many churches were involved, the Catholic Church in particular deserves mention, because their priests and nuns worked for months and years under extremely difficult conditions, providing hope for people who had lost reason to hope.

Advocacy and human rights concerns were very much a part of the response of NGOs and religious groups. They spent a lot of effort, much of it very good, documenting the violence and its effects, reporting on the ongoing situation, and keeping both the Kenyan and international communities informed. Some of these attorneys, human rights workers, and church leaders exhibited great personal courage, taking public, politically unpopular stances at a time when it was dangerous to do so. I have great respect for many of these people.

At the same time, there was a tendency for the analyses of what had happened to be narrow and divisive. Many of these people and groups believed they knew which ethnic groups were the perpetrators and which were the victims. They expended little effort examining the historical grievances of the "perpetrator" groups in order to understand the reasons for their violent actions.

They made few if any attempts to analyze the effects of their statements and work in advocacy. It often appeared as if much of their work further polarized the divisions within Kenya, rather than creating space to find ways to move forward as individual communities or as an entire Kenyan society.

Then there were the conflict resolution and reconciliation workshops. Weekly, we MCC representatives were informed of or invited to conflict resolution workshops held in expensive hotels in Nairobi. Western experts would fly in, give a week of training, and fly home. Later, different experts would fly in to a different hotel, give their week of training to many of the same people, and then fly home. And on and on. I'm sure some of the training was of some benefit, but the overall feeling it gave me was very unpleasant: "We from Europe/North America can come in and in a week of Western training enable you to solve the problems which have been brewing in your country for decades, which exploded recently, and which may explode again even more violently at any time." Recently a colleague at the Conflict Transformation Program returned from a meeting in Great Britain and reported that Africans who attended said almost with one voice that they were "sick of conflict resolution workshops."

Were there positive responses to the violence in Kenya? Definitely, yes. I met some amazing people working at resolving conflicts in their own communities. I will briefly introduce just two of them.

I came to know Rev. Korir arap Kaptich[82] while MCC worked with a large Protestant church doing relief and informal education in some of the areas affected by the fighting. Rev. Korir was a young pastor, married with several small children. He belonged to the ethnic group that committed much of the violence; his parish was in the

middle of some of the worst destruction and resulting societal upheaval,

Rev. Korir, unlike most people from any of the ethnic
groups, was able to make his way between the opposing
parties. He was welcomed in the displaced persons camp
where he worked with those whom his own people had
victimized. He worked with his own people, helping them
to come to terms with what had happened. He worked
with the "boys in the forest," the young men who had been
lured into fighting with promises of land, education, and
money. The boys received none of the promised rewards,
and they had become outcasts from both groups, living in
hiding in the forested hills in that part of the country. And
he worked with local church leaders from many denominations, cross-ethnically and cross-politically, finding ways
to address the situation in both the short-term and the
long-term. If school fees needed to be reduced for displaced children, Rev. Korir bargained with the schools and
got the children in. When seeds were needed for planting,
somehow he came up with seeds. If reconciliation, repen-
tance, and forgiveness were needed, Rev. Korir dealt with
the hurts and griefs on both sides. When Christianity could
address the issue, Rev. Korir was the pastor; when African
traditions were needed, Rev. Korir became the elder. Rev.
Korir was well acquainted with the historical injustices on
all sides. He articulated clearly his belief that new ways of
living together must be found and that the needs of all
sides must be addressed, both within each community and
within the nation.

Rev. Korir was not often consulted by the UN or
NGOs, and he was not on the lists of invited guests to the
many conflict resolution workshops held in Nairobi. For
the most part he worked anonymously, largely unknown
to Kenya and to the world community.

At the other end of the country, Dekha Ibrahim was a young Somali woman living in the middle of a devastating inter-clan Somali conflict. One day, as she relates it, she decided that, "My children were not going to grow up with violence, and I was going to stop this madness." She helped to organize a small group of women, the "Wajir Women for Peace." That group eventually became a remarkable citizens movement to stop the violence and the killing—The Wajir Peace and Development Committee (note the link between peace and development again). They succeeded in stopping the overt violence and are now working on longer-term development which they believe is necessary to stabilize the peace (see Ibrahim and Jenner, 1998). As with Rev. Korir, the work of this group is wide-reaching and varied, from working with the security forces about how to interact with Somali people, to helping the elders and chiefs define their responsibilities, to sending rapid response teams made up of government and citizen representatives to areas of outbreaks of violence. Like Rev. Korir, the work of the Wajir Peace and Development Committee was largely unknown within or outside Kenya.

It was because of these and other dedicated, selfless Kenyans, working with limited resources and support to restore peace and stability to their countries, that I came to EMU. I was eager to explore academically methods of empowering and encouraging these peacebuilders. After two years of study and reading widely in conflict resolution/transformation theory and practice, I observe that the voices of these community-level peacebuilders are not even part of the conversation. The field of peacebuilding is largely concerned with high-level negotiations, political settlements, and mid- to high-level workshops and round tables.

It's as if the entire field of development talked only about the World Bank and IMF. These organizations are important. I do not discount their value in ending violence and bringing about more stable societies. But the "recognized" story is very incomplete, and my concern is that many people in the field of peacebuilding (and development) seem unaware of that. There are exceptions to this: John Paul Lederach's writings[83] and some of MCC's work[84] (Duba, et al, 1997; Herr and Zimmerman Herr, eds., 1998) are examples of a different focus, but there are few other voices joining in this very thin chorus.

Have I made a difference?

How is it possible to know? Is this even a proper question? Shouldn't the question be about whether I was as faithful or as committed as I should have been, or whether I learned as much as I could have?

By focusing my attention (and that of MCC in Kenya) on local people and groups, I helped to enable them to continue working on issues of peace and reconciliation. I worked to make sure that these folks were not ignored and that their work was validated. By focusing on the contributions made by these community-level people, I believe I encouraged and empowered them to continue working toward bringing about peaceful, stable, and sustainable communities.

Many of the local groups that MCC supported during those years (and in some cases continues to support) have thrived and have explored new ways peacebuilding. Hearing of these continued efforts gives me great personal satisfaction, but did my work make a difference in what's happening now? I don't know.

What would I have done differently?

I would have had better academic preparation before I went to Kenya. I would have had a better starting point if I had done more study in sociology and anthropology, economics, development theory, and gender issues.

I wish I had concentrated on systems earlier on in my experience—the linking of the micro and macro, the interplay between the social, the religious, the political, and the personal. I wish I had trusted my instincts more and given more validity to my own story and history. I wish I had challenged MCC standard practice (for example, grassroots orientation is better, too much money is harmful, relationships are central, and so on) more often. I would have asked more "why" and "why not" questions rather than "how" questions.

What are the growing edges?

I am most interested in and concerned about the overlap of development and peacebuilding. How can we address these areas in a way that is helpful to people in very different situations around the world, but who share common human interests? We all want to live in a stable, peaceful, and just society and to raise our children there, safe from both the overt violence of war and the covert violence of injustice and poverty.

For me, the growing edge in the peacebuilding aspect of development is to enable local peacebuilders to have their voices be part of the conversation about peacebuilding and development. These voices are not present now, and, in the lobbies of power, decisions are made without anyone even being aware that these voices are being ignored.

The history of liberation theology expresses some of this growing edge for me. In Latin America, communities of people came to new understandings about the Bible and their Christian faith that differed in some respects from traditional Catholic theology. While the communities in Latin America grew and thrived, they did not have an impact on the powers in the Vatican until "interpreters"— Latin American priests and bishops—translated this new reality into a language that could be understood by the religious hierarchy. I believe that a lot that is happening in communities in Africa and elsewhere has much to say to the field of peacebuilding, but the voices are not heard by the powerful. How can we as Anabaptists, how can I as an Anabaptist, with our history of peacebuilding, help to interpret the work of people like Rev. Korir and Dekha Ibrahim in language that will speak to and transform the powers? For me, this is a challenge and an opportunity.

What does the future hold? What will be the main issues and themes?

I believe that the immediate future will continue to be a time of "wars and rumors of wars" (Matthew 24:6, NIV), and that both the overt violence of armed conflict and the covert violence of unjust political and economic systems will continue. However, I also believe that there will be people in all communities around the world who will continue to "seek peace and pursue it" (Psalm 34:14, NIV).

I think that Anabaptists involved in the peacebuilding side of development will face the same ongoing issues. Where will we focus our resources (financial and human)? How will we position ourselves in relationship to power? How will we bridge the gap between community-level service and top-level policy-making? How can we help to foster dialogue and communication between the various levels and the actors in each?

Can we serve as interpreters between local peace workers like Rev. Korir and institutions of power: the UN, national governments, large NGOs? Can we validate the experiences of these local actors and translate their understandings of what brings about peaceful, stable, and sustainable communities so that the powerful can learn and be transformed?

My hope is that the work of Rev. Korir and Dekha Ibrahim and many, many others will become a part of the conversation about dealing with conflict, violence, and unjust situations. My hope is that the textbooks which students of international relations and conflict transformation will read in the near future will include those who do this on-the-ground work, and that conflict transformation theory will take the understandings and knowledge of these local, indigenous peacemakers very seriously. I think that Anabaptists—and Anabaptist institutions—are well placed to make this dream a reality.

5.
Middle Ground Perspectives

Introduction

The term "middle ground" does not refer directly to a class of development experiences that are conceptually distinct. Rather, the papers in this section represent an orientation somewhere between the grassroots position and the public policy stance, both of which are more clearly defined positions in development theory. However, as will become evident, we suggest that the "middle ground" position, along with the "grassroots," may conceptually be more closely allied to the traditional Anabaptist position than the "policy position." We will expand on this issue in Chapters 8 and 9 of this volume. In this section we include papers by Vernon Jantzi, Luann Martin, and Allan Sauder.

Vernon Jantzi's commitment to development work was sparked by the way in which family and local congregational members related to needs in his home community and surrounding areas. Contact with MCC and mission-board speakers and former workers during his formative years further confirmed his interest. However, in the course of his development work, his understanding of what development was shifted from a "we have the answers" view to the perspective that development is a mutual effort, a process that affects both the "host culture" and the "sending culture."

Jantzi has worked with grassroots-oriented programs, regional efforts, and national government agencies. As a result, he stresses the importance of working to shape public sector policy but, based on his experience, notes how easily one can be co-opted. He describes the tension he experienced between his personal values and the trap of political or program expediency as he related to governmental, bilateral, and multilateral institutions. This happened when he lived separated from relationships that would keep him personally mindful of the challenges of daily life among the poor.

That tension still exists in his current work in higher education and as a consultant. He recognizes the importance of having prophetically oriented persons working within large-scale public-sector development institutions like national governments or organizations such as the World Bank whose development efforts are channeled primarily through national governments. However, he expresses reservations about how much an individual might be able to influence the way massive organizations function without being unduly shaped by those very institutions one sets out to change. His "middle ground" status means that as a university professor and consultant he works for the formulation of values-based, public-sector development policy. But he does that from a platform that is neither exclusively grassroots nor primarily national (typically, a national government ministry) nor global (such as CIDA, USAID, or the World Bank).

Luann Martin works both in the middle ground as well as in public policy. She had experiences early in life which led to her focus on women's issues and to become more keenly aware of the impact of policy decisions on the lives of individual people. Those shaping influences were time in Nicaragua on Goshen (IN) College's Study-Service Trimester and with MCC's Peace Section Office in Washington, D.C., plus seminary courses on liberation theology and women in church and society. Her statement, that "In the absence of legislation, regulations, powerful lobbying groups, or a consumer movement, manufacturers and distributors of breast milk substitutes were highly unlikely to impose restrictions on themselves," illustrates her middle ground work in infant and maternal nutrition and her rationale for working in public policy. Like some others, she wonders if a comfortable lifestyle and being separated from her community of shared values may have eroded her zeal and commitment to social justice. She wonders if she made too many compromises, and where she might be in her career if she had been more creative in combining development work and family life. But she concludes by saying that she is content with her decisions.

Long active in MEDA development after a career in chemistry, Allen Sauder turned toward business as a means of serving the poor. His subsequent career expresses his deep humanitarian identification with groups desiring development. He remains committed to the need to identify with and have empathy and respect for the culture and ethos of the client people. He defines this as ultimately a spiritual issue—"Development is essentially spiritual at its heart"—which is the only way for "true dialogue" to occur. He maintains that a deep commitment to justice and the well-being of the client must energize the development worker and his/her program. Mutually respectful relationships are a critical ingredient for successful development experiences.

Creating an environment where people can help themselves economically and socially is a prerequisite for development. This strong commitment to justice and mutual respect needs to be based on a clear and enforced accountability system between the client and the provider. When that happens, mutual respect and justice can be achieved. Sauder places equal responsibility on the client and the provider, thereby taking a middle position between the recipient and the donor.

The Accidental Development Worker

Vernon E. Jantzi

Vernon Jantzi is currently professor of sociology at Eastern Mennonite University. He completed his doctorate in the Sociology of Development at Cornell University and later worked for 12 years with private and governmental development programs as a resident in Latin America. He also served for six years as director of EMU's graduate program in conflict transformation.

Development is an elusive and oft-maligned term today. In the 1960s when I was first involved in the development enterprise, I could use the word without hesitation and be relatively certain that everyone knew what I meant. Furthermore, I certainly did not have to defend the term. It was very much in fashion. Today that is not necessarily the case. While our underlying assumptions of the relationship between rich and poor societies may remain relatively unchanged, the way we talk about it is certainly different. Peter Berger speaks about biography and history in the life of individuals. Development history provides the setting for my biography. The changes I have noted above are part of who I am. To understand who we are as development professionals, we must understand something about where we entered development's historical stream.

How did I get involved?

I prefer to address the question of *how* I came to be involved rather than *why* I chose this path. It actually happened quite by accident or circumstance. In the 1950s, a variety of reasons attracted me and my peers in our faith community to development. I was strongly encouraged by my family and congregation to consider some type of voluntary service. As youngsters, we looked up to the Pax Boys who were in Europe rebuilding, crossing the ocean on cattle ships, building the Trans-Chaco Highway in Paraguay, or doing some other such exotic endeavor. They were our heroes. What could be more exciting than doing good and having fun?

It was clear to us that we North Americans had a responsibility to help the rest of the world. We sent relief bundles, quilts and comforters, cattle, and technology, and we taught people how to do things. We did all of this in the name of Jesus and as an expression of the Mennonite church's concern for people in need throughout the world. We were needed, especially those of us who were carpenters, nurses, and engineers, or who grew up on farms and had those practical skills. We intended to meet human need at its most individual level. We envisioned ourselves linked with common people like we were.

Our commitment to practical service was so deep that we couldn't imagine serving without getting our hands dirty. Helping with Mennonite Disaster Service emphasized this for my peers and me as our parents dragged us to disaster scenes to help clean up. Service was a dirty job. As a teenager I did not know that there was such a thing as development. But I did know that many young people, men in particular, left home to do a stint of alternative service in hospitals, experimental farms, and sometimes even in other countries through PAX, and later as MCC volunteers. That is what I wanted to do.

I was especially attracted by the possibility of doing something in Latin America where I could practice and refine the Spanish I had studied in high school and college. In the '60s at EMC, as EMU was then known, I had the opportunity to meet representatives from Mennonite mission boards, Mennonite Central Committee, and a few other agencies who made regular visits to Mennonite college campuses to recruit volunteers. My professors, especially Samuel Miller, but others as well, modeled a life of service and personally urged me to consider service in Latin America. But I wondered what I could offer. I had a relatively useless major, or so it appeared to me, for work in Latin America. What good would my foreign languages major—Spanish and German—be if I did not have some skill or special knowledge to take to Latin America?

My lucky break came when my wife, Dorothy, and I were contacted by Justo Gonzalez, a Cuban refugee residing in Costa Rica, who was directing an adult literacy program known as Alfalit, which intended to serve all of Latin America. Professor Gonzalez had learned about Mennonite Voluntary Service and thought that it would be a good way to help staff the office in Costa Rica. I had what he was looking for—no special skill, but the ability to speak Spanish. Only later would I realize how fortunate I was to have the opportunity to work under the supervision of a Latin American who would also be my mentor.

Misfortune moved me from general office work at Alfalit to be the director of Rosedale Mission's voluntary service program in Costa Rica. The director had fallen gravely ill and had to return to the United States. So I unexpectedly found myself at the head of an organization involved in development work, about which I knew nothing. The program focused on agriculture, health, and education. My only skill was that I could speak Spanish. I could speak, but I had nothing to say.

This was the era in which community development was the prominent paradigm in development. I was sociologically illiterate, and I had no sound technical expertise in agriculture, health, or education, so I felt helpless with both the "community" and the "development" parts of the concept. Since development was about transferring knowledge and skills, I found Edgar Nesman, a rural sociologist with technical experience and specialized training in agriculture and extension education. I became a Nesman sponge and eventually used the knowledge I gained from him and my language knowhow to develop training programs in communication skills for the other volunteers and development workers. At last I believed that I had something to contribute to development in Central America.

Crisis of Consciousness: From Transfer to Transformation

My term of service in Costa Rica ended in 1968. At that point I was invited to move to Nicaragua to direct the new national literacy program that the Protestant churches had asked Alfalit to initiate there. This was a new challenge. It also fit well with my growing awareness that in order for development efforts to succeed and have permanence, they had to be institutionalized. The opportunity to develop a Nicaraguan organization that would make adult literacy efforts a permanent part of the church's community development activity seemed like something I could do. I felt that community development required that village-level people assume modern values and skills that would enable them to enter the modernizing sectors of society. Literacy was fundamental for this. It made cooperatives more functional and provided people with basic skills to enhance entrepreneurial activity and foster democratic governance. This was development and I could contribute to it. Literacy work could prepare people to accept modern technology, practices, attitudes, and values.

My work with adult literacy put me in several settings that began to cast some doubt over the certainty I had gained regarding development. On one occasion I was in a remote part of Nicaragua. Community folk had gathered in the evening around flickering oil-type, tin-can lamps to entertain themselves. I was in the community to teach them literacy skills so that their lives would be richer. That evening the illiterate and semi-literate folks began to recite poetry by Ruben Dario, one of my favorite Latin American poets. I marveled as I saw how they had memorized poetry and took great pleasure in reciting it publicly. I saw a self-confidence and pride that did not require literacy. Slowly I became aware of the fact that development was as much about the spirit of people as it was about skills and technology. This was a dimension that I had overlooked in my conception of development as something that came primarily from the "developed" world to these underdeveloped regions. That night in remote Nicaragua by the flickering flame I began to see development in a new light. I couldn't see perfectly clearly, but I had the distinct feeling that my understanding was inadequate.

Another group of people in Nicaragua who tested the contours of my development paradigm was the Baptist youth group and their friends mentored by Dr. Gustavo Parajon in the late 1960s. These young people, primarily in high school and university, gathered in large and small groups in lots of different venues to have fun and talk. I loved to joke and tell stories with them. We laughed a lot.

The group was also actively involved in development programs in rural and urban areas. We talked about development, studied Nesman's writings long before they appeared in books, and brainstormed about how to bring progress to Nicaragua. These young people asked hard questions: Why was I in Nicaragua? Why did development seem to be the prerogative of the North? Why would political revolution not be a more effective way of achieving progress in Nicaragua?

They accepted me as a friend, but they raised questions that highlighted the way in which biography and history intersected for me in Nicaragua. How was I, their friend, part of a larger structure that seemed to limit or condition Nicaragua's development? They did not articulate all of these questions so clearly, but, with time, their queries as friend-to-friend forced me to ask questions that had never before occurred to me.

A number of those young people, now approaching middle age, have continued to be friends and mentors to Dorothy and me over the years. Strong relationships of this sort make us aware that development which molds and enriches the human spirit while it works with technology, credit, or health is really a two-way street.

The third encounter that helped reshape my development views was a three-week block of time with Paulo Friere, Ivan Illich, Rubem Alves, and others in Cuernavaca, Mexico, in 1970. This particular experience highlighted the importance of structural issues and our consciousness of them. Reflecting critically about these issues, as well as my place in society in relation to them, began to guide my response to "underdevelopment." In thinking about my development experience, I saw that much of what I had been doing could easily contribute to making Nicaragua worse off than it was before our development efforts began. Literacy, for example, could serve to consolidate oppressive structures rather than change them, as I had previously thought. This left me in a state of confusion. I could see the issues, but at the same time I could see that much of what I had observed in the three-week seminar could also be used to manipulate people for particular political purposes. Nevertheless, enough gray activity had happened during my time in Nicaragua that I had to radically rethink my understanding of development.

One thing was clear, however. Development that was to be transformative and liberating had to take seriously people at the grassroots or it would ultimately be alienating. How is it possible to work meaningfully with structure and yet remain in touch and connected to people at the grassroots? That three-week event in Mexico, and the questions it stirred, fundamentally changed my view of institutional development. Rather than being a vehicle to institutionalize the transfer of skills and knowledge, it would need to empower people to take charge of their own development. Through critical reflection and mobilization, people themselves would transform their communities and society. For those of us committed to the institution of the church, this perspective had radical implications for church planting and church growth.

Graduate School and Enchantment with the Macro

I left Nicaragua in June 1970 for graduate study at Cornell University where I eventually ended up with a Ph.D. in the Sociology of Development. During the five years I spent at Cornell I had the opportunity and luxury to reflect deeply on my previous years of experience. When one is in the middle of day-to-day tasks it is often difficult to spend enough time thinking carefully. During my time at Cornell I came to believe that in order for societies to experience development, someone had to work seriously at the macro level in policy and programs. I became enchanted with the possibility that policy change could radically alter daily life for thousands of peasants, urban laborers, and the socially marginalized.

So in 1997, when the opportunity came to work with a bilingual education program in conjunction with Peru's Ministry of Education, I grabbed it. The program combined an emphasis on cultural revaluation with educational reform, in an attempt to address the social marginalization of large sectors of the Peruvian population. I became increasingly aware that development at the grassroots had to go hand-in-hand with macro efforts.

In the early 1980s I became involved with the issue of land tenure in Costa Rica, under the auspices of a United States Agency for International Development subcontract with Cornell University. Our task was to carry out national land tenure policy through the development and implementation of credit and technical assistance programs in the reformed areas of the country. As good as the land reform program may have appeared, I soon realized that the primary intent was not development, but rather the containment of social unrest. Even so, I thought that something good could come from our efforts.

Before long I saw that working from the position of official power could easily blind well-intentioned persons, including me, to the daily needs of people at the village and hamlet level. E. F. Schumacher's work with the "small is beautiful" concept spoke of "economics as if peo-

ple mattered." Much of my work with land tenure and reform seemed to lack the perspective of "development as
if people mattered." I kept looking for a way to work at
policy development and implementation that had "soul"
or a connectedness to the grassroots. The Christian Base
Community movement within the Catholic church, and
its concern for societal change inspired by the work of
highly committed local groups, looked to me like an attractive alternative to what I had experienced in the circles of official power.

I still wonder whether or not we from the Anabaptist
tradition are too suspicious of official power to ever feel
comfortable working from that base for any significant
length of time. Can the church play a role at the macro
level without selling out the grassroots?

During my time in Central America in the late '80s, numerous peacemaking efforts were made in the region to
stop the wars being waged there. I am particularly aware
of the peace initiatives related to the Contra War. The
church in its broadest sense was very involved in the
peace process in Nicaragua. The church at both local and
national levels provided a social space for representatives
of warring groups to meet. And it facilitated conversations for peace that contributed to the eventual accords
that ended the war. The combination of grassroots and
macro level work seemed to offer a kind of rootedness
that I did not experience in other situations. Personally, I
believe that macro level work is necessary and policy development is essential if we are to stop being ambulance
drivers. Nevertheless, I have not been able to resolve the
matter of ultimate accountability, especially because of
my experience in macro level efforts. I see need, hope,
and possibilities, on the one hand, but the danger of co-
optation on the other.

Did I make a difference?

The question itself implies a particular understanding of development that has linear or unidirectional aspects to it. Though it may sound like a lot of mushy jargon, my experience suggests that the more appropriate question is, "Did we live a difference?" or "Did we experience a collective wholeness as a result of our involvement in a particular place?" Such questions make it more difficult to evaluate a development program, but not impossible.

To adequately evaluate MCC's program in Nicaragua, one would have to track down all of the volunteers who served there, in addition to all the persons in Nicaragua who were affected by the program. The evaluation would focus on a particular time, and it would also have to ask what happened to us in North America, as well as what happened in Nicaragua. Development as if people matter is not limited to what happens in a given locality when the actors have different social and geographical origins.

So did I make a difference? I am not sure. I was a friend. I encouraged people. I tried to foster creativity in my colleagues, but those are always my goals, no matter where I am. I helped teach literacy skills, so I can say that some people can read today because of what I did. I worked to make it possible for people to be resettled on land for which they could receive title. I played a very small role in the peace process in Nicaragua. But I did not change the nature of the relationship between the North and the South. I did not eliminate the need for ambulance drivers. Economically, many of the people with whom I worked are worse off today than they were when I was there.

I helped establish institutions. Does that count? They will most likely become bureaucratically paralyzed, as is usually the case. Does that count? On the other hand, they may empower persons to accomplish things that they would never have been able to do otherwise. People with whom I worked informally gained experience which enabled them to fill important roles that they would have been unprepared to fill had it not been for our relationship.

As I reflect on the question of what difference I made, I must ask how we dare to even raise the question? Isn't it an inappropriate question if we believe that development is ultimately relational, rather than primarily a transfer of technology, skills, ideas, or even visions of the ideal society? If we insist on asking the question, then we must frame it to reflect the relational, or more circular, nature of development, rather than the linear transfer imagery that is often embedded in our talk about development.

What would I have done differently, given the opportunity?

I would probably do much the same as I did. However, I would give more priority to developing relationships. I would also try to pay more attention to the artistic expressions of the people with whom I lived. Since relationships draw on our expressive selves, I believe that appreciating the artistic expressions of the people with whom we live and work strengthens our relationships.

What have been growing edges for me?

Recently I have begun to work much more explicitly with peacebuilding. There is a close relationship between efforts to build an infrastructure for sustainable peace and what has been described as development. Peacemaking has replaced development as the fashion of the day. As such it is exposed to the temptations that attracted development efforts in the past and continue to draw us even today.

We are attracted by the possibility of transferring skills and the central role of training in the peacemaking process. In both peacebuilding and development, we are tempted to grant too much importance to outside persons and groups who are not rooted in local relationships. We are tempted by apparent success in the short term. I want to understand how the lessons we learned in the development effort can inform the peacebuilding enterprise, and vice versa. As Anabaptist persons and institutions committed to peace and wholeness of life, we have a special challenge to bring development and peacebuilding perspectives together. Our rich history should be of some help.

Reflections on
My Experiences in
International Development
Luann Martin

Luann Habegger Martin works for the Academy for Educational Development in Washington, D.C. on a USAID-funded infant and maternal nutrition project. From 1978-1991 she lived overseas and did consultant work for private voluntary organizations (PVOs), UNICEF, and USAID. From 1992-1996 she worked for the Center to Prevent Childhood Malnutrition. Martin has an M.A. degree in international development.

Why have I chosen this occupational path?

There is no short answer to this question, such as, "I wanted to work in the field of international development since I was in grade school." Nor do I have a "call" story to tell, unlike the woman Kathleen Norris describes in her book, *Amazing Grace* (1998). The young seminary student told Norris that she had been called to be a minister so that she could preach sustainable agriculture. Norris wondered if that would be a sustainable ministry.

Growing up, I wanted to be a teacher. For the most part, college-bound girls in Berne, Indiana, in the mid-'60s saw teaching and nursing as the two professions open to them. Goshen College prepared me to teach English and, as is the college's motto, emphasized Culture for Service. My positive experience during a Study-Service Trimester in Nicaragua prompted me several years later to apply to Mennonite Central Committee for the Teachers Abroad Program. I was too late for that year's program, so I applied for a position as a research assistant in the MCC Peace Section Office in Washington, D.C. I spent the next two years in Voluntary Service in Washington, monitoring legislation, writing legislative features for the office's constituent newsletter, and helping organize seminars for church groups, students, and MCC volunteers.

Three important things happened during those years that would shape my career direction. First, I became more knowledgeable of global issues and more keenly aware of the impact of policy decisions on people's lives. Second, I realized that a church concerned about issues of peace and justice should address gender inequalities in church and society. I served on MCC's first Task Force on Women in Church and Society and edited a newsletter on the subject. Third, I met Ray Martin. One day I escorted members of the Peace and Social Concerns Committee to the State Department where Ray, an employee of the Agency for International Development, spoke on "A Mennonite's View of Serving Humanity through the Constructive Functions of Government." I was the only female in the group; Ray was the speaker, so we noticed each other.

Three years later we were married, after a year of separation when I was enrolled in the Peace Studies program at Mennonite Biblical Seminaries. Seminary courses on liberation theology and women in church and society continued to keep me focused on Third-World and gender issues.

Knowing that Ray would soon be assigned overseas, I decided to prepare myself for possible career opportunities by enrolling in a Masters' degree program in international development. During this time I attended an international conference in Mexico focusing on equality, development, and peace—the three themes of the International Women's Year. I wrote a monograph for MCC on women and development and completed an internship at the International Center for Research on Women.

I did the fieldwork for my thesis in Ghana, where we lived from 1978-80. The day after I finished typing my thesis, my daughter was born. And so began another career. For the next six years, I chose to spend my time with my two preschool-age children. When they were in elementary school, I looked for volunteer and consultant work that I could do on a part-time basis. For example, I taught English to Afghan refugee women; wrote about development programs sponsored by USAID, Save the Children, and Catholic Relief Services; and did consultant work for USAID environmental, transport, and training projects.

In some respects, my decision to stay at home with my children delayed a career in international development. In other ways, it heightened my interest in infant nutrition, an area that I continue to work in today. My work in infant nutrition builds on my own personal experiences, my concerns for women's issues, and the policy/advocacy training that I received at the MCC Peace Section Office. I was angered that commercial companies mislead mothers into thinking that there is little difference between the health outcomes of breastfeeding and artificial feeding. In many developing countries, artificial feeding nearly triples the risk of infant death. I was angered that commercial companies convince many women that they are incapable of adequately feeding their children.

After seeing dehydrated babies in a hospital in Quetta, Pakistan, with baby bottles at the head of the bed, I decided to gather information on the status of breastfeeding in Pakistan. In less than one hour, I found 30 different brands of infant formula in three shops in the Quetta bazaar. Over one-third of the brands did not provide feeding instructions in Urdu, in violation of government and World Health Organization directives. I concluded that in the absence of legislation, regulations, powerful lobbying groups, or a consumer movement, manufacturers and distributors of breast milk substitutes were highly unlikely to impose restrictions on themselves.

In a paper I wrote, I proposed research on infant feeding practices of mothers in Pakistan, training of healthcare providers in lactation management, breastfeeding promotion campaigns, policy formulation, and donor collaboration. For the next year I worked with UNICEF, in collaboration with USAID, the Ministry of Health, and the Pakistan Pediatrics Association, in carrying out these activities and mobilizing efforts to promote and protect breastfeeding in Pakistan.

For the past seven years, I have worked on international infant nutrition projects, primarily in an information and advocacy role. This role is similar to the one I had when I worked in the MCC Peace Section Office. I prepare guidelines, technical articles, and policy briefs for program-planners and policy-makers, focusing on the nutritional, health, child-spacing, economic, and environmental benefits of breastfeeding. I also write on issues related to maternal nutrition.

What has been my experience (joys, difficulties, issues)?

I have been privileged to travel extensively and live for extended periods in four countries (Ghana, Cameroon, Zaire, and Pakistan). One of the joys of working in international development has been such experiences as drinking tea with Afghan women in a refugee camp, witnessing the birth of a Ghanaian child on the floor of a mud home, and traveling with Cameroonian women in the wee hours of the morning to sing Easter hymns to fellow church members.

Another pleasure of my career has been the opportunity to work on issues about which I care deeply with a diverse group of committed, talented individuals. These individuals approach development from different perspectives: human rights, social justice, community mobilization, gender equity, or behavior change at the household or institutional level. My associations with people of various persuasions have helped me grow in my own understanding of development.

Along with the satisfaction of seeing people mobilized to address different problems comes the frustration of observing the numerous obstacles that confront individuals who work for change. Whether dealing with infant-formula manufacturers in Pakistan or gun lobbies in the United States, the forces are formidable. One has to fight hard against resignation and cynicism.

Have I made a difference?

Since I don't work on the front lines of development, I am unable to tell stories of how my efforts have made a difference in the lives of specific individuals in a particular community.

Development requires a lot of ordinary and daily small acts, from frontline workers as well as those who are behind the scenes. The impact of these deeds, usually unheralded, may only be evident many years hence, as was the case in Jesus' parable of the mustard seed.

I would like to think that in Pakistan my work contributed to efforts to mobilize health professionals to address detrimental feeding practices that can result in malnutrition, illness, and death. For the past several years my job has been to provide information that educates, sensitizes, and influences program-planners and policy-makers in the areas of infant and maternal nutrition. Based on requests for various publications that I have developed, I know that there is a demand for this information. Have these advocacy materials resulted in changes in attitudes, practices, and policies? That's difficult to say.

The impact of a position paper on maternal nutrition that I co-authored was recently assessed by the funding organization. The evaluator determined that the paper had given impetus to program design for maternal nutrition activities in USAID and a major US-based PVO. The evaluation was subjective; it was also in the interest of the funding organization to show impact. Nevertheless, I do believe that advocacy materials contribute to development efforts for the following reasons:

- Informed choice requires access to clear, accurate information.
- Information can heighten awareness and enhance the policy climate for nutrition activities.
- Equitable access to information reduces the chance that information and knowledge will be used to manipulate and control others.

Having said all this, I want to emphasize that any difference that I or, for that matter, anyone else makes in development depends on a host of factors. Take my work in infant feeding. Information, policies, health services, and community-based activities all have a potential role in affecting infant-feeding practices.

I believe that it's not only *what* I do that can make a difference but *how* I go about doing it. Years ago a supervisor challenged me to find an organization that met my ethical standards. This comment was triggered by my observation that some of the office's billing practices were questionable. I am the one on a staff challenging people to support what they say or write. One colleague remarked that I help to keep everyone honest.

What would I have done differently, given the opportunity?

Sometimes I wonder where I would be if I had worked with Mennonite institutions or pursued a teaching career. Working for a big government development organization can be a treacherous path. In 1978 Ray and I left for Ghana, our first overseas assignment after we were married. My VS experience, seminary training, and development studies filled me with ideals about a simple lifestyle, liberation theology, and basic human needs. When we entered the house that USAID assigned us, Ray and I thought that it was much too big for the two of us. We found a smaller house but were told it wasn't suitable. I would have been appalled to think that 10 years later I would be living in Zaire in a complex of townhouses, complete with a swimming pool and tennis court, with nine other American families, two of them with the CIA!

What happened to me during that decade? Comfort, the duties of family, and separation from a community that shared many of my values may have eroded my zeal and commitment to social justice. I wonder at times if I made too many compromises. At the same time, I am very grateful for the opportunities I had and the friendships I formed during our 13 years overseas with USAID.

Another one of my "I wonder" moments occurs when I reflect on where I am in my career. Where might I be if I had not decided to follow my husband wherever his career took him? When we arrived at a new post, Ray immediately reported to work. I, on the other hand, spent months getting the family established and looking for employment opportunities. In the past year I met three Foreign Service wives whose marriages broke up after 20 years. As they moved with their husbands from post to post, they picked up odd jobs along the way but never established themselves in a career. They now find themselves ill prepared to support a household.

When I see peers in more senior positions, I think that I might be holding such a position if I had devoted myself to a full-time career after graduate school. Knowing my personality, I can imagine working 12 hours a day, including weekends. My family responsibilities, thank goodness, saved me. While I cared for my children, my family nurtured me in ways that no job ever could. So even though I wonder at times what would have happened to me if I had given higher priority to my career, I am content with my decision.

Having said that, I believe that I could have been more creative in combining development work and family life. Several of my personality traits limited me. For one thing, I am not a risk-taker. I prefer structured environments such as language classes and well-defined jobs. I tend toward perfectionism, so I don't like to put myself in situations where I might be embarrassed by sounding like a child learning another language or exposing my ignorance. I also don't like to promote myself, so I am reluctant to try to persuade others that I can provide a service.

I could have had more opportunities if I had been more proactive. Instead of waiting for a job, I should have been more visionary, presenting to others ideas about how I could contribute and looking for ways to make volunteer jobs more fulfilling assignments. For example, one time I approached Habitat for Humanity in Kinshasa and asked about their programs and my potential involvement. I got a lukewarm reception and little information, so I dropped it. I may not have spoken to the right person, or I may have presented myself in a way that suggested I wouldn't be of much service. I gave up too quickly.

As far as my job, there are several things that I would do differently. I wish that I had had more field experiences and fewer "academic exercises" given to conducting literature reviews and assessing the efforts of others. I also wish that I had sought more opportunities to listen to individual stories from those involved in development. My line of work tends toward one-way communication. Although I knew better, I have developed materials with little knowledge of or input from potential users of the information. Time was wasted, and the product collected dust.

At times I have been quick to apply my standards of work to others, failing to appreciate that ownership and utilization of a product by others is the primary consideration. The process of developing a product with the end users may be as valuable as the product itself.

What are the growing edges for me?

I struggle with four particular areas in my work these days: a results-oriented approach, small-scale programs, "quick fix" solutions, and ethical dilemmas.

- **Results-oriented approach**

Congress has applied a lot of pressure on USAID to demonstrate results from its foreign aid program. Before a work planning exercise, a senior vice president from the organization where I work hammered in the need to scrutinize every proposed activity to determine whether it would yield results. In a competitive environment for funds, those projects that cannot show measurable, quantifiable results will likely not be renewed.

I am involved in a behavior change project. Demonstrating behavior change within a fairly short time period and attributing it directly to project activities is very challenging. We spend hours trying to determine the indicators to measure change and the level of change that might reasonably be expected. People go through all kinds of tortuous exercises, filling out matrices and designing charts with arrows going in every direction, to assure themselves and their supervisors that what they are doing will bring results.

As we all know, in development work there are unanticipated results and hidden costs. For example, a new road may make it easier to get crops to market, but it may actually have a detrimental effect on the nutritional status of households that sell rather than consume their crops. The drive for results assumes success, but by whose standard and for whom?

- **Small-scale programs**

Many argue that results come from community-based solutions. In the early days of foreign aid, the emphasis was on infrastructure: roads, dams, hospitals, etc. Benefits were believed to trickle down to the masses. Today I hear a lot about community development, empowerment, and participation—words that resonate with Mennonites.

Although I believe that community-based activities are at the heart of development, they often seem isolated, with limited reach. I recently watched a television program titled "Rebuilding Neighborhood Communities Block by Block." One person after another told how his or her organization was restoring communities through the rehabilitation of housing and microenterprises. Finally a man in the audience stood up and said that he was uncomfortable with this self-congratulatory praise. Block by block, the picture looked encouraging, but on a national level, the supply of affordable housing was decreasing. I believe that community development must occur alongside national efforts to address systemic problems and to mobilize resources for reaching large populations.

- **"Quick fix" solutions**

On the one hand, I am concerned about the block by block, slow pace of community development. On the other hand, I am concerned about the "quick fix" approach to development. For example, micronutrients are popular these days in the nutrition community. In some respects, this represents a largely technical, often top-down solution. Working out the logistics of delivering micronutrients is a lot easier than addressing poverty and food insecurity. Quick fix solutions, beneficial as they may be, sometimes distract people from the socioeconomic and political determinants of malnutrition. A vitamin capsule doesn't fill a hungry child's empty belly.

- **Ethical dilemmas**

The fourth area that I wrestle with in my job relates to ethical issues surrounding breastfeeding and AIDS. Ten years ago the promotion of breastfeeding seemed a noble cause and a critical component of child-survival programs. It is known that breastfeeding saves millions of lives by reducing the risk of morbidity and mortality from diarrhea and pneumonia.

But now it is also known that breast milk can transmit the deadly HIV virus. Approximately 14 percent of children born to HIV-infected mothers are infected by breast-feeding. These children are often born in places where infant deaths are due to infectious diseases such as diarrhea and pneumonia. Given these realities, how should women in areas of high HIV prevalence be counseled, especially since most of them do not know their HIV status? What does informed choice mean if breast milk substitutes are unaffordable and clean water is unavailable to prepare the infant formula?

What does the future hold?

Sometimes I am tempted to leave international development work and devote my attention to domestic issues, especially while I am living in the United States. I am also tempted at times to change employers and work for an organization that views development in spiritual, as well as physical and material, terms and is faith-based rather than project-driven. Working on a project with a fairly limited mandate seems too narrow at times.

I am reminded again of Kathleen Norris's story of the minister who felt called to preach on sustainable agriculture. For the time being, sustainable development is the objective of my work. I don't know where my career will lead in the next 10 years. Maybe I will decide that development work is my true calling. But I hope that I will remember Norris's warning. In *Amazing Grace* she writes, "If a call merely confirms a comfortable self-regard, if God seems to be cleverly assessing our gifts and talents just as we would, I would suggest that it is highly suspect."[85]

Reflections on My Experience in Development

Allan Sauder

Allan Sauder is President of Mennonite Economic Development Associates. Allan previously worked with the International Development Research Centre, Mennonite Central Committee, and Home Hardware Stores, Ltd. He has lived and worked in Tanzania and Bangladesh, and his travels have taken him to more than 60 countries. Allan holds an M.B.A. from the University of Western Ontario and a B.Sc. from the University of Waterloo.

I am grateful for this opportunity to present some reflections on my journey in international development work, not because it has been particularly unique nor totally successful, but because too seldom do I take the time or discipline myself to stop and think about what I am really doing and why. Since I have recently been appointed to a new position within Mennonite Economic Development Associates, it is particularly useful for me to re-examine my own motivations and the beliefs which stand behind the activities for which I am responsible—those of MEDA's international economic development division. Before launching into a discussion of my experience in development, I offer this Haitian proverb, which sometimes seems to sum up my experience in development:

Taking the snake to school is one thing; making it sit is another.

Why have I chosen this occupation path?

Where did my interest in development begin? Was it in
the Sunday evening presentations at St. Jacobs Mennonite Church, when my family attended to hear missionaries and MCC workers returned from far-off lands? Was
it from the Sunday school mission banks where we put
our nickels? Did it come from the strong sense of community that was instilled in me at an early age? Or was it
my sense of adventure, derived in part from the novels of
Somerset Maugham and Graham Greene, which led me
to wander in Europe for a while after high school, and
then for a year and a half throughout New Zealand, Aus-
tralia, and southeast Asia in the middle of my undergraduate studies in chemistry?

In any case, after returning from Asia in 1975, I was
convinced that business makes the world go round—not
chemistry. I decided to switch streams and move into
business studies. When I applied to business school, I realized that I was not primarily interested in accumulating
wealth, but in serving the poor. Although I was not directly connected to a church at that point, I made a commitment to God that if I was accepted into the Masters of
Business Administration program, I would work for the
poor, and not for myself only. Twenty years later I am still
living with that promise.

What has been my experience?

Upon graduation from the University of Western Ontario, my wife and I signed up as volunteers with Mennonite Central Committee in Bangladesh for three years.
I set about applying my newly acquired MBA to assisting
groups of destitute women with marketing their handicrafts. I then accepted an assignment in Pennsylvania

with MCC as Assistant Director of the SELFHELP Crafts program (now called Ten Thousand Villages). Two years later, I moved to a job in Ottawa as Research Officer for the International Development Research Centre (IDRC).

Although I found the secular world of development to be fascinating, especially as viewed from the Vice President's office where I was situated at IDRC, after three years I began to yearn for a more hands-on, practical experience again. At that point I took an assignment with MEDA in Tanzania for three years, followed by stints in Winnipeg and Waterloo as Director of International Operations for MEDA. Now, after 11 years at MEDA, I have recently accepted the position of Executive Vice President, with responsibility for the international economic development division. My current duties include overseeing four departments: consulting, trade, the global investment fund, and international operations.[86]

Have I made a difference?

During a recent family trip to Bangladesh, we had the wonderful opportunity to visit a number of projects with which I worked some 18 years earlier. Some of the projects have grown amazingly and have become fixtures on the development landscape. *Aarong*, a tiny retail handicrafts store established jointly by MCC and the Bangladesh Rural Advancement Committee (BRAC), has grown to become a chain of six stores located in most of the major cities of Bangladesh. The largest is a four-story handicrafts emporium. From its 13-story office/warehouse complex, *Aarong* also ships handmade crafts across the world, serving some 30,000 producers. In another project, about 120 women produce solar-dried coconut powder for the biscuit and candy factories of Bangladesh, replacing a product that was previously imported. Annual sales of over $100,000 in this project have enabled many of these women to invest significantly in their children's education. Another project which started as a glove-making center, using treadle sewing machines donated to MCC, has evolved into a garment factory with 900 employees. On the day we visited they were making and price-tagging nylon plush pants for Wal-Mart Canada.

At MEDA I have been able to witness exciting changes in people's lives as a result of their having access to credit and/or new markets for their produce. In Nicaragua, where we were almost ready to give up on a new credit program in 1990 because of an extremely sluggish economy, a profitable micro-finance facility now exists with a portfolio of $2 million and some 7,000 clients.

While it is wonderful to see the growth and evolution of some of these projects, I find it difficult to connect my daily work with these "successes." All projects are, of course, the result of many persons' ideas and efforts, and most are also subject to the fortunes or misfortunes of happening at the right or wrong time and place within the world of macro politics and economics. However, with few exceptions, I am struck by the importance of putting management and eventual ownership in the hands of local staff and national institutions. Those projects which have remained in the hands of expatriates, however well-meaning, have too often tended to languish.

Have I made a difference? I would say a cautious "yes." In certain projects I have been able to bring some fresh, outside ideas, and in others I have perhaps brought some management disciplines. But, in almost all cases, the ultimate success of the project has depended on the local staff who, through the grace of God and perhaps the networking capacity of the project's leadership, have been inspired to join the project.

What would I have done differently?

It has become a cliché to say that I would have spent more time developing relationships with people. But I believe that the single most important activity of a development manager is finding and nurturing the best staff and the best partnerships. Nurturing relationships with committed persons is the heart of the faith/business/development nexus. It is not only where we have our best shot at making a difference, but I believe it is truly the point where God enters our work.

How does one go about spending more time developing these crucial relationships in the face of an ever pressing workload, with reports to be written, budget spreadsheets to be prepared, tour groups to be entertained, and staff complaints to be resolved? It is not easy, especially in a cross-cultural setting. Too often I have found it easier to do the task myself rather than spending time developing the relationships and understandings which permit effective task delegation. Sometimes the national staff fails to see the importance of the tasks which we consider crucial to success, and sometimes they are right! The net result of failing to develop good working relationships and understanding with national staff and partners is that too often the expatriate development worker burns the midnight oil, neglecting family and health, while national staff and counterparts feel inadequately utilized.

The starting point for developing effective relationships must be genuine respect for the strengths and skills of one's national colleagues, however different their methods may be from those with which we are familiar. I found that one of the best ways to get to know my national colleagues was to travel with them to visit other businesses and development programs within the region. Not only are the long hours together in jeeps or airports an ideal opportunity to get to know your colleagues, but they are given a chance to share in the earliest stages of developing a vision for what could be applied in their own setting.

As a corollary, we must also be prepared to analyze results with our colleagues and to make hard changes when results are not being achieved. Genuine respect includes the right to say: "I respect what you are trying to do, but the results we agreed upon are not being achieved, and something must change." Development programs are often very poor at setting measurable targets with staff and following up with a fair and effective performance evaluation. In some cultures, this Western approach is not commonly applied. Nonetheless, I believe that Christian stewardship compels us to find effective ways to be accountable for human and financial resources, and to hold our staff and partners accountable. I believe accountability to be a universal principle of human society, and that it is possible to find or adapt effective ways of demanding accountability in all settings.

In most cases, staff or partners respond extremely well when given respect, clear expectations, appropriate training, and opportunities for career and personal development. However, there are situations where dishonesty or chronic under-performance demand a change. Firing is difficult anywhere, but in a foreign culture it can be especially troublesome. Employment legislation is often designed to protect the worker despite poor performance. In some cases, the courts may be influenced by the family of the fired person. Occasionally a fired person may resort to more drastic threats. And in most cases, fired staff have very few alternative employment opportunities to support their families. Nonetheless, we do a significant disservice to development when we shy away from these tough decisions, allowing room for financial impropriety or wasted human resources. Therefore, a second thing I would have done differently is to demand more accountability and to have been bolder in making decisions to terminate staff when necessary.

What are the growing edges?

I would like to summarize what I have learned about development from three slightly tangential perspectives. First of all, I believe that development does not happen without a spiritual dimension. I do not believe development is something that one can do for another person.

Development occurs when people or communities have the *vision* and the *options* to make a better life for themselves and for their neighbors. At the heart of this process is a confidence and a belief that things can be better, a hope that is essentially spiritual in the broadest sense. My own motivation to work in development derives from my Christian heritage—a call to justice that compels us to pursue programs that offer options to the disadvantaged and that lead to more equitable distribution of wealth.

Other communities may come to these basic principles from other spiritual traditions, but I maintain that in the absence of genuine concern for the well-being of our immediate neighbors and for the global community as a whole, development is severely jeopardized. We are all too familiar with the problems created by projects which are not people-centered and are often imposed from outside the community.

Second, I believe that economic development is basic to other levels of development. Without a job or other means of securing a reasonable income, one's ability to afford good nutrition, healthcare, educational opportunities, adequate housing, and other basic human needs is severely limited in most societies, and increasingly so in our own. When we speak of grinding poverty, I think we are really referring to the grind of having no options—of having to spend the whole day, every day, gathering firewood, fetching water, and cooking what you know to be a woefully inadequate diet.

At MEDA we promote economic growth with equity to the benefit of, and in partnership with, the disadvantaged. We believe that this is best accomplished through a business-oriented approach that results in sustainable enterprises. We are therefore engaged in programs that offer credit and training services to microenterprises and that make marketing and training services available to small-holder farmers. Most importantly, these services are not offered by a "development project," but by a sustainable and financially viable credit union, farmers' association, or other such business. Central to sustainability is the principle that these services are not offered for free. If the credit, training, or marketing services are genuinely offering new options to small businesses or small farmers, they are services for which the poor can and will gladly pay—thereby assuring future sustainability. Thus, sustainable and equitable economic development is my second tenet.

Finally, development of even the most basic microenterprises, such as street hawkers who carry their entire inventory on their heads, or community-centered businesses such as marketing associations, requires an adequate enabling environment. In our global world, the farmer in the most remote village in Africa, or the slum-dweller in Port-au-Prince, Haiti, are as surely affected by global business as is the banker in London, England, or the grocery-store owner in Harrisonburg, Virginia. The global inter-relationships of trade policies, interest rates, currency regulations, and political stability are in many cases at the root of economic inequities.

Although many of us are disturbed when foreign aid budgets are targeted for cuts or realignments, we should remember that the real impact of these budgets is miniscule compared to the global effects of international trade and investment. I am not an expert in these matters. I am, however, convinced that global imbalances can only be addressed when we understand them and when we are committed to doing something about them. These are very complex issues and will require a generation of highly trained and experienced managers. I hope that some of the graduates of the Anabaptist colleges, as well as many of our overseas colleagues, will not shy away from taking positions within international businesses and organizations that interact with international businesses. I hope that we can take our faith and our people-centered development approach into this world.

To summarize, I believe that some of the growing edges of development are closely related to these three perspectives and lead to the following questions:

1. If development is essentially spiritual at its heart, how do we as development workers effectively share spirituality in a true dialogue? How do we create a process that opens development options, that does not shy away from accountability, and that supports and strengthens our own faith and motivation?

2. If sustainable economic development is best served through a business-oriented approach, how do we ensure that it is also equitable? Like most tools, business is a blunt instrument with potential for good and evil in equal measures.
3. If minor shifts in the global economy can have more significant impact than the sum of all development programming, how should we as Christians prepare ourselves for work in the global marketplace?

What does the future hold?

The *Human Development Report 1998* (United Nations Development Programme, 1998), states: "World consumption has expanded at an unprecedented pace over the 20th century, with private and public consumption expenditures . . . in 1998 reaching twice the level of 1975 and six times that of 1950. . . . The benefits of this consumption have spread far and wide. More people are better fed and housed than ever before. Living standards have risen to enable hundreds of millions to enjoy housing with hot water and cold, warmth and electricity, transport to and from work—with time for leisure, sports, vacations, and other activities beyond anything imagined at the start of this century."[87]

While this image might seem at odds with what we see in our daily work with the poor, there certainly are many countries where these changes are noticeable, even over periods as short as a decade. One of the privileges of growing older is the ability to look back on the way things were. During recent trips to Bangladesh and Bolivia, I had a chance to reflect on how things had changed in 20 and 10 years respectively.

Bangladesh is now home to nearly 60 million more people than when I first visited in 1979, an 80% increase in 20 years. In spite of this increase, I sensed that, for the most part, people really are better off. Although malnutrition is still too common, the country is better able to feed itself, thanks in large part to the "green revolution" of improved seeds and farming methods. Many of the rural poor have an extra source of income from family members working in the Middle East. Labor is one of the country's major exports, often resulting in persons within the country having better access to transport, education, and clean water, and sometimes luxuries such as television. I also sensed that many Bangladeshis are now more in control of their lives and their institutions, perhaps an almost measurable result of the legions of development programs working in Bangladesh. However, the clearest and most pervasive result of this "development," was almost unbreathable air in the cities, with some of the highest recorded levels of lead poisoning in the world.

The UNDP report goes on to state: "How do these achievements relate to human development? Consumption clearly contributes to human development when it enlarges the capabilities and enriches the lives of people without adversely affecting the well-being of others. It clearly contributes when it is as fair to future generations as it is to the present ones. And it clearly contributes when it encourages lively, creative individuals and communities."

In Bolivia I had an opportunity to look more directly at the influence that MEDA has had in the Santa Cruz area. Over the past 10 to 15 years, MEDA has creatively worked with communities of small-holder farmers and microentrepreneurs to develop whole new industries which are now sustaining those communities. In the case of rural farmers, MEDA's promotion of edible beans, and the development of export markets for them, led to the creation of an industry which has now spread to some 15,000 hectares. The economic opportunity which this industry represents to small-holder farmers can be seen in the growth of their farms, which for many began with one or two hectares and has grown to more than 50 each now, and in the access their children now have to higher education. One farmer spoke of his seven children, six of whom had completed or were in university.

Meanwhile, in the urban markets of Santa Cruz, where MEDA began offering microcredit 10 years ago, a whole microfinance industry has evolved with over a dozen competitors. Some of the furniture-makers who received $400 loans from MEDA's microcredit program to purchase their first or second piece of woodworking equipment are now running shops with 20 employees or more. Many are investing in much larger facilities. MEDA's ongoing intervention is currently in the form of an investment with an association of these furniture manufacturers to help them finance a showroom and some inventory for exporting.

I believe that business development can serve the poor, but that it does not do so automatically. As stated in the United Nations Development Programme (UNDP) report, "Human life is ultimately nourished and sustained by consumption. Abundance of consumption is no crime. It has, in fact been the life blood of much human advance. The real issue is not consumption itself but its pattern and effects. Consumption patterns today must be changed to advance human development tomorrow. . . . Human development paradigms, which aim at enlarging all human choices, must aim at extending and improving consumer choices, too, but in ways that promote human life." In a global economy, poor people and poor countries bear the brunt of unequal consumption. "The average

African household today consumes 20% less than it did
25 years ago."

The future of development holds a number of challenges, each of which relates closely to the growing edges
which I outlined in the preceding section.

- How can we promote development that fosters economic growth while preserving natural resources
  and creating less pollution and waste?
- How can we ensure that business goes to the tough
  places, where financial rewards may not outweigh
  risks, but where there is great potential to promote
  economic growth, creating jobs for poor people and
  expanding their access to social services?
- How can we as Christians offer more—an economic
  development model which enlarges human choices
  in all aspects of life?

I want to personalize these challenges. From somewhere deep in my Anabaptist heritage, which suggests
that my actions are my beliefs and vice versa, I need to
address these issues personally. One of my goals in my
new position at MEDA is to offer appropriate forums in
which to share our spirituality and our faith struggles, mi-
croentrepreneur to development worker, board member
to staff, small-holder farmer to board member, and so on.
Likewise, I am committed to finding business models that
make money *and* give away ownership to those who most
directly benefit from the service. And finally, I need to
find time and space to learn more about this complex
world in which we live, and to further explore the potential for interface between faith-inspired, people-centered,
environmentally sustainable development and the world
of big business and multinational trade and investment.

6.
Large-Scale Public Policy Perspectives

Introduction

The three papers in this section represent the experiences of Anabaptists/Mennonites working in positions of public policy. Common to all these authors is their focus on big-picture issues at national and global levels where their work and decisions typically affect large populations of people.

Ray Martin, who has spent most of his development career working in international health with USAID, and more recently with the World Bank, considers his work to be a calling—a vocation. Largely due to missionaries who visited his church when he was a young person, his own sense of adventure, as well as the Mennonite emphasis on service, community, peace, and stewardship, he began his development work in 1965 in Somalia with what is now Eastern Mennonite Missions. Through rubbing shoulders with government and embassy officials, he discovered that Christian service need not be limited to working for church organizations. Although his international experiences have led him to express many uncertainties, he concludes by saying that Mennonites and other people of faith should contribute their convictions and experiences to the evolving understanding of what development is. "Let us articulate our theology of development," he says, "and share it boldly with others."

The second paper is by Beth Heisey Kuttab and reflects her wide range of significant experiences and perspectives. Growing up in Lancaster County, Pennsylvania, one of the most substantial and traditional Mennonite communities, she has done development work from the southwestern United States, to Palestine and other Middle Eastern countries where she has spent most of her efforts, to Mexico and South American countries. Her experiences as a woman working in grassroots development work, as well as an executive in a United Nations agency, provide her with a broad view of many issues on many levels. She is concerned with the use of power, both in the agencies themselves and between them and the recipient groups in the field. She is sensitive to the need for development in specific localities, but also to the needs of the funding agencies, as well as the tensions that can emerge between the various levels of service and organization. She believes that it will require strenuous thinking and discernment in order to create, and then maintain, partnerships of integrity between funding agencies and their recipients, when the "funding agency generally possesses all the financial resources and the bulk of power and control in the relationship."

Richard Yoder mixes teaching at Eastern Mennonite University with research and work overseas, mostly with USAID-financed projects in the areas of microfinance and health. A dominant theme for him is the need to supplement traditional ambulance-driving approaches to development, which have historically been practiced by Mennonites, with public-policy and systems-change approaches that reduce the need for ambulance-driving. Anabaptist values of service, peace and justice, community, and "ethics over doctrine," along with his mission-oriented parents and initial MCC experience in Afghan-is-tan, have all been influential in his understanding and practice of development. How to get inside the "50-lay-ered cultural onion," how to use power appropriately, and how to resolve the lifestyle tensions that surround the world of development, are the major dilemmas and challenges he faces in his work.

My Journey From the Cornfields to the World Bank

Raymond Martin

Raymond Martin retired several years ago after a long tenure with USAID and more recently with the World Bank. He continues to provide consultancy services to development agencies in the area of public health. His career with a variety of private and public agencies gave him the opportunity to serve extensively in Africa and in Asia in particular.

How and why did I choose a career in international development?

Was I "called" to a lifetime career working in the Foreign Service of the U.S. Agency for International Development and as a consultant for the World Bank? My conception of a "call" has changed over the years, but I do feel that I was "called" to serve in the development of Third-World countries.

As a teenager, I wanted to go into overseas Voluntary Service with Eastern Mennonite Board of Missions and Charities (EMBMC). My dream came true in 1961 when I was 21, and the experience determined the direction of my career for the rest of my life.

As a New Holland, Pennsylvania, farm boy, I had a pretty limited world. Yet visits from missionaries to my church opened a window to exciting, faraway places. Missionaries were my heroes, beckoning me to the adventure of discovering exotic places in foreign lands.

Seeing the world was not my only motivation. Helping to build the church was also a goal. After two years at Eastern Mennonite College, I was assigned by EMBMC to southern Somalia to help in agriculture and community development. I was sent to a remote village established as a place for nomads to settle down, build schools and clinics, and learn agriculture.

My Somalia experience of living in a grass-roofed hut and coping with stinging ants, snakes, and elephants provided the drama for great stories and slide shows when I eventually returned to the U.S. What captured me even more, though, was living and sharing with a community of proud but poor Somalis, struggling to build a better life for themselves. The seeds for my lifetime career in international economic development and public health had been planted.

From Somalia, I was reassigned to Dar es Salaam, the capital of Tanzania, where I worked in the Relief and Service Division of the Christian Council of Tanganyika. Administering aid to refugees, I rubbed shoulders with government and embassy officials. I discovered that Christian service need not be limited to working for church organizations. The direction of my life's calling was further clarified.

After graduating from Goshen College and studying economic development in graduate school, I joined the Foreign Service with the U.S. Agency for International Development. My tours of duty, eventually including my wife and two children, were in Morocco, Ghana, Cameroon, Pakistan, and Zaire. After 25 years of service with USAID, I joined the World Bank as a public health specialist.

Although serving God and serving people through the government, especially in association with the diplomatic corps, was unfamiliar to Lancaster Mennonites in the 1960s, I was grateful that most of my friends and church brothers and sisters affirmed my choice of career. They understood that God could use people in many different settings. In some ways, serving people and the church through USAID was not really very different from doing so through a church organization with the title of missionary. In fact, I wondered why the church never thought of commissioning me as a missionary to work through USAID.

During graduate school, I remember debating whether I should look for an overseas position with USAID or with MCC. Although I didn't know any Mennonite models for choosing government service, I decided to be bold and give it a try. My attitude was that if the conflicts between my Mennonite-influenced values and the demands of USAID service were too great, I would simply resign.

My standard was put to a test after I completed my first overseas assignment in Morocco. I discovered that my next assignment was to CORDS, the program in Vietnam that was to "win the hearts and minds of the people." It involved the CIA and the U.S. military, as well as USAID. Despite my general commitment upon entering the Foreign Serve to go anywhere I was assigned, I told USAID that I would not accept this posting because of my pacifist convictions. USAID responded by threatening to fire me. I enlisted the help of the American Civil Liberties Union. In the end, USAID dropped its threat and I was formally posted to a Washington job.

Did my stand have any impact on Washington policy and the USAID bureaucracy? By itself, probably not. In concert with the protests of many other people with a variety of motivations, it probably did. Did my refusal to go to Vietnam deprive some Vietnamese of the help that a sensitive and caring American with religious convictions might have brought? I don't know. I would have respected someone in my position who would have decided to go. But for me, accepting that job would have pulled me too far from my moorings.

The impact of all of this on me was not so bad. For better or for worse, I stayed with USAID. The senior personnel officer who threatened to dismiss me is now a good friend. Furthermore, staying in Washington for several years as a bachelor in my early 30s opened the way for me to meet a young VSer at the MCC Peace Office in Washington—Luann Habegger, now my wife.

Many times during my USAID career, I wondered whether I was remaining true to my Mennonite values, or whether the allure of good pay, a comfortable life, important positions, and professional challenges dulled my sensitivities. I squirmed when I read internal confidential documents justifying USAID budget requests to Congress which emphasized the fight against Communism, promoted exports and business opportunities, and assured pro-Western votes in the U.N. After the Vietnam assignment episode, however, I experienced no occasions where the gap or conflict between my personal values and motivations and those of the organization were so great that I felt I had to resign.

Have I made the world a better place?

The question posed for these panel presentations was "Have you made a difference?", allowing, I suppose, for a negative difference. I just read the book *The Road to Hell*, which describes one perspective of the impact of donor agencies and nongovernment agencies, including churches, on Somalia. The book jacket says, "If you think your charitable giving is making the Third World a better place, think again. If you think that your government is trying to do good, think again."

I guess I need not only to assess whether my career in foreign aid helped make the world a better place. I also need to be daring enough to be open to the possibility that my life work, including the premise on which my "call to service" was based, was so off the mark that my influence on Third-World development was negative.

I don't really want to consider that possibility. But the longer I am in this business—and it's now been 35 years—the more I call into question the whole post-World War II foreign-aid model. On bad days I do wonder what happened to my idealistic youthful "calling" to build a better world. Have I made a difference in the countries where I served?

Somalia is much worse off now than it was in the early 1960s when I worked there. The *ujamaa* political and development philosophy of former President Nyerere of Tanzania, one of my African heroes, was a big fiasco. In the 1960s I thought of the philosophy as almost Christian. In Morocco I was helping the U.S. award King Hassan for his moderate stance in Mid-East and Arab affairs. Ghana is doing okay. Cameroon's per capita GNP plunged soon after we left in 1984, and recently Transparency International rated Cameroon as the most corrupt country in the world. Pakistan never addressed its sharp class structure, and its government is on the verge of defaulting on its multi-billion-dollar foreign debt. I realize that the USAID commitment to Pakistan, including the quarter-of-a-billion-dollar portfolio of health projects that I managed, was related more to the anti-Communist struggle in Afghanistan than it was to genuine development objectives. In Zaire I was part of the U.S.'s generosity to President Mobutu for his pro-Western, anti-Communist policies while we overlooked his corrupt and despotic ways. I watched firsthand as the country went downhill to disaster.

With that assessment, can I feel affirmed in my life's work? It isn't easy. Do I feel personally responsible for such bad outcomes? Not exactly, but I must accept that I was an integral part of the policies and programs and historical forces that resulted in those outcomes. I try to convince myself that I was a positive influence overwhelmed by powerful forces over which I had very limited control. That sounds like a lame excuse, but maybe it *is* true. Jesus made a difference, we would say, but the last 2000 years of human history are hardly what he worked for.

There are ways that I can convince myself that I helped make the world a better place. My field is public health. I can rejoice that the probability that a mother and father will lose their newborn baby before the age of 12 months has been cut almost in half since I joined USAID in 1967. Since then, global life expectancy has increased about nine years—astounding. Adult literacy increased from 46% to 70%. Although population growth remains worrisome, the doomsday scenarios that we've all heard have not led to widespread starvation. In fact, the increase in food production has outpaced population growth. Maybe my lifetime career in international development was not a waste of time. Such advances in well-being are unprecedented in human history. Our health status has gotten better, thanks to new technologies such as vaccines and improvements in our water and sanitation, and educating people about how to stay healthy.

Did I or didn't I make a difference? On Mondays, Wednesdays, and Fridays I feel that I had it all wrong—that the world has not become a better place. On Tuesdays, Thursdays, and Saturdays, I feel positive—that overall the life of Third-World peoples has improved. I guess it is evident that after a lifetime career in international development, when I should be confident that I know how to do it, I remain, instead, terribly confused. The issues are so complex. The uncertainties strengthen in me one of the oldest of Mennonite values—humility.

At a personal level I could cite many examples of how I believe I made a difference in people's lives. As a project and program manager I am convinced that my professionalism and Christian values did make a positive difference in outcomes. So I am not at all apologetic or despondent about my life's work. When I look at the big picture, however, or when I read a book like *The Road to Hell*, I am less sure.

What would I have done differently?

Given the uncertainties I've expressed, you would suppose that I would choose a far different course if I had the opportunity to go back 35 years and start over. Actually, probably not. I acted on the best knowledge and insight that I had at the time.

I definitely continue to advocate that Mennonites be active in international development. I believe that some Mennonites should consider serving through government channels or with big international development institutions. Our smaller scale, community-level efforts, such as those of MCC and Mennonite Economic Development

Associates, should continue, but we should also boldly tackle the large-scale, global challenges that governments and international organizations struggle with.

I definitely think that people interested in careers in international development should consider spending some time working on the frontlines at the community level. Voluntary Service or the Peace Corps are good preparation. Many of my USAID and World Bank colleagues lacked the perspective that such experience provides.

I do wish that throughout my career in big international development bureaucracies, I would have been bolder in speaking out from my own experience and insight rather than deferring too readily to the opinions of others. My Mennonite "quiet in the land" mentality inhibited me from courageously asserting myself.

I am absolutely convinced that our Mennonite heritage and values give us some authority to speak about effective approaches to development. I am referring to Mennonite humility, our ethic of service, our ability to identify with the poor and weak, our priority of peace, our sense of not being part of the powerful ruling establishment, our emphasis on community and equality, and our sense of stewardship.

I could have had a healthier attitude about how I saw myself in relation to the Third-World people I worked with. I had many "ugly American" colleagues who were much worse than I, but, nevertheless, I found it hard not to slip into the mentality that we from the rich, highly developed, technologically-advanced West knew the answers and were ready to give them generously to the poor backward folk of the Third World. I have become less sure that our technology, our preoccupation with material advancement, and our management methods will improve the well-being of Third-World peoples. I think we should be willing to share our techniques and experience, but we should be less pushy about advocating them as the gospel for everyone. We should be available to other countries and cultures, but we should dampen our missionary zeal to remake the world in our image. And we should remind ourselves that development is as much a social and a cultural process as it is a matter of finance and technology.

We need to change our mentality so that our First World-Third World relationships in development cooperation become much more demand-driven than supply-driven. We should not aggressively push our assistance on poor countries who may not be as eager to receive our beneficence as we are to give it to them. At USAID, we aggressively marketed our aid. The bigger our programs and the more money we spent, the better our performance evaluations and the faster our promotions. At the World Bank, despite denials by management, there is pressure to lend. Energetic, perhaps well-meaning, Bank managers and technicians (like I am) convince Third-World officials that they'll be better off with our loan money. Of course we go through the ritual of our social soundness analyses, beneficiary assessments, popular participation exercises, and impact projections. We must, however, learn to listen more. It is easy to lose perspective. We must change the incentive structure in our organizations so that true development is the measure rather than the vast sums of money we move.

A recent op-ed article in *The Washington Post* by Fred Hiatt made me uncomfortable. He wrote, "What do we now know? For one thing, that foreign aid, on average, hasn't worked. As Oxford University economist Paul Collier recently summarized current research, foreign aid on average has not raised growth rates, has not lessened poverty, and has not brought about improved economic policies. Huge sums of money, accompanied by endless hectoring, lecturing, and setting of conditions, have had, on average, zero impact."

Key challenges and cutting edges

With such a gloomy assessment, what do we do now? A happy future for all of humankind is only marginally related to development of the world's poorest peoples when one looks at the sustainability prospects of current global trends. Rather, the biggest challenge has to do with the reluctance of the so-called developed world to accept limits to growth in its use of natural resources. I still support efforts by rich countries to promote development in poor countries. That is the enterprise to which I have devoted my life. I believe, however, that the biggest challenges for our great-grandchildren, both mine and those of my friend Bashimbe who lives in Kinshasa, Congo, will be determined more by how well affluent nations adopt sustainable economies than by the development of poor countries.

The most daunting challenges in 21st-century development have less to do with the "development" that we rich countries transfer to the Third World than with changes we make in our own unsustainable, high-consumption lifestyles. We must call into question our very notions of what constitutes progress. Mennonites, with our emphasis on stewardship, community, and simple lifestyles, should be at the forefront of this rethinking. MCC's effort to develop a "theology of enough" is on the right track, I think. But when you look at the predominant lifestyles of North American Mennonites, we are not outstanding models.

I am referring to the rate at which we consume natural resources, our refusal to temper our consumption of fossil fuels, our tolerance of pollution, our contribution to global warming, and on and on. In my field of public health, it is easy to get scared about growing antibiotic resistance, chemicals that mimic hormones, population pressures, and environmental pollutants that cause cancer and other diseases. I am not a congenital worrier, but I constantly run across new things to worry about. The latest for me is discovering how polluted our environment and water supply are becoming from the excess use of pharmaceuticals. We use so many drugs that excess quantities are flushed down our drains and toilets and are now detectable in our water supply. That raises concerns about the long-term impact on our immune systems and the development of drug resistance by our major bacterial enemies.

When it comes to foreign aid, I think we need to rethink our traditional development approach in a very fundamental way. It isn't easy for me to say this, but I think foreign aid as I practiced it in USAID and at the World Bank is flawed, at least in part. I don't pretend to know what needs to be done to make it work. I must admit that on occasion I have wondered whether granting money or free technical assistance to developing countries is really doing them a favor.

I certainly do not want MCC and MEDA to go out of business. But I see little reason for Mennonites to lobby Congress for larger aid allocations. I think we have underestimated the corrupting influences and perverse incentives that result from giving money free to Third-World bureaucracies. I believe this about church-to-church relations as well as government-to-government relations. I do not advocate the immediate disbanding of

USAID and the World Bank either, but I think the development enterprise would benefit from some radical changes in our assumptions and our methodologies.

Regarding Mennonite participation in development, I think the low-key, patient, listening, and partnering approach often practiced by MCC has a lot to be said for it. On the other hand, I think Mennonites should stop being satisfied just with small-scale, even if successful, programs, often hidden from public view. Although Mennonites are not numerous enough to single-handedly make a major difference in the big picture, we should be wrestling with the problems and issues that face entire nations and the global community. We need to think about how our successful models can be scaled up to the magnitude necessary to make a widespread impact. That means that our Third-World partners and we should be involved in policy dialogue and advocacy to influence the actions and programs of national governments and global institutions. We have been too timid in this regard.

We have another challenge, and that is to help governments and global institutions understand the relevance of cultural and spiritual factors to overall development. World Bank President Wolfensohn calls churches and religious organizations the biggest nongovernmental organizations in the world. He is eager for a dialogue on faith and development with religious leaders. Along with the Anglican Archbishop of Canterbury, he hosted a Faith and Development Dialogue with leaders of nine major religious faiths. There was agreement "that the definition and practice of desirable development must have regard to spiritual, ethical, environmental, cultural, and social considerations, if it is to be sustainable and contribute to the well-being of all, especially the poorest and weakest members of society." Wolfensohn wants Bank staff to be educated about the religious beliefs in countries where they work.

Another example of deepening insight in global institutions is the recent action which the World Health Organization took to add the word "spiritual" to its definition of health. It now reads, "Health is a dynamic state of complete physical, mental, spiritual, and social well-being and not merely the absence of disease or infirmity." Mennonites and other people of faith should contribute their convictions and experience to the evolving understanding of what development is. Let us articulate our own theology of development and share it boldly with others. This EMU conference, provided that we follow up on our deliberations here, can contribute to that challenge.

It All Started with
National Geographic

Beth Heisey Kuttab

Beth Heisey Kuttab is currently the Director of Relief and Social Services in Amman, Jordan, for UNRWA, the United Nations Relief and Works Agency for Palestine Refugees in the Near East. She has responsibilities for policy development and program implementation in five areas of UNRWA operations—Lebanon, Syria, Jordan, the West Bank, and Gaza Strip. Her formal education includes a B.A. in Sociology, an M.Ed. in Counseling Psychology, and an M.A in Management. She has lived and worked in the West Bank and Jordan for 20 years, is married, and has two children.

Why have I chosen this occupational path?

Some of my fondest childhood experiences involved overnight visits to the homes of my classmates, some of whom I judged to be in a better economic class than I. I vividly remember indulging in snacks of potato chips and Coke, enjoying frozen beef pies that had been heated to perfection (all "luxury" foods never purchased by my mother), and, best of all, sitting down to read *National Geographic* magazines, an indulgence my family couldn't afford. The latter exposed me, at the age of 10, to the worlds beyond the white, Anglo-Saxon, Protestant, largely rural farming community in which I was growing up. It may have helped to lay a foundation for my increasing conviction that life outside Lancaster County, Pennsylvania, was far more fascinating.

A second influence which undoubtedly subtly shaped my emerging interest in other cultures and peoples of the world—and their needs—were the sporadic visits of overseas missionaries to the small country church I attended. They brought stories of sacrifice, simple lifestyles devoted to service, extraordinary culinary delights such as monkey meat, and color slides of travel to exotic locales. So while I grew up in a subculture and religious environment that often seemed homogeneous and oppressive to me (movies were forbidden, as was the wearing of slacks or makeup for females, for example), I also was steeped in a tradition of thought that stressed hard work and devoting one's life to serving those less fortunate. I never embraced the Protestant work ethic as intensely as others in my family or community. But somehow I did so thoroughly "catch the 'service' bug" that it became difficult for me to find meaning, and therefore satisfaction, in a career that did not include a humanitarian dimension.

I grew up on a small farm, which was an invaluable setting for learning the vagaries of nature and experiencing the calloused feet of shoe-free summers, the sweat of bringing in hay, and the backbreaking effort needed to harvest the garden's yields. I also concluded that I would go to great lengths to avoid spending my adulthood in anything remotely related to farming or hard physical labor. Curiously enough, I have been most touched while traveling around the world (to visit development projects) when I have been in peasant communities where humble people struggle to eke out a simple living—and where a successful income-generation project makes a tremendous difference in their quality of life. I carry great affection for heads of families (whether male or female) who support their families in the midst of tremendous difficulties, perhaps because I remember my 8th-grade-educated father struggling to make ends meet.

My volunteer and paid work-experience during my teenage and college years (including a painting stint on a Navajo Indian Mission Station in New Mexico and inner-city work with youth in San Francisco and Harrisburg) further cemented my cross-cultural interests and a career focus that was people-oriented. Two years of post-graduate work with young women in refugee camps in Jordan, followed by exposure to the United Nations in New York and three years as a project officer for a development agency, only intensified my appreciation for the nature and difficulties of international development. Eventually I married a Palestinian lawyer, which to date has meant that I have lived more than half my adult life in the West Bank and Jordan. That step also made it necessary for me to choose a career that was applicable in a developing country. Events in my childhood made me inclined toward a career in development, and my subsequent work and life experience have reinforced my decision to continue in this field.

What has been my experience?

My development experience, while not continuous during the past 25 years, has nevertheless progressed from grassroots work in Palestinian refugee camps to middle management responsibilities with an international relief and development agency based in New York, to the current diplomatic post I now hold with the United Nations in the Middle East. While this professional journey has its advantages (progressing from the meager pay of a volunteer to the very generous package of a U.N. salary and employee benefits, for example), it also has its disadvantages. The higher one advances on an organizational ladder, the further s/he becomes from the organization's clientele. While the increased power and control one has as an executive is welcome, increasing distance from the daily lives of the poor one is seeking to serve can risk formulating policies that are irrelevant, ill-conceived, or downright injurious.

One of the ongoing challenges I face is posed by gender. While major strides have been made over the past several decades in the U.S., women in executive positions in development agencies still often find themselves operating in a man's world. Added to that, in my case, has been the challenge of working in a conservative, primarily Islamic culture as a young, single female, and then developing a career in the same conservative culture 15 years later as a working mother.

I sought to live in one of the refugee camps where I was working outside Amman, Jordan (when I was newly arrived in the country, at 22 years of age and single), in order to understand better what it meant to live as a Palestinian refugee and to develop fluency in Arabic. While I was informed that my idea had merit, I was also emphatically told that this was quite impossible because it was culturally incorrect and would not be understood by the refugee community. While this response was entirely accurate (as I was to learn in time), I was disappointed to feel so quickly and blatantly the constraints of being female and single.

Later I was to learn that struggle shared by working mothers universally—that of juggling the demands of home and family with the day-to-day responsibilities of the office. While these types of stresses can be greatly eased by hiring domestic help and by cooperation from husbands, it is still not without its burdens. When I was on a duty trip in Lebanon last year, I got a call in Beirut from the babysitter taking care of our children in Jordan, saying that our daughter had her eyeball scratched in an accident at school. My husband was in Jerusalem, and therefore out of contact, because no calls can be made from Beirut to Jerusalem. That is only one of many frustrations—and a reminder that family members are sometimes made to pay an unwelcome price—for having a mother who works full-time, especially when that can entail travel to countries of the Middle East. Communication there is not always easy or possible, and political stability cannot be taken for granted.

A career in development requires understanding power relationships whether one works in a given community at a grassroots level, or in an NGO where there are likely to be power politics and turf battles within the staff or with the funding agency. Gender differences often add to the complexity of preventing, solving, or coping with such matters, and graduate textbooks in development do little to assist the average practitioner with this. At these points, one can learn the value of mentors and trusted professional colleagues.

I've learned how it feels to be on both sides of the funding divide. I've worked for agencies that provide funds for relief and development efforts, and I've worked with organizations that depend on the success of their staffs' fundraising abilities. I certainly prefer a job with an agency that does not require writing and marketing project proposals in order to survive. It is far easier—and more pleasurable—to dispense funds than to raise funds. Some agencies do not have to devote a large percentage of their administrative time to fundraising efforts, but all development organizations with which I am acquainted must keep their respective constituencies informed, interested in, and happy with their agencies' activities so that funds continue to flow into company coffers. No agency can ever take its funding base for granted, and in the face of decreasing financial aid levels (at least in terms of governmental allocations for international/foreign aid), many agencies have to compete more vigorously and creatively than ever in order to cover their annual operating costs.

I have also experienced the differences between working with small, nongovernmental organizations that are largely mono-cultural (that is, most core staff share similar socio-economic and religious backgrounds) and agencies that are a huge, diverse, and bureaucratic mix of nationalities and personalities. Large organizations tend to require that one learn complex and nuanced professional skills, often not needed in a small NGO. But working in large bureaucratic structures often means experiencing delay after delay while pushing or cajoling a desired decision or action on its journey through the system. Each type of organization has its advantages and disadvantages.

I rode a roller coaster, thrilling and spilling while co-founding a West Bank-based NGO for nonformal community education in the late '80s. I learned some of the complexities of entrepreneurship during the first *intifada* there, and the experience gave me a new appreciation for what it means to start and build an NGO. That, plus earning a business-oriented Master's degree in Management caused me to consider how business concepts can be brought to bear on development issues in general. I also got acquainted with basic tools of development practices, such as institution-building and microfinance activities.

I've experienced the greatest joy in my development career when I've gotten out of the office and met committed people who are activists and advocates with and for the poor. I've been enriched far beyond any childhood wish as I've traveled in the Caribbean, Latin America, Asia, Europe, Africa, and the Middle East, not as a tourist, but as the representative of an agency with resources for partnering with local NGOs. It is satisfying to be able to make a difference in people's lives by offering humanitarian aid and assisting with development efforts.

I have been touched time and time again by those who live in chronic poverty. To witness their lack of pretense, to see the crowded shacks and slums where many live with nothing beyond the most basic material goods, to learn that many do not have enough income to purchase medicine for a sick child, is supremely humbling and a powerful reminder of how rich I am and always will be by comparison. Poverty is not only the lack of adequate food, clothing, and shelter, but also the lack of access to opportunity (education, jobs that provide sufficient income, adequate transport and transport infrastructure, enjoyment), as well as the lack of basic services (such as good healthcare), and an environment that is politically stable and safe. To be part of a profession that can make any positive difference in the lives of the poor, whether on an individual, organizational, or community level, is to be privileged indeed.

At the same time, development practitioners can expect numerous difficulties, especially at the grassroots level. These difficulties may take the form of resistance to change or barriers caused by tradition or culture. Men may object to women working outside the home or studying for an advanced degree. Transportation to and from project sites may be hard. I remember riding uncomfortably for hours with colleagues over very bumpy roads and gullies in order to reach a project area in Bolivia, with two separate stops along the way to repair flat tires. Language barriers may seem insurmountable and phones may never seem to work. Are the skills you tried to teach in a training workshop appropriate or ever actually applied by the students? How long can you work in crowded, hot, smelly, dirty, uncomfortable, and sometimes unsafe, conditions? Development is not a profession for the faint of heart, especially when it is practiced at the heart of need.

Desk officers of funding agencies can expect other challenges. They may have to decipher financial reports of projects that are in foreign currencies. Trying to calculate the value of the dollar at the time of the report can be a challenge if there are unpredictable and fluctuating levels of inflation. They may need to deal with communication gaps that may arise due to long distances between the funding and implementing partners. They most likely will have to raise funds for projects based on the needs and assets of a community quite distant from the funding source. And they will need to visit projects in far-flung places even when they are ill. I remember hiking up a remote mountain in Bolivia at 6 a.m. one hot morning with my supervisor and about half a dozen agency U.S. board members in tow. We were on our way to see the progress being made on a fish pond for a family who lived at the top of the mountain. I understood the purpose of that hike, but I was in the full throes of *sirrochi* (high altitude sickness). I coped with a pounding headache and a nauseous stomach that keep revolting at several inopportune points as we worked our way up the side of the mountain.

A career in development can mean sleeping three to a sagging bed in Angola because of the lack of sufficient hotel space. It can include watching mice run back and forth across a darkened airport lounge in the middle of the night while waiting for a plane connection in Africa. It may involve being stranded for three days in a hotel room, as I was in New Delhi when Mrs. Indira Gandhi was assassinated, because of riots in the streets below and sudden political instability. Yet such a career is rewarding because one can see people in need being genuinely assisted in their struggles to survive, as well as to better their lives.

Have I made a difference?

The persons who are best able to address this question are those who have participated on the ground in the development efforts funded by the various agencies I have worked with. They are the best judges of whether any development effort has had the desired impact and for how long that impact has been sustained. I have been a link in the chain delivering financial and sometimes human resources to local organizations in foreign countries, and I would like to think I have made a difference. But any positive results should largely be credited to those who have done the basic, hard, slogging, on-the ground, long-term work that is involved in true development. On many occasions I have seen the results of development projects which have failed. Those that have succeeded have indeed alleviated human suffering and made a difference in the quality of life of those who have participated. They have made all the trials and errors worthwhile.

Upon reflection, what would I have done differently?

First, when I was in college I wish I had asked more critical questions about how I could use my sociology major in the real world following graduation. I wish I had asked college administrators about the kinds of jobs previous sociology majors were able to find and what salaries they were able to attract so I would have had a more realistic sense of what my four-year investment might yield. I would have paid more attention to opportunity cost. I would not have accepted the answer that the only professions open to people-oriented graduates were either social work or teaching. A degree in Development Studies was not available in the early '70s, at least I was not aware of such a degree, so I had to stumble upon the world of development on my own, learning what it encompassed and what skills were needed for a related career. In retrospect, I also would have taken a double major and ensured that at least one of my majors was a practical skill.

Second, when I first moved to Jordan in 1972 I would have tried harder to live in a setting that would have forced me to learn Arabic, that is, in a place where no one spoke English.

Third, I would have begun financial planning for retirement at a much earlier age. That means I would have given greater weight to being employed at a higher income level and by an employer who offered a pension plan. I would have paid closer attention to the economics of compounded interest over a period of 20 years.

Fourth, and related to point three, I would not have waited until I was in my mid-40s to conclude that I should not look to my husband as the sole supplier of my financial security. After seeing too many of my female friends and acquaintances in their 40s lose their husbands prematurely to illness or divorce, I finally realized that I could not guarantee the health of my husband. I decided to attain as much financial independence as possible so I could provide for our children and fund my retirement if anything unexpected happened to my husband.

Other than those points, my answer to this question is much like those of this year's Miss Universe finalists. When asked if they had any regrets, most responded that they didn't because all of their experience to date, mistakes and all, had shaped them into the persons they had become. Since they were content with who they were at the time, they had no regrets. My sentiments on this subject are basically the same.

What are the growing edges for me?

If I had the luxury of taking time off for concentrated study, I would focus on public administration and how it might best be practiced in particular countries. I am currently in a management position with UNRWA, a quasi-governmental U.N. agency created in 1949 for Palestine refugees, who, more than half a century later, are still living in 59 camps in the Middle East. My responsibilities—and the questions that surround them—are often similar to those faced by government ministry officials around the world. For example, how do we provide housing for the poorest refugees when agency resources are insufficient? How do we continue to attract international aid, that is, donor support (primarily governmental) and counteract donor fatigue after more than 50 years of assistance from the international community, with no political solution in sight that would allow UNRWA to be dissolved? How does one attempt to decrease refugee dependency on UNRWA services (as real budgets continue to shrink in the face of increasing population and increasing need), when the refugees cannot collect taxes and make their own fiscal decisions, and when they often live in contexts of political instability, high unemployment, high poverty rates, and hostility from the surrounding population (as in Lebanon, where refugees are banned from practicing 70 different professions), when they are unable to own property, and when their political future is still uncertain.

What does the future hold?
What will be the main issues and themes?

Development concepts and terminology will continue to evolve. What may be known as "relief services" today may be labeled "humanitarian aid" tomorrow. Gender-related projects might evolve from a "Women-in-Development" origin to a "Gender and Development" orientation. Development now should be "sustainable" and ensure that environmental protection is factored into any action or intervention. Western funding agencies that partner with local NGOs will still need to grapple with how the integrity of those partnerships can be maintained as much as possible, when the funding agency generally possesses all the financial resources, and hence the bulk of the power and control in the relationship. It requires steadfast deliberation not to have such unequal partnerships form. Without that, local NGOs end up feeling manipulated, patronized, or otherwise at a disadvantage in reaching their goals.

How to do development and be as effective as possible will continue to tease practitioners. Should one focus on advocacy and the changing of laws, or should one concentrate instead on community, "on-the-ground," development? Some practitioners believe that development starts with the individual, and they shape their programs accordingly. Others focus instead on community groups, organizations, and institutions. How can NGOs be encouraged to cooperate more extensively, thereby eliminating duplication of effort and increasing the possibility of new synergies and a greater collective impact?

The growing divide between the rich and poor of the world (whether in technology or materials goods) and the increasing impact of globalization on the far reaches of developing countries pose new challenges to development agencies. Should they focus on a macro- or micro-systems perspective?

What is the role of technology in attacking the *causes* of hunger, as opposed to the symptoms of hunger—one of the core challenges of development? Should more "Geekcorps.coms" be formed, a type of Peace Corps for tech-savvy professionals?

What is the role of venture philanthropy, and what is its future? How can more "social entrepreneurs" be shaped and rooted in communities of need? How can the fledgling attempts of visionary, activist economists, such as the Peruvian economist Hernando de Soto, be broadened to make more ownership of land possible for squatters in developing countries?

How can a human-rights approach to development be encouraged instead of a needs-based approach? Are there any new insights about how practitioners can or should work *with* the poor (as opposed to *for* the poor)? How can this be accomplished within what some may call national "cultures of corruption"?

Will a trend develop in the future whereby practitioners from developing countries will travel to Western countries for reverse professional exchanges, in which the Westerners do the learning instead of the teaching?

Will the creative use of photography, art, drama, and dance as tools for development become more widespread?

What will the outcome be of the "debt forgiveness" campaign for certain developing countries?

All of these issues and more will be firmly on the development agenda in the future. The elimination of poverty and even the widespread alleviation of poverty is beyond the reach of most development careers. Yet I hope that the science and art of development will continue to progress so that development has an increased impact on both the causes and the symptoms of poverty in the future.

From Ambulance-Driving to Public Policy

Richard A. Yoder

Richard Yoder combines international work with teaching and research at Eastern Mennonite University. He has worked in Africa, Asia, and the Middle East, primarily with projects financed by USAID, U.N. agencies, as well as MCC and MEDA. His work has been in the areas of microenterprise development and health economics. He holds a Ph.D. in public and international affairs and masters degrees in public health and in economic and social development.

Why this occupational path?

Perhaps the single most defining experience influencing my development career was in Afghanistan in the early 1970s where I worked as an MCC volunteer seconded to the Medical Assistance Program. Working as a gofer/jack of all trades in a 15-bed health center in the Hindu Kush Mountains, I helped to treat many children who were dehydrated from diarrhoeal diseases. After some time I began to notice that the same children kept coming back with the same diarrhea problems—while we kept treating them with intravenous fluids. Why was this, I wondered.

Although I didn't use this language at that time, I later came to realize that we were ambulance-driving. We were treating the symptoms rather than the causes of diarrhea. We were missing a better solution which lay in the realm of sound public policies—policies that would

have had the effect of reducing the need to cure diarrhoeal diseases. We would have been more effective had
we encouraged the construction and use of pit latrines
and wells. Then people would not have needed to use for
drinking and cooking the same river water into which
their feces and that of their cattle flowed whenever it
rained.

This same line of reasoning led me later to learn that
instead of spending $250,000 to build a 15-bed health
center, we would have saved more lives if we had spent
that same amount of money immunizing 23,000 infants.
In the jargon of economists, the opportunity costs of
building that health center were very high.

These kinds of experiences led me to do a graduate degree in *public* health rather than medicine (not that I
would have had the grades in college to get into medical
school!). Furthermore, my volunteer experiences in
Afghanistan and Jordan in the early 1970s, combined
with subsequent coursework in graduate school, taught
me that development is a complex and multidimensional
process. Consequently, I continued my formal education
and did an interdisciplinary Ph.D. that combined public
policy, public administration, and economic development.

Oddly enough, perhaps one of the more important
lessons I learned during this time was how *not* to do development, although I don't mean to suggest that I've
learned the definitively right way of doing development.

Because of what I experienced and learned early in my
career, much of my work since that time has been in the
area of public policy. I've helped to design and implement
policies and programs, both internationally and domestically, that are intended to reduce the need for ambulance-
driving. Domestically I've served on the Harrisonburg

(VA) City School Board, and, internationally I've worked in some 15 countries with organizations ranging from US-AID to the United Nations, African Development Bank, and the World Health Organization, primarily through private firms who have contracts with these organizations. Internationally my work has been primarily in two areas: microenterprise development and health.

Exhibit 3 summarizes my own development journey as I've learned to understand more about hunger and poverty and the kinds of responses available to help alleviate them. Information in the first row (Perceived Problem) shows how we tend to define a development problem. Row two (Logical Solution) shows the range of responses we typically give to the defined problem. Row three illustrates the Type of Problem we believe it to be, whether a technical need for better management, improved variety of agriculture seed, more effective vaccines, etc., or, whether the problem is more imbedded in the systems, structures, and institutions of a society, thus requiring political and macro-level changes before improvements can occur at the micro level.

I have four observations about Exhibit 3, each of which has influenced my movement from ambulance-driving solutions toward public-policy and preventive approaches. First, how one defines the problems of hunger and poverty largely determines the solution that one proposes.

Second, solutions toward the left-hand side of the Exhibit tend to be more technical and micro-oriented, while those toward the right side tend to be more systemic and structural in nature, as well as national and international in scope.

Third, while ambulance-driving and public-policy change are both important, I believe that it is fundamen-

Exhibit 3:
Responses to Hunger and Poverty: From Ambulance-Driving to Public Policy

Ambulance-driving ⟶   ⟵ Public Policy

Perceived Problem:[1]	No fish, indigent	Ignorance; don't know how to fish	No Money; can't buy equipment to fish	No, or limited, access to river or land	Poisoned fish from polluted water	Can't export fish
Logical Solution:[1]	Give fish, relief	Education and training; teach how to fish	Provide credit to buy tools to fish	Change land tenure system; remove net from upstream	Advocate for environmental laws	Establish fair trade laws; reduce tariffs & quotas
Type of Problem	Technical	Technical	Technical, systemic, and structural	Systemic and structural	Systemic and structural	Systemic and structural

Thanks to Wally Kroeker for one of the best extensions of the well-known fish story as presented in "Feed them for How Long?" in *The Marketplace,* September/October 1994.

tally better to prevent poverty than to have to cure or reduce poverty. It is better to immunize children and prevent disease than to need to treat the sick. It is better to
prevent hunger than it is to have to give food aid to people, and so on.

Fourth, Mennonite resources have been concentrated
disproportionately on the ambulance-driving side of the
continuum.

Why did I go to Afghanistan and Jordan as a new college graduate? I suspect that the answer lies in the Anabaptist family and heritage in which I grew up. Certainly praying for missionaries as a child influenced my
thinking, as did my parents' decision to fully support, out
of their small income from the family farm, a missionary
family in Puerto Rico. The Anabaptist heritage values service, simplicity, peace and justice, bringing "good news to
the poor," and community. Over time, the ideal of "community" has stretched beyond the Mennonite world to
encompass the global community that connects all of us
together. In other words, the heritage in which I grew up
placed greater emphasis on ethics over doctrine and actions over words. A poster mounted in a stairwell in the
public middle school I attended in New Carlisle, Ohio,
said it clearly: "Your actions speak so loudly that I cannot
hear what you are saying."

What have been the challenges
and rewards?

Perhaps the primary challenge I have faced in my development work has been what Harold Miller, a wise
friend and long time MCCer in East Africa, calls "getting
inside the 50-layered onion." At their roots, development
specialists are change agents. Yet bringing about positive

change while respecting a people's culture and traditions is a complex process. In many ways, development is an effort to separate what is outside one's control, and thus not so susceptible to change, from what is within one's control, and thus is susceptible to change.

I remember a conversation I had with Tabo, a clerk and driver for an organization I worked with in Africa. When I inquired how his infant daughter was doing, he said that she was very sick with diarrhea and would probably die. The village witch doctor had cast an evil spirit upon his daughter because of something his wife had done. While trying not to dismiss the power of witch doctors and traditional healers, I suggested that I doubted that his daughter was sick because of the witch doctor's evil spell. Rather, it was because of the dirty water or food his daughter had been consuming. In effect, I tried to convey that his daughter's health was probably more within his control than he suspected, that he needed to change paradigms or his worldview. Was that the right thing to say?

I remember many stories about my cross-cultural relationships that tell me that I didn't get much below the first few layers of the 50-layered onion. Those occasions have brought me more grief than I would choose, in spite of working internationally and cross-culturally for much of my professional life.

A second challenge of which I'm keenly aware is power—its presence, and its easy use and misuse. Because of the knowledge and resources, particularly the money, which we from the North bring to the development enterprise, we are in positions of considerable power. For me, simply acknowledging that power has been a challenge, not to mention attempting to comprehend power's role in what I do. This is partly due to my growing up in a subculture that emphasizes service and being a servant and, consequently, has difficulty addressing the reality of power. Reconciling my self-concept as a servant, which I strongly value and promote, while having considerable influence over the use of millions of dollars, and consequently over the lives of quite a number of people because I'm in a position of power, is hard to grasp—and humbling.

How does one manage this power without being corrupted by it, while working with many people and institutions whose first interests are strategically national, personal, or class-based.

This is further complicated by the fact that the intended "beneficiaries" of one's efforts, that is, people at the margin, are largely voiceless and powerless. A further complication is the tripartite phenomenon David Lamb has called "nepotism, corruption, and 'big-manism'" in many Third-World countries, where these forces are expressed within the broader legacy of imperialism and colonialism. Attempting to understand my role and participation in this complex web of relationships constantly challenges me.

A variety of other more personal issues disturb me. These include lifestyle differences, income and wealth differences, not taking myself too seriously, and never feeling quite comfortable at the many cocktail parties I've attended.

In spite of such challenges, I have had many rewarding experiences and positive relationships over the years. I believe, however, that the rewards of development work need to go beyond relationships, as important as they are. The rewards need to result in improvements in people's quality of life. They must include having fewer of their children die, having more food to eat, and having more and better education and better housing.

Has a difference been made?

Have I helped to make a difference? I will briefly cite cases from three countries I have worked in: Bangladesh, Swaziland, and Kenya. Each reflects a different place on the ambulance-driving to public-policy continuum of Exhibit 3.

I spent two years in Bangladesh in the early 1980s. It requires considerable stretching of the imagination to believe that I helped to make a difference there. In the country that Henry Kissinger crudely called the "basket case of the world," I was on a United Nations-financed project designed to reduce its rate of population growth. Bangladesh had one of the world's highest rates of population growth and was one of the poorest countries in the world. Without going into detail about the project, I will simply say that the "problem" implicit in the design of the project was so poorly defined that no matter how well we did our job, we would not have made any difference. Using the language of Exhibit 3, the development problem was defined as ignorance, or not knowing how to fish (that is, a technical problem). A more fundamental understanding of the problem would have defined it as the result of having limited access to resources, thus calling for a redistribution of power and resources within the country.

In Swaziland I spent three years on a USAID-financed project in the mid-1980s. Its objective was to reorient the nation's healthcare system away from its urban, hospital-based, and curative design to a rural, community-based, and preventive orientation. This reshaping involved several components, such as preparing a national five-year plan; decentralizing annual planning, budgeting, and management systems; redesigning the organizational structure and functions of the Ministry so that decision-making was decentralized to local levels; creating partnerships between the government and nongovernmental health services; and integrating Western medicine with traditional medicine. In terms of Exhibit 3, much of the work was of a public-policy nature, attempting to bring about change at systemic and structural levels.

In 1997 I returned to Swaziland to assist in the preparation of the country's national five-year plan. That gave me the opportunity to assess what progress had been made over the intervening 15 years. While many of the old problems remained, I was encouraged by a number of key health status indicators. Infant mortality rates had declined by some 45%. Life expectancy had increased by some 36%, and malnutrition rates had improved substantially. The health system was being managed by District Health Management Teams rather than by headquarters staff, and the Teams were using more timely information to set priorities and prepare plans and budgets. A larger share of the budget was being financed from internal funds rather than being dependent on donor funds. Clearly many factors contributed to these improvements. But I think it is reasonable to assume that the positive changes came in part because of a national healthcare system that was reoriented toward offering primary healthcare in the rural areas rather than hospitals and curative care in urban areas.

In Kenya I was part of a USAID-initiated institution-building project with an organization that has become one of Africa's largest and most cost-effective nongovernmental organizations. It provides credit, training, and research services to small-scale (typically one to five employees) microentrepreneurs. Since 1992 the organization is fully Kenyanized and is offering several thousand loans per month, averaging about $400 each, with repayment rates of nearly 98 percent at a low cost per dollar loaned. These numbers are significant because they have reduced dependency on donor funds through a financially sustainable organization. In addition, for every loan disbursed, one new job is created or secured. Furthermore, incomes have increased by some 45 percent, thus allowing low-income households to have more food, to pay for school fees, to improve their housing, and to obtain better healthcare. According to the framework of Exhibit 3, the Kenya work had elements of both technical change (providing credit) and systemic and structural change (advocacy for legal reform favoring low-income entrepreneurs).

Most of my other development work has been short-term consulting related to moving healthcare systems toward greater financial and institutional sustainability, while at the same time making health services more accessible to and useful for low-income groups. Some of these have made a positive difference; others have not.

Given the option, what would I have done differently?

Broadly speaking my work has been an interplay of teaching, research, and consulting, much of it happening in five-year intervals—five years in the field, followed by five years in an academic setting with short-term consulting during the summers, and then back to the field again. Teaching has given me the opportunity to read about the development enterprise and reflect on my work. Doing research and presenting papers at professional conferences has allowed me to extend my understanding of development issues and to interact with other development specialists. Teaching and research, in turn, have informed me in the whats, hows, and whys of doing development when I am in the field. Each of these activities has had a synergistic effect, resulting, I hope, in making a more positive difference in my life and the lives of people in the global community.

I have found working at national levels of public policy enormously rewarding. If I were to do something differently, I would work at higher levels of public policy where global structures and systems are created, which have impact on national-, regional-, and village-level systems and structures. I am continually impressed at the extent to which global financial activity, for example, can have enormous impact, for good or for ill, on the daily lives of villagers. It can undo almost instantaneously decades of hard work by people at the village level.

Another area in which I would do things differently has to do with relationships. I would drink more tea with my national hosts, particularly those at the grassroots. These relationships are not only very rewarding personally, but necessary for doing good development.

What have been the cutting edges for me, and what does the future hold?

I've already mentioned two cutting edges for me— peeling away the 50-layered onion, and acknowledging and using power appropriately. A third challenge before us is privatization.

One of the legacies of the Thatcher and Reagan administrations in the 1980s is the rise of the free market as the engine of development. Initially, efforts to privatize economic activity focused on transferring state-owned enterprises in centrally planned economies to the private sector. More recently, privatization efforts have spread to include the social-service sectors, such as health and education, areas which historically were considered public goods. Official development assistance typically follows the policy goals of those countries providing the assistance. That means that much of my work in the health sector in recent years has been related to privatization. I am somewhat troubled by this, since in the past, public-health services have included many spill-over benefits. The private sector is not able to provide those benefits at a price affordable to the majority of the population. Yet I am also aware that many governments cannot offer *free* healthcare services, and in many cases are unable to provide healthcare services at all.

The market certainly can play a powerful role in improving the lives of people. Yet my own published research, as well as that of numerous others, fails to find a positive relationship between countries that are more privatized and a variety of development indicators. This is not to suggest that the solution lies within the public sector. The research also shows that it is not the size of either the private sector or the public sector which makes a significant difference in and of itself. Rather, there must be additional factors, unique neither to the public nor the private sector, which affect development in a positive way. What these other factors are requires further investigation, and discovering them is a cutting edge issue for me.

In the meantime I muddle through, doing the best I can with the information I have—ironically much like the missionaries (whom I prayed for as a child) did before me and of whom I have tended to be rather critical.

A fourth cutting edge for me is the nature of the advice I give my students at Eastern Mennonite University. I'm afraid that my word to those who talk with me about development work has become like a broken record: do a double major in Peace and Justice, and in Business and Economics. The Peace and Justice major will give them the perspective they need, while Business and Economics will give them the tools. I urge each student to take an assignment with MCC for several years, do a Ph.D. in some area related to development, and then take a job that will eventually lead to a position in public policy.

I observe that students seem to find it difficult to think seriously about moving into public policy positions. A number of the international development firms I have worked with over the years have said that they would consider any of my strong students as interns. I have had many strong students, but only one has taken the opportunity.

I'm mystified by this, although I suspect that part of the reason is the way we have interpreted "service" and "servanthood." We are taught to be humble, not to have too high a view of ourselves, to think of others first, to identify with people who are vulnerable and at the margin, to have, as Don Kraybill has stated, "upside-down kingdom" values.

In terms of vocational choices, we have translated those values to include teaching, social work, medicine, and church work. These are the most common majors and professions chosen by Mennonites who graduate from college. All of these are "service" or "helping" professions; all of them are ambulance-driving professions.

I propose that we broaden our definition of service and express the upside-down kingdom values of the Anabaptist heritage in an additional way. In addition to ambulance-driving, which I believe needs to continue, we must also become part of the process of creating systems and structures that reduce the need for ambulance-driving. Liberation theology, with its roots in the Catholic church of Latin America, has helped me to understand this. I believe that when the apostle Paul talks about the principalities and powers in Ephesians, he is referring to invisible realities, such as public policies. He says that we do not fight against flesh and blood, that is, any single individual. Rather, we fight against invisible realities that express themselves through the actions of individuals or some larger entity. For example, apartheid, racism, and discrimination are not so much the evil of any single person as they are the evil of systems. The fact that women in the United States receive wages and salaries which are approximately $0.70 to every $1.00 their male counterparts receive, for doing the equivalent job, is not a problem of genetic inferiority. It is something larger and more systemic.

Why shouldn't we get our hands dirty by joining the public policy dialogue? Why shouldn't we be co-creators of the historical process? Who is better prepared to do public policy work than Anabaptists who have worked with MCC at the grassroots?

In spite of strongly advocating moving into public policy positions, I believe that doing so is risky. Fundamental among these risks is the danger that our power will go to our heads, that we will sell our souls, lose our upsidedown values, and become part of the system we are trying to change. Such dangers should not be underestimated, but the presence of risk is not a reason to refuse to enter the dialogue. If the Anabaptist faith perspective which we bring to the dialogue cannot stand on its own two feet, then perhaps we ought to re-examine our understanding of that heritage.

To summarize, I believe that there is a compelling need for alternative voices at the policy level. There, in addition to picking up the pieces through our ambulance-driving, we must become part of the process that reduces the need for ambulance-driving. Upside-down kingdom values carry a lot of power. I think that we can and that we ought to become part of the process which moves the global community toward a world that is more peaceful, just, and sustainable.

Part III

The Analysis

Introduction

In order to give background for understanding current development efforts by Mennonites, we provide an overview of mainstream approaches to development in the first part of this book by summarizing those dominant competing perspectives. We then present an historical accounting of Mennonite involvement in missions, relief, and development.

In the second part of the book we include stories and critical reflections by Mennonites who have been doing development work at the public policy level, the middle ground level, and the grassroots level.

In this final part of the book we examine the data presented in the previous two sections and elsewhere in an effort to make sense of it all, while drawing some observations and conclusions.

In Chapter 7 we review the assumptions, themes, and patterns present in the experiences of this study's practitioners and scholars. What commonalities and differences emerge across the three levels?

In Chapter 8 we attempt to identify an "Anabaptist/ Mennonite Ethic of Development" by examining the extent to which a set of common values and ethics emerge within the work of the practitioners, regardless of their organizational affiliations. We follow this with a summary of Anabaptist theology and ethics. We then draw comparisons between what are generally understood to be

Anabaptist ethics and those of Mennonite development practitioners. We also make some comparisons between mainstream development efforts, as presented in Chapter 2, and Mennonite perspectives on development.

In Chapter 9 we look at specific tensions, dilemmas, and opportunities experienced by Mennonites doing development.

Finally, in the Afterward we offer some concluding thoughts and challenges.

7.
Common Assumptions, Themes, and Patterns

Mennonites work with diverse development organizations. Do they bring the same assumptions, themes, and patterns to those organizations, whether they are public policy, grassroots, or middle ground? If so, what are those assumptions, themes, and patterns, and how are they expressed? To answer these questions, we examine the responses the practitioners gave in their individual papers. We pay special attention to the differences and similarities that emerge among the three levels.

Couched within our questions—and the practitioners' answers—may be assumptions about the nature of change and an "appropriate" approach to development. Watch for those presumptions, assumed by the questions.

The framework presented in Exhibit 2 on page 37 (which looks at who is responsible and who has control

over changing my condition) can be helpful in understanding the practitioners' expectations about change.
The quadrant that perhaps best characterizes the practitioners' assumptions is Quadrant 2: "I'm not responsible
for the situation, but I can change it." Much like the anti-
war protestors of the 1960s and 1970s, most practitioners
in our study would argue that they are not responsible for
poverty and oppression in the Third World, but they can
have a role in changing it. Some would likely argue that
by living in rich and powerful countries they are indirectly responsible, and thus could fit Quadrant 1. Development workers are, by definition, change agents and
thus would not fall into the third or fourth quadrants
which say, "I can't change it," regardless of who is responsible. Their change orientation would lead them to
assume that they have a certain degree of control over a
situation and its outcome. They would believe that it is
possible to make a difference, however the term "difference" is defined, and they would believe that change, at
least in part, can be externally induced and/or facilitated.

While most practitioners probably hold that change is
mutual, and that both parties need to learn, close examination would likely show that they expect the greatest behavior change to be on the part of the host country nationals. This expectation is greatest among public policy
practitioners. This assumption leads to the greatest re-
sentment among host country nationals when rich countries provide development aid. Nevertheless, this assumption is present in most development work.

Do our questions imply a certain model of development? The "Have I made a difference?" question assumes
that it is at least possible to make a difference, although
it does not suggest whether that difference is positive or
negative. Presumably, if the practitioner felt that s/he

could not make a positive difference s/he would *not* have chosen development as a vocation. Our questions may not assume the superiority of any of the particular models of development described in Chapter 2, but we have assumed a linear view of life. That is consistent with a Western worldview where it is believed that life can be improved, however defined, rather than a traditional or tribal worldview.

Why have you chosen this occupational path?

Perhaps the most common reason practitioners gave for choosing their particular occupational paths is the influence of their Anabaptist faith and its emphasis on service, justice, and peace, along with its related heritage which places greater emphases on ethics over doctrine and action over words. Stories told by visiting missionaries and MCC workers in their churches left strong impressions. Parents, Mennonite college professors, and others who modeled a life of service were influential. Adventure and an opportunity to do good while having fun were certainly factors as well. These elements are common to all the practitioners included, regardless of whether their work focuses on the range of public policy matters or grassroots issues. Additionally, all the practitioners, regardless of their current work, began at the grassroots level—most with MCC.

While these were common experiences among all the practitioners, certain factors influenced whether they finally chose a grassroots, middle ground, or public policy path. Those who stayed with the grassroots seemed to be drawn by its orientation toward strong relationships, along with the belief that development work is best done when working directly with the poor, rather than the top-down approach of public policy workers. Middle ground workers, some of whom worked earlier at both grassroots and public policy levels, liked the option of reaching in both directions to make connections.

All of those doing public policy work had an experience, usually in their first development-related jobs, which indicated that factors beyond the local community were affecting the well-being and wholeness of individuals who lived there. Something bigger than any single individual or the community itself seemed to be influencing the quality of life at the local level. Often the practitioners were not able to identify this "something" until later in their lives (often during graduate school) when they had an opportunity to read and study in a more systematic way.

For example, one practitioner who did Voluntary Service with the MCC Peace Section office in Washington, D.C. as a research assistant became exposed to the impact of public policy decisions on individuals' lives. Another discovered that Christian service need not be limited to working for church organizations while rubbing shoulders with government and embassy officials as part of his voluntary service work with a missionboard in Somalia. Still another observed while an MCC volunteer in Asia that the same children kept returning to the clinic with diarrhea—and wondered why. From conversations with his friends in Nicaragua, one practitioner who went to Latin America as a mission-board volunteer fresh out of college began to suspect that he was perhaps part of a larger structure that was limiting Nicaragua's development.

Each of these practitioners eventually faced a question about the extent to which systemic, structural, and institutional factors at the national and global levels are barriers to individuals and communities experiencing health and wholeness. All of the practitioners currently doing development work at the public policy level worked at the village level early in their careers and experienced the systematic and structural nature of the problems they worked with. Consequently, each moved into development work at the public policy level, although not without feeling ambivalent about their choice.

At the same time, others keep on working at the grassroots and middle ground levels, clearly articulating the systemic roots of many of the problems they work with regularly. They have decided to continue their efforts at the grassroots for a variety of reasons. Moving from grassroots work to public policy work should not be seen as normative. In fact, some middle ground workers have intentionally chosen to stay at that level, in part because they have become disillusioned with public policy work.

How do practitioners experience doing development work?

The most common theme among workers at the grassroots is the rewards and joys they experience from their relationships with people from the countries where they work. It is this very ingredient that public policy people found most lacking in their experience. Perhaps because grassroots development workers interact daily with people living in poverty, they seem particularly able to see the world through the eyes of the poor. Similarly, they become acutely aware of these persons' demeanor and dignity and generally become convinced that development has as much to do with the spirit of people as it does with skills and technology.

Frequently grassroots and some middle ground workers use language that is somewhat more explicitly religious in nature, referring for example, to "the biblical basis of service," "the deep faith of [people]," "the wisdom of relying on and trusting God," or "looking at Scripture through the eyes of the poor." In addition, and unlike public policy and middle ground workers, grassroots workers typically link with local churches rather than with governments or private sector organizations.

Middle ground workers often see themselves as a bridge between the macro and the micro. They tend to have a results orientation similar to public policy workers, while at the same time they frequently establish connections with villagers, which grassroots workers commonly do. Middle ground workers interact with policy-makers and can influence policy. By having a foot in both worlds, these people, it can be argued, bring greater benefits to all. Several middle ground practitioners in this study had experience at the public policy level but, for a variety of reasons (such as yearning for more hands-on, practical experience, or becoming disenchanted with the compromises of public policy work), opted to concentrate at the middle level.

Public policy workers' ideals are dominated by ambiguities and paradoxes, and to a much greater degree than those of workers at the grassroots or middle ground. Perhaps the grayest area for Anabaptists/Mennonites has to do with lifestyle. Those in public policy have the highest incomes, the best housing conditions, and the greatest material disparities between them and their local counterparts, not to mention persons in the local society's lower income groups. How does one live in these realities while remaining committed to Anabaptist values of simplicity, justice, and equity? "Have we succumbed to the 'good' life?" is the tormenting issue.

Beyond that are more ambiguities of faith and practice for public policy workers. For example, given the positions they hold, do they sufficiently acknowledge the power at their disposal, both its use and misuse? How do they maintain a servant perspective while having control over substantial sums of money and people? In addition to wondering if they've fallen for the good life, they're haunted by the question, "Have we sold our souls, as well?"

Many of those who work for bilateral and multilateral organizations are ambivalent about whose interests they serve—the rich or the poor, the weak or the powerful? One practitioner doing USAID-funded work observed that the major force driving the distribution of his agency's resources is what benefits the United States. He noted that this helps to widen the gap between rich and poor rather than reduce it. Another practitioner working for large donors stated that his faith makes him critical of the globally dominant mainstream (or neoclassical) development economics because they serve the interests of rich countries. So while he advocates for more sensitive voices at the public policy level, he argues that these must be prophetic voices.

Paradoxes abound. Those countries which experience increasing wealth usually also have increasing corruption. The wealth is distributed unequally and unfairly. Globalization can create common interests, while at the same time it decimates local culture. As countries "modernize," family structures, culture, and traditions significantly weaken.

A final observation. Not only is the nature of the work done at the grassroots markedly different from that done in public policy, so, too, is the final "product." One works on the front line delivering services. The other enables or advises people charged with making policy or developing systems to improve the delivery of services. The "product" that one sees is very different, both in content and in time.

Have you made a difference?

With few exceptions, public policy workers generally expressed positive feelings about the contributions they have made, although they were usually careful to articulate their particular roles in a limited way, indicating that they are part of a broad process that is multidimensional and complex. They acknowledged that the "long run" expresses the nature of policy work, and that that is also one of the frustrations of the work. Furthermore (and as described in greater detail in Chapter 2), most public policy workers have a "results" orientation. They pointed to global improvements such as declining infant mortality rates, increasing life expectancy, declines in population growth rates, increases in food output per capita, increases in incomes, reductions in illiteracy, and the empowerment of women. On the other hand, these public policy practitioners expressed mixed feelings and uncertainties about many bad projects or programs which occurred along with many good ones. Interestingly, few authors spoke of bad projects that they have been a part of, although all could point to bad projects elsewhere.

Grassroots workers, on the other hand, typically defined the differences they made in terms of relationships, particularly relationships at an individual level. People were mentored, encouraged, and empowered; trust was built and spiritual communities created.

"Drinking tea with MCC," while an oversimplification, perhaps captures how the notion of "making a difference" is characterized by these persons. Stories appear to play a prominent role among grassroots workers, most of which reflect the one-to-one and person-to-person emphasis of grassroots work. It is also the grassroots workers, along with some middle ground workers, who wondered whether "Have you made a difference?" is the right question to ask. Rather, they suggest, the question should be about faithfulness, commitment, or learning: "Did we 'live' a difference?" "Is development ultimately relational, or is it primarily a transfer of technology, skills, ideas, and visions?"

Middle ground workers, like public policy workers, tend to integrate business principles into their understandings of development more than grassroots workers do. For example, most have a fairly strong results orientation. Like public policy workers, many place a major focus on institution-building, and, consequently, are concerned about matters of financial and organizational sustainability. While middle ground workers may be inclined to comment that "it is easier to make a buck than it is to make a difference," many of them are concerned about fostering creativity, being a friend, encouraging people, and empowering individuals.

Workers in this study at all three levels expressed humility, wonder, and honor about being associated with such a vocation. Many acknowledged that they are engaged in a special kind of work, a "calling," in fact, whose focus, regardless of the means, are the least advantaged of God's creation. For many, issues of life and death, rather than the model of car they own, are what inspire their work and give them a sense of responsibility, challenge, and awe.

What would you have done differently, given the opportunity?

The most frequent response to this question is that they would have spent more time with people, building relationships. While this answer was common across all three levels, it was particularly dominant among the public policy workers, perhaps because it is the level at which building personal relationships is neither emphasized nor highly valued, and it is where distance from the common people is the greatest. The wish for more relationship-building may also reflect the strong results orientation of public policy workers and the pressure they feel to meet the programs' objectives and spend the money allocated for those efforts.

Why this emphasis on relationships? One middle ground worker may have spoken for many practitioners in our study when she said, "Nurturing relationships with committed persons is the heart of the faith/business/development nexus. It is not only where we have the best shot at making a difference, but I believe it is truly the point where God enters our work."

From all three levels came these common themes of what-might-have-been: more listening, more cross-cultural understanding, and more emphasis on systems approaches and multidisciplinary perspectives, while at the same time being as highly skilled as possible in particular areas of expertise.

We also note with interest that being "more bold, more confident, more assertive, and more proactive" are ideals identified by several people across the levels. While humility, and the associated phenomenon of being the "quiet in the land," are values traditionally maintained and promoted by Mennonites, these qualities can also impede other Mennonite values of service, such as identifying with the poor and weak, and fostering peace, community, and stewardship.

What are the growing edges?
What does the future hold?

Power is an issue that runs through all three levels—acknowledging it, understanding it, using and misusing it. The subject—and its practice—are uncomfortable for Anabaptists/Mennonites who, on religious grounds, have historically placed a high value on service, servanthood leadership, putting others before oneself, not having an inflated view of oneself, and identifying with people at the margins of society. Because of this, the practitioners in our study do not regard themselves as equals with their colleagues, although they want to perform their tasks with excellence. The contradictions they experience around these issues continue to be a challenge.

The middle ground and public policy workers in this study speak of straddling two worlds—the sacred and the secular, or the church and the state. Taking faith-inspired motivations and perspectives into a donor-funded world which generally does not share the same perspectives, and doing development in countries whose culture and traditions are also faith-shaped but not necessarily in keeping with Mennonite faith and practice, are other sources of tension.

Grassroots workers often do development alongside a local church. How can they approach development holistically and, at the same time, how can they support the local church? Middle ground workers tend to build institutions among private sector businesses or NGOs; public policy workers tend to build institutions within government or in the private sector. Grassroots workers help build institutions among local churches. So while a common theme of institution-building is present at all three levels, how, where, and with whom it happens, varies.

One theme dominates all three perspectives in relation to the questions, "What are the growing edges?" and "What does the future hold?" It is the emphasis placed on spiritual and religious values. The pattern is quite common among grassroots workers, but less so among middle ground workers. We are interested to observe that it is strong among public policy workers, a place where stereotypically we would least expect it. What is not clear, however, is whether our respondents hold a common set of assumptions when they speak of religious and spiritual concepts. They use phrases such as: "pursuing the spiritual journey," the "increasing relevance of the religious values of honesty, compassion, conviction, character," the need for "universal values," a "theology of enough and a theology of development," working for organizations that "see development in spiritual, as well as physical and material, terms . . . that are faith-based rather than project driven," promoting "upside-down kingdom values," or "having faith in God and trust in the common sense of ordinary people to work through and overcome the paradoxes of development."

Another theme which is most prevalent among public policy workers, but is also present among some practitioners of both grassroots and middle ground perspectives, is a call for Mennonites to be more involved in public policy positions. These voices want to increase the proportion of Mennonites working at public policy and to have their numbers begin to balance those at the grassroots and at the middle ground.

We lift out comments from four practitioners: First, "We need more prophetic voices asking questions from an Anabaptist/Mennonite perspective." Second, "Mennonites and other people of faith should contribute their convictions and experiences to the evolving understanding of development. Let us articulate our theology of development and share it boldly with others." Third, "The combination of these influences . . . have led me to desire being a bridge, a connection between worlds that do not know or understand each other, . . . and I now feel ready or able to encounter the policy world I once shunned." Fourth, "I believe there is a compelling need for alternative voices at the public policy level where, in addition to picking up the pieces through our ambulance driving, we become part of the process that reduces the need for ambulance-driving. Upside-down kingdom values carry a lot of power. I think we can and ought to become part of that process that moves the global community toward one that is more peaceful, just, and sustainable. Who is better prepared to do public policy work than Anabaptists who have worked with MCC at the grassroots level?"

From our own experiences—and theological rootings—we propose that one can attempt to change systems and do public policy work in places other than large donor organizations or governments. Powerful people's movements have evolved from grassroots initiatives, both violent and nonviolent, and have changed national systems (Marcos' Philippines, Samoza's Nicaragua, eastern Europe in the early 1990s, Iran under the Shah, British India, as well as the Civil Rights and anti-Vietnam War movements in the U.S.) and international systems (the anti-globalization and anti-World Trade Organization movement). If one decides that working in government or with big donors involves too much compromise, or if protest movements are not where one wants to be active, there are other options. Research institutions, newspaper and magazine editorial pages, political action committees, and lobbyists groups are all places to invest oneself in affecting public policy issues.

Building bridges, creating partnerships, and making connections and linkages can also be guiding themes. Can peacebuilding, called the newest development fashion by some, benefit from the lessons learned in development efforts, and vice versa?

We noted above that grassroots workers have a pattern of using religious and spiritual language, while public policy and middle ground workers do less so. Yet spirituality is emerging as a central theme among public policy workers, and among middle ground workers to a lesser extent.

Grassroots workers traditionally have tended to look somewhat askance at public policy work. Yet several grassroots and middle ground practitioners in this study expressed an interest in moving toward public policy work. Others observed the need for a greater emphasis on public policy approaches.

Public policy workers typically say that you can't change systems by raising goats—a not very veiled criticism of grassroots work. Yet most public policy practitioners in this study, as well as middle ground authors, have expressed regret that they did not give relationship-building sufficient attention, nor did they invest adequately in building communities.

What we observe here is a partial role reversal. The historic concerns of grassroots-oriented people are being articulated by public policy people, and, vice versa. Alternatively stated, throughout the continuum the macro and the micro may be discovering that they need each other, that they are two sides of the same coin and each a part of a seamless web. Indeed, conversations at the development conference held at EMU reinforced this observation. It was unusual to have persons representing the range of development perspectives sitting at the same table and talking with each other. Myths and stereotypes were reduced and a common ground began to be identified.

Once there was a clear separation between the values of the state and the values of the church, as reflected in the two-kingdom theology. Now there seems to be a graying or weakening of this clear separation. There are an increasing number of questions about whether such a clear divide is helpful for knowing how to live and function in this world. Building bridges and creating partnerships, networks, and linkages are more and more attractive concepts. The two-kingdom model, perhaps best exemplified today by the Amish, no longer seems as useful for those doing development work, for those trying to combine the macro and the micro, for those who are aiming to be bridge-builders, and for those who are attempting to deal creatively with the ambiguities and paradoxes of "being in this world without being of this world." We will explore what this alternative framework is in the next chapters.

8.
Toward an Anabaptist/ Mennonite Ethic of Development

Ethics and Ethical Frameworks: A Brief Definition

At the beginning of this book we noted that 30 years ago, Denis Goulet wrote that the basic questions for both developed and underdeveloped societies are neither economic, political, nor technological, but moral. Many experienced development practitioners support Goulet's assertion. But what do we mean by "moral" and its associated term, "ethical"?

Since in this chapter we will attempt to identify an Anabaptist ethic of development, we will begin by clarifying briefly what we mean by "ethics" and an "ethical framework." At a basic level, "ethics" are characterized as principles of conduct that govern moral judgments. A simple

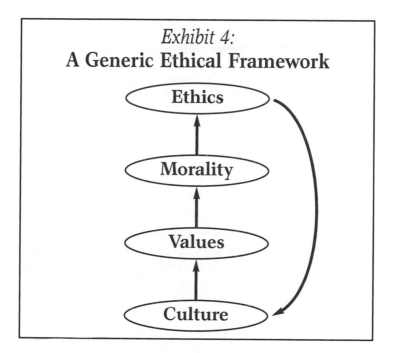

Exhibit 4:
A Generic Ethical Framework

Ethics

Morality

Values

Culture

model for understanding these concepts and their linkages is shown in Exhibit 4.

Ethical principles are undergirded by systems of morality, values, and culture. A particular culture is at the foundation of each of these systems. Different cultures give rise to value systems which, with few exceptions, are not universal.[88] These values, or enduring beliefs, are often unexpressed or not articulated. Rather, they take the shape of assumptions which tend to be commonly understood by those within that particular value system. These values and assumptions provide a sense of right and wrong, good and bad—that is, a system of morals or rules of conduct.

Ethics, on the other hand, are generally characterized as *reflections* on morality, that is, reflections on the continua of what is right and wrong, good and bad. Social ethics, in turn, can inform and influence culture, as shown by the feedback loop in Exhibit 4. Thus, ethics are principles of conduct governing moral behavior for individuals, groups, and societies.

Ethical systems can generally be categorized as primarily: (a) consequentialist or teleological[89] (ends-oriented; greatest good for the greatest number); (b) rules-based or deontological (means-oriented; do unto others as you would have them do to you; the rightness of an action depends on whether it accords with a rule, regardless of its consequences; popularized by Kant's categorical imperative); or (c) subjectivism/egotism[90] (moral judgments are impossible because of the human inability to think rationally; hence, ethics are self-evident or emotionally desirable).[91] It is out of this context that development ethics can be defined as ethical reflection on the ends and means of global development.[92]

Goulet reminds us that the notion of ethics assumes the existence of choices; if there are no choices, then there are no ethics. Thus, the possibility of ethics is conditioned by a prior possibility of freedom and accountability for that freedom. The presence of choices is what leads to ethical dilemmas when in cross-cultural settings we experience different, if not clashing, value systems.

In light of this generic ethical framework, we will address in this chapter the extent to which Anabaptists doing development hold common values and ethical principles regardless of their organizational affiliation. All the practitioners in our study have their roots in the same sub-culture, that is, the Anabaptist subculture. At the same time, all the practitioners are part of a larger society that influences and shapes their values and ultimately their ethical principles. What does this mean for the normative questions of what *ought* to be with respect to development ethics—the ends and means of development?

Elements of an Anabaptist Ethic of Development

The analysis in the previous section suggests that "value free" development is impossible. Indeed, ample evidence exists to document that development as implemented in poor countries and in poor areas of rich countries reflects a clear set of explicit value assumptions regarding what and how to achieve specific desired outcomes.

Michael Todaro, author of a widely used text on economic development, claims that development attempts to realize three values: (a) to provide people with the ability to choose, (b) to have sufficient resources to survive, and (c) to enjoy some semblance of democratic government.[93] Some (non-Western) observers will quickly claim that these development values are not universal, but rather an expression of the values underlying Western society and economies. Todaro and other theorists do not explore to any extent the often-unarticulated values that support or accompany the development process.

Recent research in Africa and Latin America supports the view that people in developing countries are clearly aware of the explicit values undergirding development as described by Todaro, as well as those unspoken values such as rationality, efficiency, problem-solving, and efforts to control natural and social forces, all of which shape how international and national governmental and nongovernmental development organizations operate.[94] For example, these organizations often consider traditional culture as an obstacle that must be overcome or used as the vehicle through which modern values and practices can be introduced and institutionalized.

Anabaptists throughout their history have committed themselves to serving the most disadvantaged groups in society, a clear value orientation. Menno Simons, the 16th-century Dutch Radical Reformation leader, cited earlier in this book, claimed that true faith or religious commitment is real only if expressed in action; it clothes the naked, comforts the sorrowful, feeds the hungry, shelters the destitute, cares for the sick, and becomes all things to all people.[95] This core value of "service to the poor" still orients the broad Anabaptist movement today. Over the years it motivated Mennonite involvement in relief, refugee and reconstruction work and, most recently, development and peacebuilding. However, only in the past 50 years has development become a specialized activity for nongovernmental organizations, including Mennonite groups. As a matter of faithfulness, Mennonite development practitioners have tried to bring together Anabaptist values and the socio-economic development efforts promoted by their development-related organizations, MCC and MEDA in particular.

Deriving the Ethic

We noted earlier that an ethic can be derived from the values held by a society or subculture, and that a society's goals reflect the values it embraces. The means used to achieve the goals must also be consistent and in harmony with the espoused values. Drawing on Kreider's earlier summary of the MCC approach, on our own experience, and on the accounts of Mennonite practitioners at the conference on Anabaptist/Mennonite Experiences in International Development, we have identified a Mennonite ethic of development with a set of values, means for their implementation, and ultimate development goals that these values and means seek to attain. The components of this ethic are summarized below in Exhibit 5.

The chart in Exhibit 5 contains three columns: the set of **values** identified in the analysis, a sample of the **means** to make the values real in daily life, and the **ultimate goals** or ends emanating from the values and means.

We identified eight mutually reinforcing values: people-centeredness, service, integrity, mutuality, authenticity, humility, justice, and peace. Not only are many of these values mutually reinforcing, they have an order or priority among themselves. For example, the claim that there can be no peace without justice would suggest that one condition must exist prior to the other. However, the list does not preclude nor require that this be the case. On the other hand, one could propose that the eight values represent a number of types, such as values that provide a basic orientation toward life (service, people-centeredness), others that represent traits necessary to carry out that orientation (integrity, mutuality, authenticity, humility), and valued states or conditions (justice, peace).

While these possibilities present interesting questions for future research, we need to note that this study limited itself to identifying the values that make up a Mennonite development ethic, as reflected in actual practitioner experience, and to reflecting on the implications of such an ethic.

The second column in the chart sets forth actions that can help put into practice the eight values from column one. In other words, the actions are concrete expressions in life of the abstract values. Hence, they must be of the same quality as the values. As such, they should not contradict what the values represent, but rather serve as a way to express or operationalize those values in daily life. Thus "means" become specific, practical incarnations of the various abstract values. Returning to the oft-cited statement by Menno Simons, the actions in the column entitled "Means" are to values what Simons says feeding the hungry, clothing the naked, and caring for the sick are to "true evangelical faith."

In the third column the chart identifies four Ultimate Goals of a Mennonite development ethic: a world that is more just, peaceful, and sustainable, and where the quality of life is more truly human and life-enhancing. These goals are "outcomes" which Mennonite development practitioners, scholars, and church constituents desire, even though they may differ on how to achieve them.

Exhibit 5:
An Anabaptist/Mennonite Ethic of Development

Values	Means	Ultimate Goals
1. People-centeredness	• Listening actively • Viewing relationships as important in and of themselves, e.g. for their human value • Committing oneself to cross-cultural understanding in order to humanize all parties in the development enterprise • Engaging in practices that enhance personal dignity of everyone	• Justice • Sustainability • Quality of life • Peace/ salaam/ shalom— from the personal to the global

Values	Means	Ultimate Goals
	• Decentralizing power as a basis for people to act as subjects in development rather than as objects • Developing culturally appropriate participatory structures and systems	
2. Service	• Defining work as vocation or calling • Being accountable to all stakeholders • Promoting the interests of others rather than just one's self-interest • Viewing all stakeholders as persons to be served because of who they are, rather than for what they can contribute • Practicing cycles of reflection and action • Giving preference to the disadvantaged • Exercising "Servant Leadership" • Justice • Sustainability • Quality of life • Peace/*salaam*/*shalom*— from the personal to the global	• Justice • Sustainability • Quality of life • Peace/ *salaam*/ *shalom*— from the personal to the global
3. Integrity	• Engaging in clear and honest communication with all parties	

Values	Means	Ultimate Goals
	• Eliminating hidden agendas • Accepting responsibility for mistakes • Granting recognition for others' accomplishments, e.g. proper attribution • Recognizing one's strengths and weaknesses	
4. Mutuality	• Building relationships • Trusting others • Committing oneself to mutual accountability • Sharing resources in ways that enhance the common good • Assisting, as well as learning from, those served • Structuring organizations to be learning organizations	• Justice • Sustainability • Quality of life • Peace/ *salaam*/ *shalom*— from the personal to the global
5. Authenticity	• Appreciating one's own culture in order to more fully appreciate another's • Minimizing invidious markers of difference • Interacting with others guided by the recognition that everyone is both teacher and learner	
6. Humility	• Willing to let others take their due credit for achievements • Thwarting the drive to misuse power	

Values	Means	Ultimate Goals
	• Recognizing another's true merit without comparing him/her to someone else • Encouraging the development of others' gifts	
7. Justice	• Sharing burdens and benefits fairly • Working for policies that promote the common good • Acting ethically based on life-enhancing values • Taking a stance on ethical issues rather than claiming neutrality • Committing oneself to work from a systems-perspective rather than from particular interests • Creating systems that are open to input from all stakeholders	• Justice • Sustainability • Quality of life • Peace/ *salaam*/ *shalom*—from the personal to the global
8. Peace	• Practicing nonviolence as an expression of the value of human life and dignity • Working to create and maintain just relationships • Recognizing and promoting social, economic, and environmental interdependence • Cultivating respect for the physical, social, and spiritual aspects of all persons	

Values are the abstract concepts that orient our behavior. Means represent the way we put abstract ideas into action in daily life. Ultimate goals are the social constructions built by concrete actions, in this case a particular kind of community, nation, or world. Thus, at every level, abstract values will be evident, but always in different forms; they are embodied as concepts, actions, or discrete social constructions.

Let us illustrate in some detail the elements of the development ethic we have identified. We recognize that this is an idealized construct, extracted from the imprecision of personal practice and classified into categories that may appear more definitive than they are in real life. Multiple feedback loops and linkages also exist that cannot be depicted in the chart. Nevertheless, even though the chart does not capture the dynamic complexity of the ethic, it allows us to examine a reality that we believe exists. That reality, we acknowledge, is in constant evolution. For example, in 1950 we may not have so clearly identified mutuality as a value in a Mennonite development ethic as we do today. The difference between then and now is that diversity, multiculturalism, ecumenicity, and inter-religious dialogue are all much more a part of today's dominant North American, if not global, value system in which Mennonites freely participate, though often somewhat haltingly.

Values and Means

The first concept in the Values column, *people-centeredness,* reflects a commitment to have human beings front and center in the development enterprise. People are subjects rather than objects. As objects they function merely as factors of production; part of the land, labor, and capital trilogy. As subjects, even though they may provide labor for production, their ownership in the development process endows them with greater dignity and general well-being.

For persons to be subjects rather than objects of development, all parties must willingly listen actively to each other. Active listening indicates the importance of all individuals in a development process where people matter. Relationships are valued as ends in themselves rather than for instrumental purposes, like creating ways to increase production, promoting a willingness to change, or building better health or communication infrastructure. These activities are important, but they are not valid reasons for instrumentalizing human relationships.

For the development process to be people-centered, everyone involved must be able to understand and appreciate the different cultures from which the various parties come. If some are from outside, they must appreciate and understand the local culture, just as local parties must do the same for cultures from the outside.

People-centeredness means that development is not unilateral, but a collaborative effort by all parties. Decentralization, or the devolution of power, is essential to the process. This will be reinforced by jointly created, culturally appropriate, participatory decision-making structures and systems. Mennonite practitioners who work more with policy than at grassroots-level practice readily recognize that policy needs to be person-centered and informed by the grassroots contexts in which it will be applied. The subtitle of E.F. Shumacher's book *Small is Beautiful: Economics as if People Mattered* summarizes well how macro-oriented development workers approach their work: "policy as if people mattered."[96]

The value of *service* is central to an Anabaptist lifestyle in general, so it figures prominently among those values undergirding a Mennonite development ethic. Many practitioners characterize their work as not just a job, but as a vocation—perhaps even a sacred calling. They see themselves as primarily accountable to marginalized people who have little access to the basic necessities of life. The service motif means that the practitioner or the development agency will act in preference toward disadvantaged groups, rather than promoting their own self-interest.

All stakeholders—donors, development agencies, practitioners, and marginalized populations—need to be called to mutual accountability as they together pursue their ultimate goals of people-centered development. The challenge is to facilitate the proper balance among the interests of the various parties. Praxis—acting and reflecting on one's actions—becomes an ongoing and important activity in maintaining an appropriate balance because each party is learning while making its particular contribution to development, whether funds, technical assistance, labor, or other local resources. The service value calls for a leadership style known as "servant leadership." This approach emphasizes the leader as servant, building shared vision and maximizing stakeholder value and humility, and is more in harmony with servanthood and praxis than that of the more typical "command and control," so prevalent in many development efforts.[97]

Integrity, the third value in the chart, often appears among the attributes of Mennonite development practitioners when their co-workers describe them. For example, oral history in some Bolivian communities where Mennonite development workers lived and worked has made nearly legendary the openness and honesty that characterized their lifestyle and practice. These practitioners believed that they could contribute to the devel-

opment process, but they quickly recognized those contributions that only community persons, local government representatives, or other technicians could make.
These practitioners came with no hidden agenda. Communities are frequently suspicious of such workers who
come under the auspices of an international church-relat-
ed development agency (or of a foreign or home-country
government agency, for that matter), which presumably
has a hidden religious or political agenda in addition to its
publicly stated purpose. Nevertheless, eventually the Bolivian communities came to value the "untied" contributions made by these practitioners.

The value of *mutuality* does not easily fit into development language and frameworks. By definition, development has traditionally tried to make poor countries more
like Western rich countries, although changes have occurred to mute or alter that in recent years. However, cultural lag still means that development language and organizational structures often have an imperial feel, though
many individual practitioners struggle to resist that tone
and style. Many Mennonite practitioners explained that
they entered development work because they felt they
could provide something that "beneficiaries" needed in
order to solve their problems.

Earlier in this book, Raymond Martin reflects on his
experience by saying, "It was hard not to slip into a mentality of thinking that we from the rich, highly developed,
technologically-advanced West knew the answers and
would generously give them to the poor backward folk of
the Third World." Comments like this suggest that not
only were practitioners highly motivated to serve, they
were frequently tempted to believe that as international
development workers they had what poor people needed
in order to improve their lives, whether in health, agri-

culture, education, or business. However, nearly all practitioners noted that they quickly discovered that local people had more to teach them than they could ever hope to teach local people. They soon recast their work as an undertaking characterized by mutuality rather than as a unilateral, unidirectional transfer of knowledge, resources, or skills. As mutual learning occurred, everyone benefited, outsider practitioners as well as local people.

Most grassroots workers realized rather quickly that developing and maintaining relationships was as important as any scientific advance their expertise could achieve. With this came a new appreciation and respect for local culture. Practitioners often noted that at first they wanted to understand the local culture so that they could figure out how best to couch the innovations they were bringing, so that local people would more quickly accept them. However, with time, they came to view culture as the framework for living that highlighted the importance of relationships and the aesthetics that enriched life. Practitioners drew inspiration from the local culture to form new patterns for living which they hoped to take with them when they returned home. They began to see culture not so much as something that needed to be changed in order for new technologies and perspectives to take root, but rather as the framework for judging the appropriateness of those technologies and perspectives. They learned from, as well as contributed to, the culture in which they worked. At the same time, host culture communities would say that they also expanded their understanding through contact with the culture the development practitioners represented.

Authenticity appears as a distinct value in the Mennonite development ethic, even though it may seem closely related to integrity and mutuality. In this book we distinguish authenticity from other values by focusing on matters of self-perception and presentation. Development work involves the coming together of two or more cultures, irrespective of where it takes place. Commonly it involves crossing rural and urban cultural boundaries, class divides, or even ethnic and national cultures. We are better able to understand who we really are when we discover more fully our own culture. This in turn enables us to interact more authentically with persons from the host culture in which we are doing development work. The better we understand our own culture, the more we appreciate the host culture. We are also able to eliminate or reduce the invidious markers of class, ethnic, and national differences. Authenticity enriches our relationships with others as we recognize that everyone is both teacher and learner in every situation. Authentic development embraces this principle.

Humility begins at home. True humility requires that we recognize our own true merit. Once we recognize our own worth, we will be better able to thwart the personal drive to increase our power, which ultimately results in the absence of authenticity, in a breakdown of mutuality, and in the loss of integrity. Humility in development work means that we encourage others to take due credit for their accomplishments. We encourage others to develop their gifts further. Of course, this also applies to us and our own gifts. Humility is the recognition of the true worth of others and of ourselves.

Justice and peace, the final two values in the chart, are core values for Anabaptist/Mennonite development practitioners, whether they work with grassroots organizations or with public policy organizations. These values not only inform the actions (the Means in the chart) used to achieve development goals, but they must be present structurally in the social entity which development ultimately seeks to create. Justice-inspired actions focus on fairness and equity in personal relationships as well as within the larger system. Promoting the common good, taking an ethical stance where appropriate, that is, not claiming neutrality on ethical issues, and sharing fairly both burdens and benefits, are all actions that make justice concrete. Actions for justice seek to develop policies that make fairness and equity the norm, rather than leaving them to be negotiated on a case-by-case basis. This ultimately has political implications for how the voices of all stakeholders are systematically heard.

Peace interfaces closely with justice but focuses more on questions of dignity and wholeness. Justice actions and structures greatly enhance efforts toward peace, but they are different. Nonviolence as a lifestyle, rather than a social-change tactic, addresses the value of human life and dignity. Peace-inspired actions are oriented toward promoting whole persons; they seek to foster the physical, social, and spiritual well-being of all members of a group, community, or society. Peace activities also involve creating an awareness of social, economic, and environmental interdependence and a respect for the integrity of creation.

Ultimate Goals

Anthropologists claim that every culture orients its people about how to relate to each other, to nature, to time, and to one's own personhood. The Mennonite development ethic suggests a guide which should orient development work. Undeniably, the goals in the framework reflect a Western-value orientation, but that does not necessarily invalidate them. Given these values, and the means used to carry them out, what are the implicit or explicit ends in the work of Mennonite development practitioners?

Our analyses of practitioners' experiences, reflections on the MCC development style, and our own involvements, suggest that the ultimate goal of the Mennonite development ethic is the creation of a world that is more just, sustainable, and peaceful, and a world in which the quality of life has improved. In other words, the values and means embraced by the Mennonite development ethic will orient development efforts to construct families, communities, societies, and a world characterized by:

- Justice,
- Sustainability,
- Quality of life,
- Peace/*salaam*/*shalom*—from the personal to the global.

Actions must implement distributive justice rooted in fairness and equity, so that burdens and benefits are shared fairly. *Justice*-oriented actions will also foster reciprocity, an expression of distributive justice that dignifies all parties in the relationship. Our commitment to taking a moral stance on ethical issues demonstrates that we are not neutral. We guide our actions by a moral code, in our case, a faith-based code. Faith-based action means that the moral stance we take is derived from a faith tradition that emphasizes fair and equitable treatment for all.

Sustainability means that we believe in taking the natural and social environments seriously. We stress being in harmony with each other and with the natural environment. We recognize the systemic nature of the environment and its ability to replenish itself if it is not pushed beyond its carrying capacity. The same is the case with the social environment. For example, social organizations should be in harmony with the social environment and should not require more social resources to sustain themselves than the system can supply. In other words, social organizations must be compatible with the skills and knowledge available in the context.

Quality of life focuses not just on *"having more,"* a necessary but insufficient condition for ensuring physical survival, but also on *"being more."*[98] Thus, there are physical, social, psychological, and spiritual needs that must be met. To achieve this we need to implement the value of people-centeredness by developing participatory structures and systems that make it possible for people to be subjects in their own development. In other words, we strive for equity in the distribution and use of power. This requires that we implement the value of justice, which leads to trusting others, and listening to and identifying with others, typically known as empathy.

Peace, understood holistically as *salaam* or *shalom*, pays attention to the quality of relationships, whether personal, international, or anything in between. Peace relates directly to international structures and systems that promote interdependence, respect for the other and creation, nonviolence, and valuing human life. A commitment to peace affects how we engage in trade, tourism, international relations, and development work. It is helpful to reflect again on the comments at the conclusion of Chapter 3 made by Ron Mathies and Tim Lind. They highlight the importance of viewing service as learning and understanding servanthood as an approach in which one comes not with answers or solutions to the needs of others, but rather with one's self and puts this at the service of the context it encounters.[99]

Servanthood emerges from combining the values of mutuality and service. The former underscores the reci-

procity of the relationship and the latter the value of helping. However, since all "helping relationships" are problematic because of the inherent differences in power that
typically accompany them, it is important to explicitly
recognize this disparity in power. Fusing the values of
mutuality and service, along with a dose of integrity, humility, and people-centeredness, produces servanthood.
This is character required of all development workers, especially those who are attempting to bridge boundaries of
class, nationality, ethnicity, religion, and location
(rural/urban/suburban). As such, it is part of the Anabaptist ethic of peace for living, equally applicable to "outsiders" or "insiders" in a situation, irrespective of who the
categories apply to. For example, a specialist from Nairobi and an expatriate development volunteer, both of
whom are working in a rural Kenyan village, should each
exhibit the same respectful behavior and attitudes.

Concluding Thoughts

We close this section with a few summary comments
in relation to the Mennonite development ethic. First, we
believe that "value free" development is impossible, regardless of our organizational or religious affiliation.
Therefore, it is important to be aware of the explicit and
implicit values that shape how we understand and do development.

We recognize that the ultimate goals may sound rather
ethereal and idealistic. However, they do allow us to identify clear outcomes or ultimate goals for evaluating alternative courses of action as development practitioners.
These goals are global. They go beyond personal, organizational, ethnic, or national interests and thereby recognize the interdependence of all creation. What difference

would it make if international development decisions were filtered through the "justice, peace, and sustainability" lens, rather than the more common lens of maximizing personal, organizational, national, or regional interests?

Even though we identify what we call a Mennonite development ethic, we are aware that other organizations or individuals may share many elements of the framework. The values are not necessarily unique to persons coming from the Anabaptist/Mennonite faith tradition.[100] However, until other groups or development organizations generate their own ethic of development, using inductive methods rather than deductive methods, it will be difficult to determine the extent of overlapping values.

It can be argued that the development ethic ideal as we present it may work well in one-to-one relationships, typically experienced in village-level development work, but that it is not relevant at the macro level and in the public policy world of bilateral and multilateral aid, where raw politics and strategic national interests prevail. Certainly the challenges differ depending on the institutional and contextual settings. We want to clarify, however, that the elements of the development ethic which we set forth here were derived from practitioners working in a range of organizational settings, including large bilateral and multilateral development institutions where national or regional strategic interests are thought to hold sway. We are confident that the ethic clearly serves to orient individuals, irrespective of the particular setting in which they work.

On the other hand, our data does not allow us to address the question of impact at the organizational level. One might hope that the World Bank has kinder and gentler development policy because of individuals working there who are guided by an Anabaptist-like ethic of development, but that would be merely speculation at this point. However, if one takes into consideration all the forces that operate to effect change in an institution like the World Bank, it would seem appropriate to claim that the presence of persons with an Anabaptist/Mennonite development ethic within the Bank could contribute to the overall process of change as it occurs.

There are, of course, questions left unanswered in our discussion. Does an Anabaptist/Mennonite ethic of development, and its attendant values, serve the goals of the larger development effort? If the ethic is not useful to engage and evaluate larger development goals and practice it should be discarded. On the other hand, if the Mennonite development ethic helps more than hurts, then it should be further shaped and promoted. While we have addressed the issue of whether or not the development policy benefits the human condition, we have not addressed the issue of scale of impact, which seems to be part of the discussion. The question of whether or not working at a higher level necessarily has a greater impact, either in development or mission outreach, remains to be debated further. We alluded to this issue in relation to whether or not the ethic applies to macro level policy work, but we will take up the topic again following a discussion of the ethic's relationship to a general Anabaptist theology and ethic for life.

Summary of an Anabaptist Theology and Ethic

Mennonite scholars still argue about whether a widely accepted systematic Anabaptist theology and ethic exist.[101] Others argue that a cohesive theology and ethic which all members could agree to is not possible because the locus of authority in Anabaptism is within the congregation. Regardless, we believe that it may be helpful to try to state a theology and an ethic that include the essentials that shaped the Anabaptist movement. We grant that it may be presumptuous to try to establish an Anabaptist development ethic in order to compare practitioners' experiences in doing development while following it. But we shall try. First, we offer minimal definitions of theology and ethic.

Paul Tillich explained, "Theology is the methodological interpretation of the contents of the Christian faith."[102] As such, theology moves back and forth between two poles: the eternal truth claimed as its foundation and the temporal situation in which that eternal truth must be received. Theology consists of both *form* (methodology) and *content* (the specific analyses of the subject matter). In reference to *form*, Anabaptist/Mennonite theology is more specifically "a dialogue carried on in the church [which] explores the implications of the church's experience of God in Christ for its ethical decisions, worship, organization, and mission strategy."[103] Mennonite theology, according to Robert Friedman, arises and is carried out primarily within the community of faith in an attempt to articulate the presuppositions, content, and consequences of Christian faith. This approach emphasizes the role of all the members of a local congregation in the creation of the doctrines (the content of the theology) and application of the religious tradition (ethics). This methodology has been termed the "hermeneutical community," in which the worshiping community, claiming the presence of God's spirit, is involved in interpreting the meaning of the Christian scriptures.

Methodologically then, Anabaptist/Mennonite theology emerges continually as a product of ongoing discernment among the community of believers as they attempt

to follow Jesus' example in daily life. By consulting practitioners and observing the broader dialogue expressed in
published materials and documents by Mennonites, and
then comparing their praxis with what they say, one
should discover substantial insights into an Anabap-
tist/Mennonite theology and ethic.

Scholars have exerted an immense amount of effort to
discover the essential nature, that is, the content, of the Believers Church, of which the Anabaptists are a central constituent. There is increasing agreement that the Believers
Church is "not primarily a community of explicit belief. In
a way, the term 'Believers Church' puts an unrepresenta-
tive stress on belief and implies incorrectly that the given
[established] churches are, in contrast, weak in believers.
Actually, it is the given churches which historically have
placed the greatest stress on creedal belief. The Believers
Churches, so-called, really stress far more than belief;
namely obedience, purity, simplicity, discipleship,
covenantal accountability, mutual support, mutual discipline and mutual, though also exclusive, love."[104]

A similar statement was made by the findings committee of the Believers Church conference in 1968: "Believers Church, therefore, points first of all not to the doc-
trinal content of beliefs held, nor to the subjective believ-
ingness (sic) of the believer, but more to the constructive
character of the commitment in defining the visible (in
other words, ethical) community." The committee continued, "The believer in Jesus Christ manifests a new quality of life which many of us have preferred to call discipleship."[105] Again, these later statements stress the "doing" aspect of the Christian gospel, rather than creedal
minutia. Discipleship refers to ethical behavior.

In spite of the existential nature of Anabaptist theology, and the historical difficulty in codifying a theology of

Anabaptism that satisfies the diversity of Mennonite experience, North American Mennonites have been able to produce evolving statements of faith, principles, and practices. The most recent was published in 1995—*Confession of Faith in a Mennonite Perspective* (CFMP).[106] In addition, numerous statements and position papers have been generated by MCC and other Mennonite institutions.

The 24 articles of the CFMP identify a number of faith-practice guidelines characterizing Anabaptists. A sampling of the most relevant ones include discerning God's will and the ethics that flow from it as a church, following the example of Jesus (discipleship) rather than conforming to the world, pursuing the will of God rather than individual happiness, living simply and laying aside materialism, acting peacefully and with justice rather than with violence or military means, making one's first loyalty to God's kingdom rather than to any nation-state or ethnic group, telling the truth rather than relying on oaths, performing deeds of compassion and reconciliation, loving one's enemies, forgiving those who persecute, living a holy life, living out one's faith within the church community, and practicing spiritual disciplines and stewardship.

Walter Klaassen's *Anabaptism: Neither Catholic nor Protestant* details a number of elements of an Anabaptist ethic, many of which overlap with what we have already identified. He emphasizes a radical and uncompromising discipleship; relationships governed by truth and love; refusing to participate in warfare, including the non-payment of taxes which support war; non-swearing of oaths; fostering community and sharing possessions; and the separation of church and state with one's primary allegiance to God.[107]

An analysis of the content of writing by leading contemporary scholars of Anabaptism produces a list of Anabaptist/Mennonite beliefs and doctrines which suggest a coherent set of interdependent and interacting themes. Chief among them are a disciplined community committed to following the teachings of Jesus, separation from the world (the idea of two kingdoms), a voluntary church (based on adult believers baptism), ultimate obedience to God and the scriptures, discipleship (following the example of Jesus), love and nonresistance, mutual sharing/communalism, and religious liberty (freedom of conscience).[108]

What relevant historical sources might we point to for this theology? Some historians and theologians maintain that Anabaptism is only an historical phenomenon, dating from its beginnings in about 1525 through approximately 1650 when the persecution basically ceased. They maintain that the movement has no contemporary significance, that the beliefs and ethic expressed during the active period of the movement may have once been defined as "normative Anabaptism," but that it is not applicable today. This position holds that what evolved from the Anabaptist movement into what is now known as "Mennonite" cannot be defined as "Anabaptist." Rather, "Mennonite" is descendent and derivative of Anabaptism which has gone its own way. Others argue that it is appropriate to use the term "Anabaptist" to refer to the ideals that the original movement espoused, and so "Anabaptist" can be normative for the present age, although adaptations must be made, as for example in specific forms of nonconformity.[109] In this book, we take this latter position, and we use the terms "Mennonite" and "Anabaptist/Anabaptism" interchangeably.

Five major principles emerge from the work of scholars which can be considered as the broad framework of an Anabaptist theology and ethic. The first principle is the ethic of love. For example, J. Lawrence Burkholder proposes, "The central idea of the Christian ethic according to Mennonites is love (Luke 10:27)."[110] The CFMP states, " . . . Our faithfulness to Jesus is lived out in the loving life and witness of the church community" (65-66). Defining Anabaptist beliefs and practices emerge from this ethic of love. These include nonresistance, brotherhood (mutual responsibility for the welfare of the entire community), community life, and communalism.

The second principle of the ethic includes peace, justice, and nonresistance. The CFMP states, "As followers of Jesus, we participate in his ministry of peace and justice. Jesus empowered us to love enemies, to forgive rather than to seek revenge, to practice right relationships, to witness against all forms of violence including war among nations, hostility among races and classes, violence between men and women, abortion and capital punishment"(82). The scope of this mandate is not simply local, but global.

A third principle is stewardship. "As stewards of God's earth, we are called to care for the earth and to bring rest and renewal to the land and everything that lives on it. We are called to be stewards in the household of God, set apart for the service of God." (CFMP, 78). The material world is in God's hand, who "is the owner of everything." "Economic justice is an integral part of the Sabbath cycle. The effect of the Sabbath-Jubilee laws was a return to relative economic equality every fifty years" (CFMP, 79). Christians respect the earth and benefit from its generosity; consequently, they are commanded to share it with all peoples everywhere in the world, regardless of race, nationality, or beliefs.

A fourth principle is "helping neighbors join the community under the reign of God." This means following

Christ and sharing "kingdom of God" life with one's neighbor, known in Mennonite circles as mutual aid. The "kingdom of God" comes, as Jesus taught, by implementing Christ's great commandments, namely by loving God and one's neighbor, and by doing good to all others, including one's enemies. "Jesus proclaimed both the nearness of God's reign and its future realization, its healing and its judgment. In his life and teaching, he showed that God's reign included the poor, outcasts, the persecuted, those who were like children, and those whose faith is like a mustard seed. The church is to be a spiritual, social, and economic reality, demonstrating now the justice, righteousness, love, and peace of the age to come" (CFMP, 89-90). Again the scope is worldwide.

A final principle is a mission impulse at the heart of Anabaptism. Most scholars agree that this is a key ingredient in the movement, but they do not concur about the shape, content, or methods of this mission thrust. The CMFP asserts, "We believe that the church is called to proclaim and to be a sign of the kingdom of God." It goes on to state, "In his mission of preaching, teaching, and healing, Jesus announced, 'The kingdom of God has come near; repent, and believe in the good news'" (42).

No coherent "Anabaptist theology of development" exists, and, if one did, it would probably not be very different from one derived from a good general Christian theology and doctrine. What would be distinctive in an Anabaptist theology of development would be an "obedience" or discipleship emphasis, focusing on ethics, which are so clearly at the heart of Anabaptism. We find it more useful and accurate to talk about a set of Anabaptist principles of behavior, which can be termed an "ethic" as defined in the earlier section, "Ethics and Ethical Frameworks: A Brief Definition." This orientation frames our discussion of Anabaptist ethics in general and development ethics in particular in the remainder of this chapter.

Are these ethical principles, derived from the various sources of Anabaptist theology, related to the ethical principles of Anabaptist/Mennonite development practitioners? We will investigate that question in the next section.

Convergences and Divergences Between Anabaptist Theology and Ethics; An Anabaptist Development Ethic

Is there a linkage between Anabaptist theology and ethics, as summarized in the previous section, and the values and ethics of Mennonite development practitioners, or are they largely unrelated? Are the values and ethical principles of the practitioners largely uninformed by Anabaptist theology, or are they nearly synonymous with Anabaptist values?

At the risk of substantial oversimplification, Exhibit 6 summarizes the key values and ethics of the Mennonite development practitioners involved in our study, and those derived from Anabaptist theology. The development practitioners included among their values and ethics: people-centeredness, mutuality, service, integrity, servant leadership, peace, and justice. Anabaptist theology includes values and ethics such as love, nonconformity, community, simplicity, truth-telling, discipleship, mutuality, holiness, and forgiveness.

What can be observed from this comparison, particularly in terms of convergences and divergences? Clearly, while there is not a one-to-one correlation between the two sets of values, there is certainly more convergence than divergence.

Exhibit 6:
Comparing Values and Ethics Held by Development Practitioners with an Anabaptist Theology

Development Practitioners' Values and Ethics	Anabaptist Theology Values and Ethics
• People-centeredness	• Love
• Service	• Peace and justice
• Integrity	• Stewardship
• Mutuality	• Discipleship
• Authenticity	• Nonconformity
• Humility	• Simplicity
• Peace	• Pursuing the will of God
• Justice	
• Servant-leadership	• Proclamation of God's kingdom on earth
• Empowerment	• Forgiveness
• Listening	• Truth-telling
• Promoting the common good	• Reconciliation
• Nonviolence	• Holiness
	• Community
	• Spiritual disciplines
	• Mutuality/mutual aid

As we noted before, love has often been identified as the primary ethic in Anabaptist theology. "Love" as a term does not turn up in the Mennonite development practitioners' ethical framework. But the values present in the ethical framework are ways of expressing or doing love: mutuality, service, humility, honesty, peace, justice, and so on. These are similar to the values embedded in Anabaptist theology. Other values such as simplicity, practicing spiritual disciplines, holiness, and stewardship are not identified as values held by all the practitioners, yet all have been identified in the various theological sources.

Thus, we may suggest that there is a considerable, if not striking, congruence between the values and ethics of the practitioners and of Anabaptist theology and ethics. In fact, this may be true to a fault. For example, we Mennonites have basically been trusting people who tend to see the best in others (that of God in others?), so much so that we may have at times been naive. Similarly, our "people-centeredness" may have tilted us toward listening and identifying with others so much so that we've failed to recognize the issues of power that are often involved. Perhaps our "service" orientation draws us to provide too much assistance in ways that lead to dependency.

At the same time, there are divergences between the Mennonite ethic of development and mainstream Anabaptist theology and ethics. Perhaps the most significant area of divergence centers around the role of Mennonites in the world. Historically, some Mennonites have emphasized a posture of not conforming to the world. Theologically, they have described that as the presence of two kingdoms: the world and the church. They have held that the values of the world (the state and society) and the values of God's kingdom (the church) are so different, that one cannot be involved in the world without compromising one's faith. This dichotomy is represented in Exhibit 8.4.

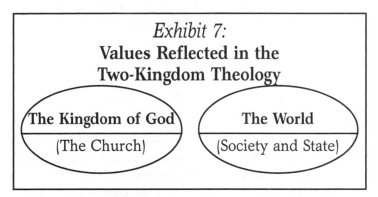

Exhibit 7:
Values Reflected in the Two-Kingdom Theology

The Kingdom of God
(The Church)

The World
(Society and State)

The "two-kingdom" worldview has generally been considered one of the basic foundations of Anabaptist theology and practice; it is first stated clearly in the *Schleitheim Confession* of 1527. Historian James Juhnke states, "At the heart of the Anabaptist view of the state, as it grew out of the left-wing of the sixteenth century reformation, was the doctrine of the two worlds."[111] In a study of Mennonite relations with the state, Driedger and Kraybill affirm that "the two-kingdom theology that pitted the kingdom of God against the kingdom of the world was foundational to Mennonite theology from its earliest expressions."[112] They suggest that the *Schleitheim Confession* "stated the ethical dualism in stark terms." Thus the Confession avers that "all those who have fellowship with the dead works of darkness have no part in the light."[113] Driedger and Kraybill conclude, "The basic theological task, it seems to us, requires careful reflection on the consequences of these divergent world views of the kingdom of God."[114]

In a recent study, Perry Bush presented the account of the two-kingdom ethic and how it expressed itself in relation to war and peace during a substantial part of the twentieth century. He states categorically that "[Mennonite] nonresistance must be viewed in light of a two-kingdom ethic and theology that lies at the heart of Mennonite attitudes toward outside society."[115]

James Halteman, a Mennonite economist teaching at Wheaton (IL) College explored the relationship between church and state in his book *The Clashing Worlds of Economics and Faith*.[116] Unlike the case we make here for greater involvement in public policy, Halteman argues that Mennonites have gone too far in this direction and need to return to more of a separatist practice.

Guy F. Hershberger, probably best known for promoting the idea of the "kingdom of God" as distinguished from the secular social order, treated the relationships and conflict between the two realms eschatologically; that is, he believed that the ultimate harmonization of the two realms will take place when Jesus Christ returns to declare victory. He proposed that the nature of the relationship which members of the "colony of Heaven" should have with the kingdom of this world is one that needs to be redeemed by way of discipleship, that is, by following Jesus. Ultimately this means rejecting violence, coercion, and power, and instead suffering for righteousness and justice, as Jesus himself did. This also means that a Christian does not have final responsibility for the world's structures and attendant injustices. "The man-made kingdom without a cross has proved to be a mirage. Social responsibility which exchanges the way of the cross for the lesser evil is not too sure of a kingdom at all."[117]

Different Mennonite groups have a variety of attitudes and practices in relation to the two-kingdom theology.

Many Mennonites from Canada, as well as from the midwestern U.S. (more specifically, those of Russian descent, or those from the branch of Mennonites formerly known as General Conference Mennonites) have historically been active in affairs of the state—including holding national political offices in the U.S. Congress or as a Minister in the Canadian government.

Those Mennonites who have held tightly to the twokingdom theology and have been reluctant to be involved in public policy or affairs of the state point to the persecution that sixteenth century Anabaptists experienced in their search for religious freedom at the hands of the governing authorities. These accounts are extensively documented in *The Martyr's Mirror*.

What implications does the two-kingdom theology have for Mennonite development workers who adhere to it? Stated briefly, they would believe that they should first live as disciples of Christ, making every effort to do what Jesus teaches, namely, loving God, and then one's neighbor. Next would be concerns having to do with societal injustices, conflict, peace, and power. As a consequence of this separation between church and state, Mennonites historically have been reluctant to be "unequally yoked with unbelievers," to get their hands dirty and work in public policy positions. Mennonites have found it natural to do relief work as described in Chapter 3. Where their work has had a development orientation, it has largely been at the grassroots level, often with local churches, at a considerable distance from state authorities.

Yet, from the papers of the practitioners, as well as from the common themes identified in Chapter 7, we hear a clear call for greater involvement in public policy to supplement the historical grassroots emphasis. Not only did this call come from those doing public policy, as we would expect, but it also came from those working at the grassroots.

For example, research done among MCCers by Merrill Ewert supports this call. In a sample survey of 461 active MCCers in 1995, he found that the largest share of the sampled MCCers identified injustice as the primary cause of poverty. In addition, he found that the largest share of MCCers stated, "Development occurs when 'unjust structures are changed' or when there is 'structural change.'"[118] What we note here is that the largest share of MCCers are working at the grassroots level, yet it is this same group who define the primary cause of poverty as injustice and the primary solution to be at the structural level, that is, through public policy approaches. It is also interesting to note that the strongest pressure in favor of structural change comes from the MCC home office.[119]

Over time, and for a variety of reasons, the clear separation between values of the church and values of the state became muddied. In the area of development, contributing factors to this were the involvement of Mennonites in relief efforts in Europe following World War II and in relief and development work in low-income countries with Mennonite Central Committee. The traditional two-kingdom theology seemed not to provide adequate answers, particularly for those working outside institutional church settings where confrontations with moral dilemmas tends to be more frequent and intense.

For example, J. Lawrence Burkholder, while administering public relief programs in China in the late 1940s, found the absolutist ethical positions arising from a two-kingdom theology difficult to maintain. Building on the tensions he experienced in China, and while doing his doctoral work at Princeton Theological Seminary, he examined *The Problem of Social Responsibility from the Per-*

spective of the Mennonite Church. Questioning the relevance of the two-kingdom theology, he called for a greater identification with and role in the world:

No one can be *actively* responsible for all of society's problems. *Social responsibility does, however, imply a general attitude of identification with the world.* The socially responsible person believes that he is a participant in the human struggle for truth and justice as these values are manifested in the social and political realms. He identifies himself with the stream of secular history and feels obligated to the world. The problems of the world are at least in a general way his problems . . . . [120]

Although Mennonite authorities did not warmly receive Burkholder's thinking and writing, his opinion was influential in the continuing evolution of official Mennonite statements and practices. As we will show, much of the thinking about an appropriate "witness to the state" was articulated by Mennonite theologian John Howard Yoder. Some of the outcomes of his thinking and influence include the formation of MCC's Capitol Hill office in 1968, their Ottawa office in 1975, and the MCC Liaison Office at the United Nations in 1991. In addition, the American war in Vietnam, the Civil Rights Movement, the nuclear arms race, as well as the American war in Iraq, all had substantial impact on the evolving relationship of Mennonites to the state.

The shift in language in Mennonite publications during the second half of the twentieth century also reflects the evolution from separatism/quietism to activism. The language of justice, development, politics, and peace largely replaced language of nonresistance, nonconformity, and relief work. [121]

More recently, and much like some of the practitioners included in this collection, John Paul Lederach,
when reflecting on his years of work in international
conciliation and peacemaking, stated that he "no longer
feels comfortable with the easily defined two-kingdom
theology" with which he grew up in the Mennonite
church. He finds "this stance too easy and rarely honest. In hundreds of ways, we do participate in the life of
society. It is never possible to fully withdraw, and I do
not believe we are called to withdraw."[122]

We should note that, in spite of many Mennonites being reluctant to engage in political processes, not all
have been unwilling when their own interests have
been threatened, and not only when those interests are
matters of faith and practice. For example, while one of
the authors of this book was serving on a public school
board, it was observed that Mennonite parents who had
sons or daughters in the public school system were
quick to attend school board meetings and advocate for
certain programs (such as a reading program) from
which their child was directly benefiting, thereby taking an "activist" position. However, these same parents
were not among those attending school board meetings
dealing with systemic issues, such as eliminating the
military recruitment and training program (Junior Re-
serve Officer Training Corps) from the school, an activity by which their child was not directly affected. Nor
were the local church conference leaders willing to tes-
tify or write a letter to the school board on this issue,
citing their "separatist" position.

Similarly, during the period when the "separatist" position was more widely accepted among Mennonites,
many were willing to actively petition the U. S. Congress
to obtain exemption for their young men from joining the

military and to obtain conscientious objector status instead, taking an "activist" position.

The question these paradoxical practices raise is how is this different from the American Medical Association, the National Rifle Association, Big Tobacco, or any other lobbyist group who becomes active when their own interests are at stake? The fact that, for Mennonites, these interests are matters of faith and life, rather than profit, does not change the principle. Historically, we seem to have been more willing to become engaged in public policy issues when our personal or institutional interests are at stake, but not so willing when the broader public interest or common good is at stake.

Thus, for a variety of reasons, many Mennonites seem to favor greater involvement in the public policy process. This movement is set within broader historical continuums which could be described as "quietism-activism" or "separatist-engagement." (Driedger and Kraybill provide a fascinating account of this in their *Mennonite Peacemaking* book where they argue that a new generation of Mennonites pushed church-state relations to center stage beginning in the 1950s.) Exhibit 8 summarizes this evolution of thinking by highlighting four key areas on the continuum.[123]

At the separatist end of the continuum is Guy Hershberger who, in advocating the way of "love and nonresistance," argued for an uncompromising New Testament ethic that was faithful to the way of the cross but wary of political participation. John Howard Yoder, arguing for "*agape* love," called for witnessing to the social order while maintaining a somewhat sectarian stance in the disciple community. But it was also love that led Lawrence Burkholder to "social responsibility" for the larger social order with all of its ambiguities, compromises, and dilem-

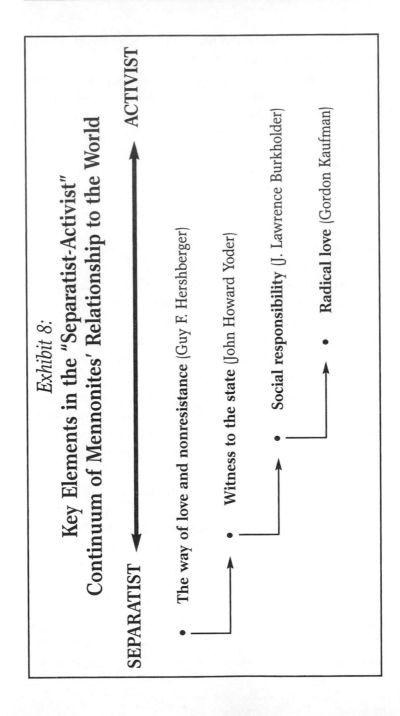

Exhibit 8:
Key Elements in the "Separatist-Activist"
Continuum of Mennonites' Relationship to the World

SEPARATIST

ACTIVIST

- The way of love and nonresistance (Guy F. Hershberger)

- Witness to the state (John Howard Yoder)

- Social responsibility (J. Lawrence Burkholder)

- Radical love (Gordon Kaufman)

mas. At the activist end of the continuum, Gordon Kaufman argued for a position of "radical love" that places Mennonites in the very heart of the sinful situation, even when support of the outcome differs with his or her personal beliefs.[124]

Clearly, the call for greater involvement of Mennonites in public policy would result in being much closer to the "engagement" side of the continuum than to the "separatist." Dual standards of morality, one for the church and one for the state, are being replaced by a paradigm which recognizes overlapping values, or, as detailed by Driedger and Kraybill, a paradigm in which both church and state are under the "lordship of Christ." The values of the church and state seem not to be so mutually exclusive as they once seemed to be and now seem to be better represented by the overlapping circles of church and state as shown in Exhibit 9.

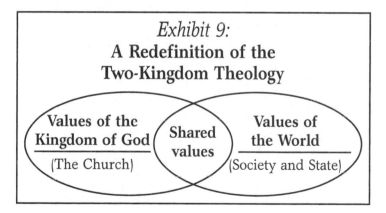

Exhibit 9:
**A Redefinition of the
Two-Kingdom Theology**

Values of the
Kingdom of God
(The Church)

Shared
values

Values of
the World
(Society and State)

The issue of globalization, along with trade and finance, presented initially in Chapter 2, is a specific example of the rationale for greater involvement in public policy and the theological justification for this. Ephesians 6:12 states that, "For we wrestle not against flesh and blood, but against the principalities and powers, the rulers of darkness of this world, against spiritual wickedness in high places."

One interpretation of this verse from the New Testament, particularly the concept of *principalities and powers*, is that it is referring to invisible realities—something that is difficult to identify but which you know is there and affecting you. Laws, systems, structures—and public policies—can all be such principalities and powers. The verse also indicates that our struggle is not against a single individual, but against those invisible realities that express themselves through the flesh and blood of individuals. The WTO and globalization are invisible realities that impact, for good or for ill, on the flesh and blood of millions of individuals. The Asian financial crisis of 1997 is a dramatic example of this. Apartheid in South Africa was less the evil of a single person and more the evil of a system.

Trade, an underlying force behind globalization, can, in principle, be beneficial to all, including the poorest. It depends largely on the rules and the terms of individual trade agreements such as NAFTA (North American Free Trade Agreement) or the WTO. Thus, in order to have more justice in the world, persons who are motivated by their Christian faith to be both prophetic and effective should focus their efforts on making the rules fair.

9.
What Kind of World?
Realities, Visions,
Dilemmas,
and Opportunities

Realities

Forty-five years ago, the United Nations declared the 1960s the "development decade." Now after nearly a half-century of development work, what kind of world has development brought. Is development still a valid enterprise in today's world? Does a Mennonite development ethic have anything to contribute to the development field in the face of current world realities? Does development, as we have known it, even have a future in our globalized world? If so, how will development need to change to be relevant and helpful?

As usual, the answers likely depend on who answers. An HIV-positive Zambian, an international banker in Hong Kong, a Colombian displaced person, a Palestinian scientist, the CEO of a multinational computer company based in North America, and an Indian community organizer will each have a different opinion about what our world is really like, if the life it offers is better today than it was a decade or two ago, and what the prospects for the future are. How any one of us answers is further affected by whether we are male or female, young or old, rural or urban. Irrespective of who we are, we would probably agree that ours is a post-modern, globalized, conflict-riddled world in which natural resources diminish steadily while inequality, poverty, and United States political hegemony appear to grow exponentially. Increasingly we believe that certain problems or issues today require global action in order to address them adequately. For example, concerted action across national boundaries is necessary to confront problems like environmental degradation, HIV/AIDS, international debt, nuclear testing, large-scale drug trafficking, global economic inequality, war, international terrorism, and globalization itself.

We may agree on the need for united action to address these global problems, yet each of us likely experiences our twenty-first century world differently. We probably disagree about which of the processes and trends are positive and negative. How we make the best of this world for the greatest number of persons is the challenge before the development field as a whole.

Mennonite development practitioners face the question of what their individual and collective contributions might be to accomplishing this task. Our world and the dilemmas it presents are daunting. That massive challenge provides the opportunity for us Anabaptists to demonstrate how our faith perspective empowers us to engage the world.

Poverty and Economic Inequality

Globalization represents either the world's best hope for a better future or the harbinger of greater gloom and doom, depending on one's perspective. Broadly defined, globalization is merely the removal or reduction of barriers to human interaction across national boundaries. Its economic manifestation is sometimes termed "marketization," since globalization is often thought to be synonymous with expanding markets or increasing international economic integration. At this point, there is greater debate about the politics related to the removal or reduction of those barriers than about whether globalization would be beneficial if realized in its ideal form.[125] Questions like the following make the issue of globalization polemical and of interest to development practitioners and organizations. Who decides? Who cannot decide? Who benefits? Who is harmed? Who bears the short-term costs? Who carries the long-term costs? These are essentially development questions.

The dilemma of economic globalization, as the questions suggest, lies in the tension among effectiveness, efficiency, and fairness. Heated debate continues, even while globalization's impact is not clear. Most parties agree that in the best case, everyone should benefit from the liberalization of national economies and their international integration. The global economic system itself should be strengthened. The efficiency argument holds that, if barriers were removed, each national economy would be free to maximize its comparative advantage by focusing its production on the abundant resource that produces the largest return for the input. A given country would be able to achieve the maximum benefit from its resource mix, thereby making more goods and services available to all partners in the trading relationship, which would increase the welfare of all parties involved.

Economic liberalization does not occur in a vacuum. It requires explicit economic policy to support the process at all levels of social organization—local, national, regional, and global. Multilateral financial and trading organizations like the World Bank, International Monetary Fund, and World Trade Organization, along with powerful bilateral organizations like the United States Agency for International Development and Canadian International Development Agency, several North American examples, play vital roles in promoting liberalization-friendly policy at the global level. Trade, especially in its liberalized form, is a powerful impetus driving globalization in all its complexity.

Technology advances, not just to meet demands for greater production, but also to facilitate trade. Progress in transportation and communication technology spurred the burgeoning growth of trade in the past quarter century. Electronic communication technology radically revolutionized international finance by essentially eliminating the constraints of time and space on international financial transfers.

Economic globalization makes production ever more efficient as it builds on and reinforces international capitalism and its reliance on the unfettered operation of market forces. Some authors prefer to refer to this process as "marketization" rather than globalization. Irrespective of what the current process may be called, international trade has always held great potential to reduce world poverty. For the past 20 years, poor countries have been calling for "Trade, Not Aid," which would require rich countries to reduce their tariffs and other barriers to trade. This is precisely what free-market globalization proponents have been advocating in recent years. An OX-FAM study supports the claim that increased trade can, in fact, aid poor countries. It asserts that if the non-industrialized countries in Africa, East Asia, South Asia, Latin America, and the Caribbean could increase their share of world exports by just one percent, the income gains produced would lift 128 million people out of poverty.[126] In fact, an MCC publication reports that evidence exists that international economic integration reduces poverty, but the impact is not uniform.[127]

Benefits from the increased trade which results from economic globalization are distributed unequally in geographic terms and are selective in impact. For example, since 1980, three regions often known as the "Triad"— Western Europe, North America, and Japan, along with the newly industrializing countries of South/East Asia— benefited disproportionately from international trade. Their share of the total world exports of manufactured goods increased by nearly 10 percent, a greater percentage than any other group of countries. In addition, and as an example of the selective nature of trade, 90 percent of the trade related to knowledge and technology, both high wealth-producing areas, took place *within* the Triad. There is little dispute about the potential positive impact of increased trade from economic globalization. There is also near universal agreement that major population groups, and even *continents* in the case of Africa, find themselves increasingly marginalized in the race toward global economic integration. The growing gap between rich and poor appears not only among nations, but has grown more acute within nations and regions as well.

The growth of global inequality, some would claim, hides behind progress made in certain regions. In a study

criticized by anti-globalization groups for being too optimistic about the benefits and possibilities derived from
free trade, OXFAM discusses the effects of unfair trade on
the poor in a globalized economy. The study particularly
underscores the problem of inequality and the apparent
ineffectiveness of poverty alleviation efforts, often a key
component in development activity. It notes that the global economy ended the 1980s in a state of greater inequality than at any other time in the century. But in the 1990s,
global inequality increased at rates unprecedented in the
post-1945 era. The study goes on to say:

> Northern governments rightly stress the need for de-
> veloping countries to give the poor a bigger stake in
> national wealth, but they have a different approach
> to global wealth. In the global economy, high-in-
> come countries make even the most avaricious na-
> tional elites of highly unequal countries like Brazil
> look generous by comparison. It is almost unthink-
> able that the patterns of income inequality emerging
> under globalization would be tolerated by any gov-
> ernment. Indeed, most would regard such extreme
> inequalities as a recipe for social breakdown and
> conflict. Yet in the case of the global economy and
> the process of globalization, what would be unac-
> ceptable at a national level is regarded as an im-
> mutable fact of life.[128]

Even though significant disagreement exists about
whether or not inequality among nations or regions is
growing or has stabilized, there is considerable agreement that inequality has undermined the benefits of globalization by failing to reduce poverty more uniformly.
The matter of whether growing inequality is a passing
phase in development or a permanent legacy has occu-

pied development policy-makers and practitioners for decades. The debate about inequality and globalization follows the same lines. But might the "discourse of inevitability" obscure the possibility of seriously considering alternative approaches, or, one could add, more radical commitments to removing barriers in order to realize greater equality?[129] The development task, particularly for those who work from a justice perspective, is to propose and to pursue alternative models and actions that benefit the poor, rather than to try to make economic globalization work for them through national and international structures that have long worked to their disadvantage.

We began this section by noting that people experience economic globalization in different ways depending on a range of factors. Irrespective of whatever evidence exists regarding the positive or negative effects of globalization, we know that the impact of globalization is unevenly distributed. In addition, barriers such as internal national inequality and policies with regressive impacts on the poor minimize whatever positive impacts globalization might have. Furthermore, the raging globalization debate will continue to generate conflict, as well as action and reactions, which will challenge poverty-alleviation development efforts over the next decades.

Culture and Identity

We have just noted that populations in many places are growing apart economically. The gap is widening. The same seems to be true culturally and socially. A man from Mali mused recently that the challenge he faced living in a remote region of the country was how to remain connected to Africa.[130] This development worker could start his generator, position a satellite dish, and be watching news and entertainment from Paris, London, or New York in a matter of minutes. As a result, he felt more connected to Europe or North America, and better informed of events in those distant lands, than he did with his African neighbors who, though they lived separated by less than 50 miles, were a whole day's journey away. Being African and Afro-centric in his worldview required more effort than allowing himself to be shaped by his "satellite community." When CNN first arrived in Kenya in the early 1990s, a billboard in a busy intersection of Nairobi boasted, "Watch CNN. It will change your life." That has been true for many Kenyans, but has it been for the good?

These stories replay themselves in many places, though details vary from situation to situation. Cultural globalization raises tensions between uniformity inspired by Western—often blatantly American—values, on the one hand, and diversity that preserves local identity and perspectives, on the other. The globalization of Western culture is problematic because it is so powerfully unidirectional. The development worker in Mali only *receives* the cultural package. Unlike his interaction with African neighbors, he is unable to help shape what is transmitted to him by satellite, which ultimately influences how he makes sense of his life and the world.

Ritzer describes what he calls the "McDonaldization" of global society, both literally via the proliferation of the burger chain throughout the world and figuratively as the bearer of Western cultural values based on individualism, rationality, and progress.[131] Global integration gains strength as universalizing Western values take primacy over the particularizing tendencies of local and traditional cultures that help maintain identity. African, Asian, and Latin American participants who recently gathered in North America to explore the relationship between conflict and globalization all pointed to the loss of identity caused by the prevalence of globalized Western culture in their societies as a major contributor to conflict. They saw this growing dominance as one of the major forces generating fundamentalist reactions to modernizing Western influences in their respective societies.[132] The presence is pervasive and often nearly irresistible. For example, local staff provided lunch as part of a one-day workshop in a Middle Eastern country by bringing in Kentucky Fried Chicken rather than the more nutritious and tasty Arabic food. When asked why, they explained that KFC is more convenient, nicely packaged, and nearly as cheap as local food!

Religion and Cultural Resistance

Religion has increasingly become the currency for fighting the battle against the globalization of Western culture. Religion provides the framework, energy, and commitment necessary to promote a new identity or to protect a threatened one. Evidence of religion's power in culture wars abounds on every side, whether in the radical white supremacist, culturally Christian militias in the United States or among militant culturally Islamic groups in other parts of the world.

Religion enters the political debate because of how it shapes national polity and group identity. Today, liberal democracy and theocracy struggle for dominance as nations wrestle with the effects of economic and cultural globalization. Theocracies, principally Islamic states in recent years, fuse religion with the political system. Under this arrangement, actions by the state easily equate to "God's will" for both the public in general, as well as for public officials. Clergy and political officials often speak interchangeably and carry equal weight. Western nations criticize theocracies for their perceived fanaticism inspired by religion.

Liberal democracy embraces the diversity of religion, but it shapes a kind of *cultural* religion that fosters both a unity and a commitment to the nation that a political system needs to function effectively. This civil religion, as sociologists refer to it, infuses national symbols, heroes, holidays, legends, and myths with sacredness.[133] It enables all religions in a given country to find a common reverence embodied in the nation that transcends their differences. As such, civil religion mobilizes a population to be willing to die for their liberal democratic state just as much as religion does for a theocracy. The West accuses Islamic states (theocracies) of exploiting their populations by sending them forth to die, blinded by religious fanaticism in the battle against the globalization of Western culture. However, the West does the same with regards to liberal democracy, but under the guise of patriotic nationalism sustained by a powerful civil religion.

Some in the West claim that fanatical Islamic theocracies inspire terrorism because terror, whether sponsored by the state or insurgent groups, lies at the core of the religion that controls the state. Whether terrorism lies at the heart of any religion or not, in the next several decades religion in the form of theocracy or civil religion will certainly be a driving force in state- or insurgent-movement-sponsored terrorism.

The "discourse of inevitability," employed so freely by Western proponents of economic and cultural globalization and its local supporters, serves equally well for those who see globalized terror as "the only option" available to withstand the tide of Westernization. In the West, leaders steeped in civil religion often resort to similar language. They describe state-sponsored terror in the form of massive waves of bombing as "the only option" to free enslaved populations from tyranny, to bring democracy, and to make the world safe. Huntington says:

> Alignments defined by ideology and superpower relations are giving way to alignments defined by culture and civilization. Political boundaries increasingly are redrawn to coincide with cultural ones: ethnic, religious, and civilizational. Cultural communities are replacing Cold War blocs, and the fault lines between civilizations are becoming the central lines of conflict in global politics.[134]

Many people throughout the world appreciate and admire elements of Western culture. Gender equality, distributive justice, efficiency, and a respect for law, although not universally applauded, are among the things that persons from non-Western cultures identify as positive characteristics of the West. Tension comes when the Western cultural package expands and then threatens personal, community, or cultural identity. Whether we like it or not, development is an important conveyor of that cultural package.

Political Democracy and Power

Politics is about power and its distribution in society. How a particular society goes about institutionalizing the distribution of power varies and is ultimately a cultural question. Politically at the global level, the dilemma we face today is between the hegemony of the industrialized countries, especially the United States as the sole superpower, and the relative disempowerment of the rest of the world.

Much development work done today assumes that liberal democracy is the preferred political expression, and so the presumptions of democracy are embodied in that development work. Economic liberalization, individualistic cultural values, and liberal democratic governance structures go hand-in-hand with many of the development models we employ. Even the heavy emphasis on broad-based participation in development is inherently structured to be more successful if the cultural milieu receiving it values individual responsibility and action.

Social movements that focus on environment, gender, peace, human rights, and even anti-globalization typically draw heavily on political models derived from a liberal democratic tradition.

While liberal democracy may be the preferred form of governance because of its compatibility with a globalized economic system, it should not be assumed that such a political system will eliminate war. Fukuyama suggests that to be successful, liberal democracy must demand the allegiance that ordinarily might have been pledged to religion or ethnicity. It demands a civil religion for which individuals are willing to fight and die. Liberal democracy is central to civil religion in the United States; hence the ease with which the nation equates "making the world safe for democracy" with sacred duty.[135] One can reasonably assert that in the United States and in other Western democracies, citizens may willingly sacrifice themselves to defend and promote democracy. The extent to which that is true for "newly democratizing" nations, however, is open to question. Development, and in more recent years the peacebuilding field, appear to have wittingly or unwittingly taken on the responsibility of mov-

ing emerging democracies into fuller "democratic" operation. Many post-war reconstruction development efforts,
often framed as working to build or strengthen civil society and to build capacity for good governance in the public sector, are inseparable from political packaging.

Discovering and supporting culturally appropriate political models that meet the aspirations and needs of persons
in a highly diverse world appears to be the development
challenge we face. This is a particularly difficult dilemma
for Westerners, because we must deal with the power we
bring to the situation, and face how development will affect the distribution of power within that context.

Global Citizens' Groups and Justice Advocacy

International terrorism as a response to economic and
cultural globalization captures our collective attention
and sends a bolt of insecurity into the towns and villages
of even the most powerful nations. International citizen
movements are emerging in response. Some rise out of in-
dignation and concern for justice. Some take on violent
forms. Ethnically defined movements formed by indigenous populations in Latin America, Asia, and Africa were
among the earliest efforts in which local concerns were
addressed by global action joining their local initiatives.
Indigenous groups marginalized by Western colonization
became the focus of individuals and organizations around
the world, who mobilized in an effort to alter national
and international policies and behavior. The goal was to
enable these populations to regain or retain their identity
and dignity as they developed ways to relate to the new
society taking shape around and within their communities.[136]

Over the years a number of new social movements, concerned with peace, the environment, gender, and now globalization, have developed to focus the energy and commitment of people across national boundaries. They intend to help shape the way in which national governments and civil societies address local issues. These movements typically seek to develop international networks and to derive legitimacy from them. They promote an ethos of internationalism and favor simultaneous action at the local, national, and international levels. They operate differently from their predecessors of several decades ago who primarily gathered information about a given issue and planned local action.

Today movements gather information (evidence) locally, share it with other activists around the world via the internet, and plan concerted global action on the basis of pooled information. They have transformed the slogan, "Think globally, act locally," into "Think locally, act globally," or a combination of the two. This change enables international citizens' movements to pressure even the largest international organizations like the World Bank or the United States government to make specific policy changes.

By calling for global solutions to local problems, this global associational revolution at the end of the twentieth century and into the twenty-first may prove to be as important as the rise of the nation-state at the close of the nineteenth century.[137] Irrespective of the long-term impact of global citizens' movements, development in the first quarter of this century must find new ways to remain effective and responsible in a world beset by changes and challenges that increasingly require global responses to local manifestations.

Tensions, Dilemmas, and Opportunities

Development, as we have said, navigates in a highly complex world where multiple forces produce social realities that some persons experience as quite positive and others as highly negative. How, then, should we as Anabaptist development practitioners engage such a world? In previous chapters we introduced a number of dilemmas, paradoxes, or ambiguities that confront us. On the following list we highlight some of the more dominant ones which we want to explore in more depth.

- Where to place limited resources—raising goats or changing systems;
- Lifestyle differences—income, housing, insurance, and so on;
- The role of cultural, spiritual, and religious values;
- Holistic development—physical, mental, spiritual, environmental;
- Power—acknowledging it, understanding it, using or misusing it;
- Straddling two worlds—the sacred and the secular; and,
- Development and development policy—where to locate it.

Other practitioners, both past and present, echo these same dilemmas. John Paul Lederach, for example, writes of the compromises that come too easily when working with high-level political processes and people. How does one relate to powerful people who perpetuate unjust structures and systems while, at the same time, seeing that of God in them? How does one authentically respond to a call to bring the message of reconciliation to people at high levels when one has the opportunity, while keeping the experience from becoming a triumph for one's ego, "fed by recognition, prestige, and power"?[138]

Much like Lawrence Burkholder found the absolutist ethical positions arising from a two-kingdom theology difficult to maintain in the complexities of administering public programs in China in the late 1940s, development practitioners today, from the grassroots to public policy levels, are bumping into similar dilemmas. Yet because they are committed to living an ethic of love in the secular world, many accept the challenge to deal with the moral dirt, as well as the moral high ground. Unlike John Howard Yoder, whose position on public policy can be interpreted as primarily limited to "witnessing" to the state, many seem interested in and willing to join with the state in an effort to be co-creators of the historical process. They are selecting this way of "doing justice, loving mercy, and walking humbly with . . . God"—in spite of the ambivalence expressed by many of the practitioners.

Raising Goats or Changing Systems? Bridging the Gap

A dilemma raised frequently by Mennonite practitioners is the tension they feel between working either at the grassroots or in public policy. Is development best promoted by teaching people to raise goats or by changing structures and systems? The tension is intensified, as noted earlier, by the belief held by many practitioners that a fundamental cause of poverty is "unjust structures" and that "good" development occurs when these unjust structures are changed. However, the largest share of Anabaptist resources (people and money) work at the grassroots level. What should we do about this?

We can begin by first classifying development work by type of action (curative to preventive) and by where, geographically, the action takes place (local to global). Is the action like ambulance-driving—fixing a problem after it occurs—or is it preventing the problem from occurring in the first place, or something in between? Is the work being done at the local level, for example, a village or community; or at the global level, for example, the World Trade Organization; or somewhere in between? Such a classification of development work leads to the matrix shown in Exhibit 10. From the matrix, we can make five broad observations:[139]

Exhibit 10: **Types and Levels of Action**			
Types of Action	**Levels of Action**		
	Local	National	Global
Curative	**A**	**B**	**C**
Preventive	**D**	**E**	**F**

1. Action at "A" (curative and local) benefits primarily those at "A" and has minimal impact on people in other areas. Examples of this include a village clinic with no outreach program or a food distribution program in a village.
2. Action at "F" (preventive and global) reduces the need for action in all other areas. An example of this

is writing trade agreements for the World Trade Organization so that the rules of world trade are fair and just. Then, to further illustrate, surplus U.S. wheat, generated through U.S. government subsidies, could no longer be dumped into low-income countries at prices below what it costs Third-World farmers to grow wheat and feed themselves.

3. All levels and types of action are needed and important. Grassroots and public policy work represent two sides of the same coin. They should be mutually reinforcing; each needs the other. Pointing out what should be obvious, a practitioner in Part II asked somewhat rhetorically, who is in a better position to do public policy work than an MCCer who has experience at the grassroots? These principles of "needing each other" and "our work is mutually reinforcing" were revealed and modeled at the EMU development conference itself where, in a far too rare occurrence, practitioners and scholars representing the range of development experiences gathered at the same table for three days to share stories and experiences. As was stated by more than one participant, walls and stereotypes were broken down and there was a clear recognition that we should be part of a seamless web.

4. The largest share of Anabaptist resources (money and personnel) tends to be at "A," the curative and local level. There is a portion also at cell "D" where there is a preventive focus. The relational orientation of the Anabaptist ethic tends to be applied at the community or village level where harm and suffering is most clearly experienced and observed. It is generally accepted that Mennonites do a good

job at this, but Mennonites have been less involved
at addressing the root causes of poverty and injustice.
5. Thus, more faith-inspired peace-and-justice people
are needed at cell "F," where the twin interests of
being effective and faithful merge. Here there is
less need for ambulance-driving. The work is for-
ward-moving, rooted in faith-motivated, life-giving
values of peace, justice, and sustainability.

What options exist to be involved in public policy at
the national or global level with a preventive orientation,
and with an interest in influencing the current dominant
model of development? The stories in Part II demonstrate
how some Anabaptist practitioners have done this. To
generalize from the experiences of these practitioners and
others, at least three options are available.

- *The prophetic option as outsider.* Being a prophet, particularly in an Old Testament sense, generally
  means working outside the system and critiquing it
  from the outside through writing, protesting, speaking, research, and so on. This is the option most
  closely aligned with that advocated by John Howard
  Yoder.
- *The advocacy option as outsider-insider.* The advocate
  is primarily an outsider, but with enough inside
  knowledge, perhaps as a former employee, to be an
  effective advocate for change. Lobbyist groups fit
  this option, as does research and writing or speaking.
- *Direct involvement as insider-outsider.* Being directly
  involved can mean working for a global institution
  as an employee or, one step removed, as a contrac-
  tor. You are primarily an insider, but also an outsider, a participant-observer. You have not necessar-

ily sold your soul to the system, and you are attempting to be both effective and faithful. J. Lawrence Burkholder's *social responsibility* ethic and Gordon Kauffman's *radical love* ethic would both fit closely with this option.

It is upon considering doing public policy work, especially as an insider, or when planning to channel more resources to the preventive and global levels (cell "F"), that one faces the need to redefine the traditional Mennonite view of how a faithful Christian should relate to the powers within society. This is the point at which one may move from holding a two-kingdom theology to adopting a different schema—one in which sacred and secular realms overlap and share many values. To return to Ephesians 6:12, and linking this to the work of Walter Wink,[140] our task, as faith-motivated people with goals of global justice, peace, and sustainability (as presented in Exhibit 5), is to:

- *Name* the invisible realities: the principalities and powers,
- *Unmask* the invisible realities: the principalities and powers,
- *Engage* the invisible realities: the principalities and powers, and,
- *Transform* the invisible realities: the principalities and powers.

Mennonites have done reasonably well at *naming and unmasking* the powers of globalization, and *engaging*, through advocacy work, the powers of the global economy. What they also need to do is to engage, through direct involvement, and to *transform* the powers from without *and* within. In other words, people with an "MCC perspective"—grassroots understandings, peace and justice orientation, people-centered commitment—need to be inside the powers, writing the rules. We are not urging Mennonites to move into positions of public policy or to work in large-scale projects as a value or goal in itself. Rather, we believe that those positions present opportunities to be faithful to the call of Jesus, to "bring good news to the poor . . . to proclaim liberty to the captives and recovery of sight to the blind, to set free the oppressed" (Luke 4:18) and "to do justice, to love mercy, and to walk humbly with our God" (Micah 6:8) to large numbers of people.

How does one work in public policy and with the powers without being co-opted by the very system one is trying to change, without losing the original reason for going there? As we saw in the first-person accounts in Part II, many grassroots volunteer organizations and workers are suspicious of their colleagues who work for organizations that pay well and who devote a lot of their time to working with people in the seat of power. There are many temptations in those systems and organizations which promote models of development that are (a) anti-development in their ultimate effect when viewed through the lens of the development ethic, that are (b) contrary to the interests of most grassroots people, and (c) whose ultimate effect is to reinforce a structural status quo in international economic and political relations that disproportionately benefits international capital and the North. Many of us have observed that persons who were once quite clear in their critique of these organizations become more nuanced in their opinions after they have worked with these organizations for some time.

On the other hand, with more experience and as an insider, one does become increasingly aware of the complexities and constraints faced by these organizations. This should not serve to separate grassroots and policy people, but rather be a basis for formulating a more comprehensive and accurate critique of these institutions and for developing better policy proposals for which to advocate. Policy persons represented in the cases in this book urged conference participants to join with them to meet with the respective presidents of the World Bank and the International Monetary Fund to address issues of justice for the grassroots, an encounter that subsequently occurred. How to continue this advocacy work in a collaborative manner that will keep the discussion alive is now the challenge. It is this type of work that many Africans who participated in the MCC Africa Listening Project called for the church in the North to join with them to accomplish.

Those who enter the secular world as a way of being faithful and as a way of engaging the powers often find themselves alone when they encounter ethical dilemmas and look for solutions. While this is true across the range of development practitioners, it seems to be particularly true for those working with large donors or governments. Perhaps it is because so few people have modeled this way of doing development. Certainly there must be alternatives to selling their souls or resigning when ethical dilemmas arise and when a course of action is considered or chosen that is clearly inconsistent with their Anabaptist value system. John Driver and others have suggested that "in addition to contributing to the development of underprivileged peoples, we might somehow contribute to the freeing of our own people (and ourselves) from those systems that enslave us and to the transformation of those authorities who promote the self-interests of the economic empire in which we are all implicated."[141] But we cannot do this individually. Each of us—all of us—require some sort of accountability or support structure.

Historically, Mennonites have looked to three sources for guidance in being faithful and living right: the Bible, tradition, and the hermeneutic community. While these sources remain relevant, we may be finding new ways to use them. The Scriptures are always there to examine, although the way we interpret and apply them continues to change. Ted Koontz's use of the terms "first language" and "second language" may help us with our tensions.[142] Being able to understand and speak the second language of public policy, he says, is important in order for us to communicate with the world. The first language, that of Christian theology, is necessary to remind us of our ultimate commitments.

Tradition expresses itself through oral means, as well as through the printed text and other media. Let us urge those people who move into public policy positions to write material that can offer all of us a perspective on doing public policy in the secular world. This can complement the existing Mennonite literature on doing development from a grassroots perspective.

The hermeneutic community, as presented in the earlier section, "Summary of an Anabaptist Theology and Ethic," is perhaps the most dynamic and useful source for development workers who are dealing with dilemmas and tensions. It is the community who conceptualizes and interprets both the Scriptures and tradition in light of current realities. The values that form the ethic of development articulated in Chapter 8 emerged from the hermeneutic community and provide a source of reflection and guidance. Attempting to deal with ethical dilemmas individually may be the most sure-fire method for losing your soul.

The internet presents some excellent possibilities for being a useful tool of the hermeneutic community. Many people are members of internet-based discussion groups or listserves. What if, for example, there was a discussion group for development practitioners, and others who are interested, with whom we could raise ethical issues and dilemmas across countries and continents and obtain fairly immediate feedback? For example, one of the book's authors was asked to be part of a USAID-funded project following the 2003 war in Iraq that was designed to reconstruct Iraq's educational system—in a context where the Pentagon is in charge of all U.S.-funded reconstruction efforts. The gut-level negative response this writer was inclined to give was offset by realizing that had he accepted the invitation, he may have been able to weave peacebuilding and conflict transformation content into the educational curriculum.

Responses to such dilemmas should be done within a hermeneutic community. Access to a "development ethics" listserve would have been enormously helpful in making such a choice. The decision could have been examined for its consistency with the values, means, and goals shown in the framework in Exhibit 5. If we are part of a seamless web, as we argue is the case, both goat-raisers and systems-changers should have voices in this electronic hermeneutic community.

To summarize, what we propose with respect to the tension between raising goats or changing systems, along with their accompanying ethical dilemmas, is this: (a) all types and levels of action are needed, and all are part of a seamless web reflecting the call to be both faithful and effective; (b) the largest share of Mennonite resources tends to be concentrated on curative work at the local level, but a larger share of resources ought to be allocated to national and global work that is preventive in nature; and (c) the ethical dilemmas encountered by development workers can be faced better by building on, or adapting, the traditional Mennonite methods of discerning and practicing right living, including the use of internet resources such as listserves and discussion groups that facilitate communication, accountability, and community among geographically dispersed people.

Furthermore, in the same way that a new generation of scholars pushed church-state relations to center stage during the 1950s,[143] a new generation of development practitioners in the new millennium are pushing Anabaptist/Mennonites to view direct involvement in public policy and systems-change as not only a legitimate, but as a necessary, way of engaging the powers of war, poverty, and injustice. Being co-creators of the historical process through engagement in public policy is relatively new territory for Mennonites. We are learning new concepts and categories in an area where history suggests the risks are substantial, and where there are few models to emulate. Because we have few examples to follow, we find there is a considerable need for thinking and writing that addresses this praxis of ambiguity and paradoxes.

Living Well While Doing Good?

"It's uncomfortable when you know that your weekly or monthly salary is more than your colleague's annual income—and many times that of the so-called 'beneficiaries' of development." This confession by a professional development worker, once a volunteer but now working in a poor country with a bilateral international development organization, surfaced in a discussion a number of years ago about the challenges faced in professional development. Many professional development workers are often accused of living well while doing good. Is it ethically questionable to work for development (that is, the poor) while drawing a high salary and enjoying the security that comes with it, especially when one's host-country colleagues typically receive none of those advantages?

This issue is further illustrated by the ballad below. The biblical quotes from Micah and Luke, which follow, call Christians to do justice, love mercy, and walk humbly with God, and describe how Jesus related to the society in which he lived. These passages contrast with another type of development ethic, presented in "The Development Set." Here are the dilemmas faced by many faith-inspired practitioners, especially those in the Anabaptist tradition.

The Development Set

Excuse me, friends, I must catch my jet—
I'm off to join the Development Set;
My bags are packed, and I've had all my shots,
I have travelers checks and pills for the trots.
The Development Set is bright and noble,
Our thoughts are deep and our vision is global;
Although we move with the better classes,
Our thoughts are always with the masses.
In Sheraton Hotels in scattered nations
We damn multinational corporations;
Injustice seems easy to protest
In such seething hotbeds of social unrest.
We discuss malnutrition over steaks
And plan hunger talks during coffeebreaks.
Whether Asian floods or African drought,
We face each issue with an open mouth.
We bring in consultants whose circumlocution
Raises difficulties for every solution—

Thus guaranteeing continued good eating
By showing the need for another meeting.
Consultants, it's said, believe it no crime
To borrow your watch to tell you the time.
Their expenses, however, are justified
When one thinks of the jobs they might later provide.
The language of the Development Set
Stretches the English alphabet;
We use swell words like "epigenetic,"
"Micro," "macro," and "logarithmetic."
It pleasures us to be so esoteric—
It's so intellectually atmospheric!
And though establishments may be unmoved,
Our vocabularies are much improved.
When the talk gets deep and you're feeling dumb
You can keep your shame to a minimum:
To show that you, too, are intelligent
Smugly ask, "Is it really development?"
Or say, "That's fine in practice, but don't you see:
It doesn't work out in theory!"
A few may find this incomprehensible,
But most will admire you as deep and sensible.
Development Set homes are extremely chic,
Full of carvings, curios, and draped with batik.
Eye-level photographs subtly assure
That your host is at home with the great and the poor.
Enough of these verses—on with the mission
Our task is as broad as the human condition!
Just pray God the biblical promise is true:
The poor ye shall always have with you.

—*Source unknown*

The Biblical Call

What does the Lord require of you, but to do justice, to love mercy, and to walk humbly with your God.

Micah 6:8

For the Spirit of the Lord is upon me, because he has chosen me to bring good news to the poor. He has sent me to proclaim liberty to the captives and recovery of sight to the blind, to set free the oppressed.

Luke 4:18

Historically among Anabaptists, service was a voluntary activity that grew out of a discipleship lifestyle. It had its own rewards and lost some of its luster if it was done for remuneration. More recently, a term of voluntary service with a church organization like MCC often introduced young persons to development or to other service occupations. The professionalization of social service and development work, especially after World War II, introduced a lifestyle dilemma for those in the Anabaptist tradition who were attracted to the development profession because of their commitment to a service ethic.

Why is this difficult? Why not choose to live simply with the minimum needed for survival? Compared with local standards, the simple lifestyle of MCC volunteers is still plush. Their ability to travel internationally—probably drawing on personal savings or family generosity—with their food, housing, healthcare, and other basic needs supplied by MCC puts them in a class quite apart from the majority of people with whom they work.

The dilemma is similar for professional development workers from poor countries who are employed by local development organizations. Differences in salaries and benefits between them and persons employed in other sectors within the local economy are often quite marked. Local development organizations frequently fund their activities through grants or contributions from external/international organizations or foundations. This enables them to pay higher salaries than the prevailing local rate, although they are still relatively low when compared to what expatriate development professionals earn who work with international nongovernmental organizations such as CARE and OXFAM or multilateral organizations such as the U.N. and the World Bank.

This difference is even greater in the case of professional development workers employed by multilateral and bilateral organizations that pay substantial salaries and generally offer sizable allowances for housing, education, hardship posts, and annual trips to their home country. The cases in this book reflect some of the ambivalence Anabaptist development workers feel regarding this issue. Finally the question becomes, are the contradictions so great that we are unable to engage in development work with integrity and so, consequently, cannot undertake it as a profession?

Job security issues further complicate the situation. For example, one of the recommendations from the MCC Africa Listening Project was that development personnel—especially expatriates, but local workers as well—should commit themselves to working long-term in a particular context since this enables them to gain more experience, develop broader networks, and become more knowledgeable of the issues to be addressed. It also enables development workers to be better advocates for policy and program changes at all levels that will directly affect the local, regional, or national situation for the betterment of all concerned. In order to retain workers for the long-term, organizations must pay adequate salaries and provide acceptable benefit packages that are competitive at least in that context. When international government funding comes to local projects, it usually comes with requirements from the funders that all program personnel be paid at international salary levels. This certainly introduces great disparities in pay among persons who are working together for development in a given place but who happen to be working with different organizations, not all of which can pay the same salaries. This is true for MCC-type organizations that are staffed primarily by expatriate volunteers and workers hired locally.

Even when the remuneration and benefit packages are similar, the international volunteers are frequently not able or willing to work for long periods of their lives at volunteer wages because of family and retirement costs in their home settings. By contrast, local workers may be willing to work for salaries that are more in line with typical local salary scales. But within their local world, they too have advantages. Because of family and retirement reasons they will also find it attractive to use the experience they gain by working in development with a "volunteer-oriented" organization to eventually seek employment in more lucrative positions with internationally-funded NGOs or national governments.

We have identified both grassroots work and macro policy work as extremely important in development. Those who want to work at macro policy issues usually find such positions with multilateral or bilateral organizations. These organizations pay relatively high salaries compared to the majority of NGOs. Because of the Northern or international orientation of these agencies' work, their staffs usually stay less in touch with the grassroots.

Comparatively high salaries and lack of contact with the grassroots tend to make development workers at lower income levels, or within less well funded agencies, look askance at colleagues who work from these macro policy platforms. This is true no matter if the well-paid, somewhat-removed person is from the North or the South. What is often overlooked is what such persons do outside their official employment to work at issues in their local communities. We do not have documentation on this from the practitioner cases in this book, but we know personally a number of policy practitioners who are quite active in their respective communities or congregations, keeping strong grassroots connections there.

While the issues surrounding the dilemma of "living well while doing good" are not simple, this is not a reason to relativize the issue and maintain the status quo. There are, in fact, frameworks in which we can examine the lifestyle issue and specific measures that we can take to promote greater peace, justice, and sustainability, in order to live the ethic of development with more integrity. In addition, while lifestyle issues bear on the full range of development workers, they are particularly applicable to those who are most highly compensated.

Discussions around income and lifestyle issues generally involve three elements: a.) how you get your income, b.) how much you get, and c.) how you spend it. The emphasis usually is on the "how you spend it" element, perhaps because this is what is most easily observed. Extravagant living—big cars, big houses, expensive and frequent trips for skiing or sightseeing, and so on—is the problem. What about others who are in need? What about the biblical critique of riches, which emphasizes the misuse of wealth and income more than it criticizes earning a good income.

Most development workers have incomes beyond what they need to live reasonably comfortably. This is particularly the case for those employed by large institutions like the World Bank or private sector firms; it is also true for those employed by NGOs and, in fact, most in non-volunteer positions.

So is the "living well" dilemma resolved best by following the example of Mother Teresa and insisting on a lower salary? Or should one take the salary established by the organization's salary scale and give away, to charitable or other worthy causes, amounts that are significantly beyond what one needs? For example, is it better to refuse part of a $150,000 World Bank salary or to accept it all and give half of it to a microenterprise loan program that would ultimately generate 100 new jobs and increase incomes of those borrowers by 50 percent?

While taking a lower salary is certainly an ethical option, we propose two actions: accepting the higher-than-needed salary, so long as the gap between your salary and that of the lowest paid employees does not exceed some acceptable ratio (such as, perhaps, 10:1),[144] and using the "unneeded" amount in ways that promote the values, means, and goals of the development ethic presented in "Elements of an Anabaptist Ethic of Development." How might such a plan be put into operation?[145]

Theologian Ron Sider, in his book *Rich Christians In an Age of Hunger*,[146] proposes a graduated tithe (10 percent) calculated on a given base figure. For each thousand dollars earned above the base, an additional five percent is given on that thousand so that, at some income level, all the additional income is given away. The base figure one chooses is important, and there are many variables that need to be considered. The Sider family, who reside in Philadelphia, decided to give 10 percent on a base figure that included: (a) the current U.S. poverty level for a family their size; (b) Christian education and college/university expenses; (c) taxes; and (d) genuine emergencies. On income above that base, they applied the graduated tithe. While this is what the Siders aimed for, they freely acknowledge they didn't always make it. Sider further states that his "proposal for a graduated tithe is a modest one, so modest in fact that it verges on unfaithfulness to the apostle Paul.[147] But at the same time it is sufficiently radical that [if done by Christians] its implementation would revolutionize the ministry and life of the church."[148]

One of the important elements in this model is the decision by a household, in the context of a broader hermeneutic community, about the amount of money members believe they need in order to live, and then their decision to give increasing percentages away. This contrasts with the more typical approach in which one gives away some fixed percentage of income and then keeps the rest.[149] Considered this way, the issue is not how much you give, but how much you keep for yourself. We observe that if Sider thinks his proposal is modest in the North American setting, determining a base figure in a global context and living by those standards would be radical indeed.

Economist James Halteman presents a similar model in his book *The Clashing Worlds of Economics and Faith.*[150] He examines the lifestyle issue by looking at one's choices related to income generation (your job and how you get your income) and choices regarding consumption (what you do with your income). Like Sider, he emphasizes the importance of having a broader community be part of making these decisions. Halteman proposes that one's income should not determine how much one spends on oneself; rather, he suggests that faith-inspired people should make their spending decisions while acknowledging four major uses of wealth and income: (a) present consumption or spending on oneself, (b) future consumption or hoarding for the future, (c) charity or giving it away, or (d) investing it in productive capital.

Asserting that "the area of [personal] consumption is the most serious blind spot contemporary Christians have in the exercise of their faith," Halteman proposes that "the amount a typical family spends on itself should be within some carefully conceived range around the average of the community in which it is called to minister."[151] So, for example, if the average family consumption in one's community is $40,000, then one should aim for a consumption level within a range of $30,000 to $50,000. One's remaining income would go not only to charity, but also to productive investment (hoarding, except for a reasonable amount for retirement, is not condoned).

MEDA, CARE, and ACCION International are among a growing number of development organizations that have social investment funds (the Sarona Global Investment Fund and MicroVest Fund, in the case of MEDA). These provide capital to financial services companies which serve microenterprises in low-income countries and to processing and marketing companies in the agricultural and handicraft sectors that work to bring products to market.

As an economist, Halteman emphasizes the importance of productive investment in a modern economy because it is an essential component in generating economic growth and employment, both of which are critically needed in low-income countries. Presumably, the returns on one's investment, whether as dividends or capital gains when sold, would be regarded as income and treated according to the principles discussed above.

There are other models, most of which are variations on these themes. What is most noteworthy is that each proposes spending less on oneself and more on others. There are interesting and legitimate differences between them related to specific methods and numbers, but all reverse the conventional norm in which one's marginal propensity to consume goes up as one's income goes up. In that, each of these models leads to greater consistency with our proposed development ethic.

Building On or Destroying Local Culture and Natural Resources?

"Economic growth will be impossible until we can free persons from their strong ties to the extended family and the obstacles it creates for development." These words, written by the director of an international development organization in Latin America a number of years ago, starkly pose the dilemma addressed in this section—to build on or to destroy local culture and environment.

This is not to deny the fact that all cultures are constantly adjusting to external influences and internal contradictions. Nevertheless, like many development organizations and professionals, the NGO director quoted above believed that the extended family, as found in many places throughout the world, promotes values that lead to anti-development behaviors. These traditional families are geared to distributing resources across the entire family system rather than favoring the accumulation of individual wealth that can eventually be invested in productive entrepreneurial activity. He recounted several cases, each with dynamics similar to this classic sit-

uation: a young man accumulates financial or other resources and is expected to contribute to his extended
family by sending his relatives to school and helping
them get land, food, shelter, or solutions to whatever other needs they might have. The destruction of the extended family and its basic values may not be the only alternative to these situations. Some microenterprise projects
have found ways to encourage saving by appealing directly to communal values often found in traditional settings. But the dilemma is now more acute than ever as
the globalization of Western culture threatens those local
cultures that could provide alternatives.

Culture shapes everything we do. It constrains us as
well as frees us. Its systems of values and norms determine the appropriate behaviors and attitudes necessary
to be part of the society in which we live. This is the con-
straining aspect of culture because it limits our attitudes
and behaviors to a particular set of options selected from
all of the possibilities open to humanity; for example,
monogamy rather than polygamy, and so on. What is desirable, right, and wrong is determined in the cultural
arena. Religion, as an integral part of culture, infuses values and norms with qualities of good and evil.

Culture also frees us because we do not constantly
have to choose our behaviors and attitudes from all the
possibilities. We do not even consider some things because they are too far outside our cultural choices, for example, infanticide. All cultures provide answers to five
important questions which determine how their respective members should live in the world:

1. *What is our relationship to time?* Are we past-, pre-
   sent-, or future-oriented?
2. *What is our relationship to nature?* Is it mastery over
   it, harmony with it, or subjection to it?

3. *What is the nature of the preferred personality orientation?* Are we oriented to being, becoming, having, or doing?
4. *What is our relationship to others?* Do we see ourselves as relating hierarchically, collectively, or individually?
5. *What is the nature of human nature?* Are we by nature evil, a mixture of good and evil, neutral (neither good nor evil—*tabula rasa*), or good?

Cultures provide answers to these questions through beliefs, attitudes, values, and norms. Since cultures are constantly changing or dealing with forces that might bring change, any cross-cultural contact potentially has moral connotations. Assumptions about social change undergirding models of development and missions determine the relationship of these efforts to local cultural systems.

In other words, our work becomes a cultural question. That is, what beliefs, attitudes, and behaviors will create a *better* society or community? More specifically, what constitutes *better* in each case? These considerations should concern not only organizations that are formed and financed in rich countries and work in poor countries, or, who work, as well, with marginal populations in their own countries. The same holds for organizations founded by local entrepreneurs in large urban centers of poor countries that work with local groups that do not share urban values, even though they may live on the margins of major cities. In other words, any work that involves reaching across cultures must demonstrate expectations, attitudes, and behaviors that are appropriate for the culture of the communities or countries where development will be carried out, whether working from one country to another, or from one culture to another within the same country, including in North America.

As noted earlier, Denis Goulet defines development as going beyond the material aspects of life.[152] He recognizes that meeting subsistence needs is essential, but notes that people "need enough to be more."[153] Physical survival needs must be met, but the ethical and aesthetic are also vital for strengthening human dignity and identity.

He asserts that development is both the bearer and the destroyer of values. Historically, development has been a Western invention in that it has typically viewed Western culture—beliefs, values, and behaviors—as a prerequisite for improvement to take place in any given society. In other words, a cultural revolution has to occur, enabling whole societies to move from a past or present orientation to a future orientation that can then serve as a basis for rational long-term planning. Chinua Achebe, the renowned Nigerian novelist, poignantly portrays in his novel, *Things Fall Apart,* the cultural—clearly *moral* from his perspective—clash in rural Nigeria when traditional and modern cultures meet.[154]

Goulet's assertions resonate with Max-Neef's claim that development must address not only questions of *having*, but also questions of *being*, by identifying human needs and those activities and relationships that truly meet them in humanizing ways. He notes that pseudo-satisfiers appear to address the issues of *having* and *being*, but in the long-term lead to alienation because they do not address ultimate human questions beyond survival.[155] The familiar adage, "Money can't buy happiness," captures the pseudo-satisfying character of money in relation to deep satisfaction and contentment. Money is certainly essential in Goulet's "having enough" terms, but it alone is not a sufficient source of happiness. Much of what happens in development is of this nature. Ultimate human needs are only partially addressed, or, in some cases, development activities may actually be inimical to their fulfillment.

The connection between human values, dignity, and well-being is what development must address. Sociologists, anthropologists, and other social scientists such as Goulet and Max-Neef argue that human dignity is rooted in a culture's value base, from which personal dignity and purpose in life are derived. As we have seen, the models for social change espoused by development organizations have historically assumed that traditional cultures and their values need to be replaced by modern cultural patterns and values in order for development to take place. So it is important that we consider how we view local culture, its values, and behaviors. Earlier in the book we described various perspectives on development. Each one embodies an understanding of social change in relation to local culture and its system of values. Should that culture and its values be built upon or replaced with others?

Some voices within the development community argue that development efforts should build on local values, which other voices consider to be outmoded obstacles to the forces of modernization and "progress," and even at times abhorrent as in the case of cultural values that condone practices such as female infanticide, slavery, or female genital mutilation. Nearly three decades ago Goulet noted the impact of development on values and behaviors when he wrote, *"Development,* as normally understood, alienates even its beneficiaries in compulsive consumption, technological determinisms of various sorts, ecological pathology, and warlike practices." He goes on to assert that truly humane development seeks to free persons "from nature's servitudes, from economic backwardness and oppressive technological institutions, from unjust class structures and political exploiters, from cultural and psychic alienation—in short, from all of life's inhuman agencies."[156]

Alienation often follows in the wake of development efforts because, as noted above, development is both the bearer and the destroyer of values—bearer of values of Western industrialized societies and destroyer of traditional values held in poor countries and in many marginalized areas of North America. Among the principal Western values borne by development are *rationality* (a commitment to verifiability as the basis for truth), *efficiency*, *problem-solving*, and a *Promethean view of the universe* (everything is controllable).[157] Lest we believe this to be an outdated view, McMichael observed in 2000:

> Development is a longstanding European idea, woven from two related strands of thought. One is the Promethean conception of European civilization, stemming from a combination of the Aristotelian association of change with a theory of nature, St. Augustine's projection of the Christian theology of salvation as a historical necessity, and the Enlightenment belief in unlimited progress . . . . The second strand took root in this global endeavor. The inevitable, and unreflective, comparison Europeans made between their civilization and the apparently backward culture of their colonial subjects produced a particularistic conception of modernity that they universalized as human destiny.[158]

Today those persons calling for *sustainable development* are more likely to envision broad-based participation in the process by all social groups and a valuing of local cultural and ecological diversity. So we face the dilemma of how development efforts should relate to local cultural systems.[159] Sustainable development by definition implies that wherever it takes place, not only will the culture, the social structure, and the values and behaviors derived from them be affirmed and nurtured, but the ecology (the web of life) will as well. As it is now widely understood, a society's, or a region's, social institutions—including the economic and cultural—are highly interdependent with the geography, the natural resources, and ecosystems of that area.

The fragility of the global environment has become an increasingly urgent issue in recent years. Development theory and practice have become increasingly responsive to this concern. Today many lending agencies stipulate that the environment be included in the plans for sustainable development, so most economic development projects require an assessment of their potential environmental impact. This, as well as the gender analysis that accompanies most Western-sponsored development projects, often clashes with the culture of the context. Rural peasants in non-Western settings and in remote areas in Western countries do not define their relationship to nature, nor to each other in terms of gender, in the same way that dominant Western and international urban societies do. The ability of these "marginal" local societies to choose whether or not to assume Western values and behaviors becomes increasingly constrained before the inevitable march of economic, cultural, and political globalization forces.

The practitioners' stories in Part II of this book do not emphasize environmental issues extensively. Many refer to the issue, but usually in passing. Mennonites in their early involvement in development typically took a mastery-over-nature view of the environment. They would have expressed it as good stewardship leading to improved production. They were not unconcerned about the environment. On the contrary, the histories of Mennonite missions, MCC, and MEDA document activities and policies that promoted conservation, stewardship, and restoration of the environment. For example, the various agencies' activities in Haiti addressed reforestation, soil conservation, and the use of natural material for fertilizer as a matter of course.

The practitioners' stories in this volume often refer to the crucial importance of the environment in sustainable development. Raymond Martin states in "Key Challenges and Cutting Edges" that demography, that is, population growth, "and the pollution of our environment and water supply [among other things]" will force us to "rethink our traditional development paradigm in a very fundamental way." From a more relational perspective, Susan Classen repeats the same theme: "Ultimately, development work is about being kind, being gentle, and walking compassionately on this earth that God has given us to share." These quotes signal a shift from viewing the environment in strictly stewardship terms, with positive consequences for production, to a more systemic perspective, focusing on the value of natural and social interdependence for enhanced quality of life and long-term sustainability.

Could the fact that most practitioners' stories in Part II allude only indirectly to the centrality of the environment in development, and demonstrate an attitude of taking it for granted, be a result of the Anabaptist heritage out of which they come? Clearly the land and the natural world have been very important in the survival and prosperity of Mennonites and their faith. However, the relationship between the environment and Mennonite values has not been closely examined nor rationalized socially or theologically.

Concern for the environment has always made a certain amount of sense intuitively to rural-based Mennonites because of what they learned while growing up, rather than what they learned from instruction in the sciences. Nevertheless, growing consciousness about the environment in the public mind has led Mennonites to think more carefully about how working to sustain the environment relates to world peace and is integrated with development. MCC has made environmental well-being one of the lenses through which it does all of its work. Mennonites are engaging in more discussion and scholarly work on environmental concerns. Among their most recent statements are *Creation and Environment: An Anabaptist Perspective on a Sustainable World*[160] and the new *Confession of Faith in a Mennonite Perspective,* which states, "We therefore are called to respect the natural order of creation and to entrust ourselves to God's care and keeping. God has given the earth to human beings to care for as God's stewards."[161]

Mennonites will need to discover what they can contribute to bringing development into harmony with sustaining vibrant cultures and a healthy ecosphere. For this to happen, significant changes will need to occur in the way Mennonites and others think about development. Earlier we pointed out that most development frameworks or models assume that local time-honored cultural patterns and values are obstacles to development, which means that they must be replaced by others more attuned to the modern values of rationality, efficiency, problem-solving, and the controllability of nature and social forces. This commitment to the destruction of traditional values and maximum exploitation of natural resources contributes significantly to the erosion of a sustainable environment and to broad cultural alienation and anomie, a state of ethical and practical disorientation or normlessness. McMichael concludes that development in

a world marked by the globalization of a Western understanding of progress is problematic. Its prescriptions are
double-edged because its conceptions of the future erase
the past.[162] Thus, a view of *development as if values mattered* poses the thorny question of how values form part
of the development equation.

Mutuality is one of the values identified from the practitioners' stories (see Exhibit 5). Mutuality inclines us toward a development ethic that respects and takes local
values seriously. From that perspective, organizations and
practitioners would commit themselves to development
whose objective is to meet human need in ways that enhance human dignity in the process. The values held by
both the practitioners and the people with whom they
collaborate are at the core of the development endeavor,
irrespective of whether or not the work takes place at the
grassroots, middle, or societal level. Those two value systems—the development organization's and the local setting's—should reinforce each other in ways that make it
possible for all involved to have security, sustenance, dignity, and freedom from life's inhuman forces and processes, so that all may "have enough in order to be more." The
challenge is to use the cross-cultural contact that the development process provides, whether urban-rural within
the same society or contact across more distant cultures,
to build on the respective strengths of all participants.
The goal—and the possibility—is to "become more" together than would have been possibility had one of the
parties' values been destroyed in the process. Thus, mutuality is an important value in safeguarding the respective cultures of all parties involved in the development
enterprise to ensure that healthy, life-enhancing change
can take place without undue cultural costs being borne
by any of the parties.

How does an Anabaptist development ethic shape our practice with respect to culture and natural resources? Remember that practice takes a variety of forms. First of all, it is individual. Where do I work? How do I work? We also respond at the collective level. What should Mennonite and other faith-motivated agencies do, and how should they carry out programs? What about nonreligious organizations with which we work in the private and public sectors? Does the Anabaptist development ethic provide any guidance for how we should relate to these organizations as they engage local cultures?

We suggest here some principles that can guide us as we face the cultural dilemma posed by development work. They may also apply to the church's mission activity.

1. We need to acknowledge that the international and domestic development enterprise is largely an expression of Western and middle-class values. This will enable us to have a clearer understanding of who we are as we cross cultures and classes in our work. A strong relationship requires that all parties have an honest understanding of their respective identities and their unique contributions to the relationship.

2. We must recognize and transcend the "conversion impulse" energizing development activity that leads us to cross cultures and classes to bring about change. We need to acknowledge that we are part of the development enterprise that considers change to be good and necessary, especially as it moves individuals and groups toward greater involvement in global society. Hopefully this explicit recognition will enable us to be more acutely aware of this unspoken and often unrecognized value that infuses

the development process. This awareness will help us hold less tenaciously to the belief that others must accept our view of change, thereby opening the possibility for mutuality to become the basis of our relationships.

3. Mutuality in relationships is a core value of development according to the Anabaptist development ethic articulated in this book. Therefore, cross-cultural and cross-class contact based on mutuality opens the possibility for something to emerge that is novel for all parties involved. This is possible because true mutuality values what all parties bring to the relationship and emphasizes mutual discovery and reciprocity, rather than unilateral transfers that tend to characterize dependent relationships.

4. As individuals we must be wary of placing ourselves in organizational contexts that sacrifice the relational understanding of development for the illusion of shaping public policy by dramatically altering the world for the poor and marginalized. We want to avoid fostering a dependency-creating trap of "doing for" rather than the mutuality of "doing with" that comes from a more explicitly participatory approach.

5. Public policy work is essential to address global problems. We should not dismiss this work simply because it is difficult to establish relationships of mutuality with people at the grassroots. We must recognize that organizations, like individuals, have different ways of working. Taking organizational partnerships seriously by maintaining relationships based on the values that undergird mutuality is one way that organizations can approximate the quality of relationships that we value so highly at the indi-

vidual level. As we consider positions in organizations that would enable us to work with public policy issues, the Anabaptist ethic calls us to give as much weight to the way an organization works—the cultural sensitivity, transparency, accountability, positive use of power, and so on, that it embodies— as we do to the opportunities it provides for affecting public policy.

6. Mennonite and other faith-motivated organizations are not by definition more sensitive to the need to respect local cultures than secular organizations. Both types of organizations are subject to the dominant Western impulse to act in a unidirectional manner. As individuals within these organizations we must constantly call these institutions which carry a disproportionate amount of economic and technological power to demonstrate authentic mutuality by taking the position of learning, by growing through mutual discovery and accountability with their partners. We must urge them to resist functioning as instruments for the unilateral transfer of knowledge and goods, even though those elements may be part of what the organizations might bring to their relationships.

Connect or Disconnect with the Missiological Thrust of Religious Organizations?

Mennonite missiologist, Wilbert R. Shenk, claims that two nineteenth century religious happenings, the Protestant missionary movement and the evangelical revivals in Europe and North America, redefined the concept of witness in Mennonite missiology. The traditional Anabaptist perspective of witness as discipleship was replaced by the understanding of witness as proclamation with a heavy emphasis on preaching and conversion. While not denying the importance of declaring a commitment to Jesus, witness as discipleship stressed that believers needed to practice Jesus' radical teachings in daily life in order to give substance to the invitation for others to join them on the journey. By the late 1800s, caught up in the rising tide of Protestant mission enthusiasm, Mennonites began sending missionaries to engage in full-time professional missionary activity—internationally, as well as within North America to large urban centers, to Appalachia, and to Native American reservations.[163]

Mennonite mission efforts attempted to combine "word" and "deed" to be true to the integrated message of the gospel. Like many other mission groups in the late nineteenth and early twentieth centuries working in colonized areas, they were particularly active in agriculture, education, and medicine. Thus, elementary and secondary schools, agricultural demonstration farms, nursing schools, and hospitals were commonly found in areas where Mennonite and Brethren in Christ mission agencies worked, even though their primary emphasis was clearly evangelistic and proselytizing. With the emergence of the Mennonite Central Committee in the 1920s and 1930s, refugee support, relief and service, and agricultural improvement increasingly became the work of MCC and less a part of the mission agencies' portfolios. In time, this led many persons to perceive a division of labor in the organizations that carried out the mission of the church—some did evangelism and others did service.

MCC came on the scene in 1920, at the same time that Anabaptist-derived groups in North America, along with the rest of North American Christianity, were caught up in the modernist-fundamentalist controversy that ended up compartmentalizing Mennonite theology. Mennonites who had come to define themselves as "people of the Book" resonated with the view of scriptural inerrancy held by fundamentalists. But Mennonites typically ignored their strong support for war. Modernists were generally opposed to war but did not accept the inerrancy of Scripture. Therefore, anyone who advocated commitment to a pacifism that called for more than nonparticipation in the military was suspect in many Mennonite circles.[164] Shenk states:

> Discipleship and peacemaking were dubbed Mennonite "peculiarities" and set aside as secondary concerns. The gospel was reduced to fit either a "social gospel" or an "evangelistic" model. We still have not fully recovered from this thinking.[165]

MCC's commitment to service, peacemaking, and refugee resettlement—all "in the name of Christ"—kept the agency focused on activities that did not result in establishing congregations where its personnel worked. In fact, the motto, "in the name of Christ," meant that MCCers' witness was through a life of service characterized by a radical Christian discipleship in daily life, rather than by explicit programmatic evangelism. The distinction between evangelism and service was not limited to the organizational division of labor between MCC and the mission boards. In relation to the evangelism-service continuum, many Anabaptist professionals in service occupations such as education, health, and social services would have seen themselves as working from the same perspective that guided MCC volunteers. The quality of their service in the workplace, church, and community was a powerful witness to their "Jesus way" lifestyle.

Mennonite development workers faced a tension represented by two different ways of understanding evangelism—lifestyle or programmatic, or being the leaven whose presence enlivens the atmosphere, compared with being a fulcrum that leverages a person to convert. MCC development workers would typically place themselves more toward the "lifestyle" end of the continuum because of their discipleship emphasis. That approach is characterized more as an "invitational lifestyle," in which the quality of personal relationships attracts persons to follow Jesus, rather than as a "persuasive proclamation," more descriptive of the programmatic proselytizing approach of evangelism. In the former, at the personal level, individuals' salvation and authentic well-being are linked to that of their fellow humans. In radical Anabaptist theology, Driver proposes, salvation takes on a collective character in addition to that of individual transformation.[166] Transformation at both the individual and societal levels becomes important.

At some places where MCC or similar programs worked, congregations formed, even though that was not part of the programs' explicit objectives. MCC personnel saw themselves as serving "in the name of Christ." Still today, irrespective of their organizational identity, development workers from the radical Anabaptist tradition face the same issues, especially when they move in circles which embrace evangelism of the persuasion and proselytizing variety which are typically not rooted in a radical discipleship ethic. The radical Anabaptists of the 16th century blended "word and deed."

The tension between evangelism and service, and the division of labor among Mennonite organizations working in evangelism and development, are less distinct now than in the past. In recent decades, mission boards have been more explicit about the integrated nature of the gospel and have supported activities that may be viewed as development or peacebuilding work.[167] In Africa, especially West Africa, and in Latin America we can cite examples of mission board support for peace and development work in regions of conflict and in urban areas that focus on the most marginalized sectors. At the same time, MCC has more explicitly committed to partnering with the church in areas where it is responding to human need. Mennonite World Conference (MWC) and MCC are cooperating to facilitate these relationships and carrying out programs jointly or collaboratively in situations where that seems mutually beneficial.

The call for the church to carry out more faithfully its broad mission in an integrated way compares with what the Latin American church would describe as *misión integral* rather than specialized proselytism.[168] The difference between integrated mission and proselytizing is at the heart of what it means to recover the Anabaptist vision in the twenty-first century. It also hints at the blurring of the boundaries between mission boards and development agencies such as MCC and MEDA.

The concept of integrated mission includes a call to personal commitment to Jesus, but not separated from a call for and involvement in work for a more just and peaceful society. The church, through its agencies as well as through the lives of its individual church members, makes itself present in all spheres of life unapologetically and does not limit its work specifically to proselytizing. The key to this distinction is that the church's involvement in the social arena is not simply an instrumentalist approach, in which the social has legitimacy to the extent that it leads to new persons becoming members of the church. Its involvement in development is part of the church's mission, irrespective of whether or not new persons become church members. Of course this is not to suggest that they will be turned away if they are attracted to the church, nor does it preclude a place for proclamation activities. It simply erases the sharp distinction between the "social" and the "spiritual."

Latin American Christians in particular, but also Christians from other parts of the world, have helped restate the legitimacy of the radical Anabaptist vision of a church that embraces all of life and does not allow itself to accord more importance to one aspect or another of its mission in the world. Therefore, development from this perspective is an important part of the broad mission of the church. Development practitioners guided by a radical Anabaptist-inspired ethos will assess their involvement in the profession not so much in terms of instrumental effectiveness, but rather in light of their ability to be prophetic in discipleship terms. This is true, no matter their region of national origin—North or South—or where they may be situated organizationally, whether in a faith-motivated initiative (mission or development); a civil society, non-governmental organization; or a public-sector bilateral or multilateral agency.

We recognize that by asking Mennonite development practitioners who participated in the Eastern Mennonite University conference to reflect on the differences they made in the course of their careers, we may have nudged them to think of their experiences primarily in instrumental rather than prophetic terms. If that indeed is true, we may have lost the opportunity to gain additional insight into how one might be prophetic when working within organizations like USAID or CIDA, which carry out large-scale development projects in addition to helping shape international and national-level economic and social policy. On the other hand, the question about personal effectiveness may still be relevant because if a prophetic voice is not making any difference, it would seem that either methods or objectives may need revision.

A number of individuals whose stories provide some of the background for this book described specific stands they had to take when asked to participate in implementing large-scale development projects that they judged to run counter to their personal values. But we have less information about particular stands persons may have taken in relation to high-level public policy formulation, a subject of particular interest to us. This is an area that merits further research, given the radical Anabaptists' historic suspicion of formal organizations and these agencies' tendency to further their own interests at the expense of the persons they are called to serve. In this regard, contemporary Anabaptist/Mennonites may sense a disjuncture between the need to be both instrumentally effective and prophetically faithful.

We have been addressing a tension between development and missions. And we have acknowledged a division of labor within Mennonite churches that has unintentionally led to an artificial division between development and missions. We must also recognize that at a foundational level there is an almost total overlap in the ideological underpinnings of the two enterprises. We believe that they are, for all intents and purposes, two different expressions of the same ideological framework. We have failed to understand that when we urge the church to be prophetic by calling for justice in the world, it often rings hollow because our missionary efforts have frequently and unwittingly been part of a larger imperial project. To recognize this does not mean that we accept the inevitability of that participation. The church needs to focus its prophetic call on itself. It ought to examine its concept of conversion and its mission efforts to see if they run counter to its other goal—that of being a community of persons committed to radical Christian discipleship. The church has fostered many prophetic calls—for an upside-down kingdom, for military tax resistance, for ecological integrity, for alternatives to violence, for an openness to diversity, and more. Behind these important voices, we have generally identified our understanding of conversion as the source energizing these expressions of faithfulness, rather than as the core of the problem.

We use the word "prophetic" to describe the church's witness to the state or secular society. The prophetic church points out what is wrong and calls for change. However, the state of the world at the beginning of the twenty-first century requires that we review our understanding of the term. Though they themselves may not embody what they call for, radical fundamentalist, political, cultural, and religious responses to the globalization of Western culture and neo-liberal economics may actually be a "prophetic" call to the Western church. It is a call to create alternative development and missiological models that respect cultural identity, local knowledge, and mutual learning. Our world, which is becoming a global village, needs models that counter the imperial impulse embedded in the globalization process. The development and missiologal models that are currently most dominant emphasize conversion to Western culture and Christianity. In so doing, they mirror one of the most objectionable aspects of globalization, rather than offer an alternative. (The radical call in some countries for the creation of an Islamic state and society, in response to Western expansion, seems to fall into the same conversion trap that grips our current Christian missiology and development theory.)

We may be discouraged by the current state of the world, but signs of hope can be seen in small ways in many societies. In areas where conflict divides communities or societies along ethnic, religious, or class lines, individuals and small groups reach out to each other across those lines to develop or maintain relationships, thereby reconnecting people who have been classified as the enemy and dehumanized by war, hatred, and mistrust. Glimpses of such actions of hope appear in Northern Ireland, Eastern Europe, Rwanda, West Africa, Israel, and Palestine when "enemies" behave as "friends." Missiologically, Mennonite and Anabaptist Centers in London, Brussels, Paris, Chile, Korea, and Australia-New Zealand function as places where diverse religious traditions come together to share of themselves in order to create a basis for mutual transformation. They aren't perfect, but they emphasize two steps: 1.) sorting out a clear identity of who we are and what contributions we could make to a relationship, and 2.) learning from those with whom we relate in that setting.

Surely congregations also exist that live out a missiology of mutuality. In a world deeply divided along religious, ethnic, and economic lines, we have no option but to develop alternative ways of interacting that take others seriously. As Anabaptist Christians we can contribute uniquely to these efforts, but we must recognize, too, that the contributions of all religious groups are needed to create a world that functions as more than a stage for economic, cultural, and political wars.

Are such ideas practical or even desirable? What can an Anabaptist ethic of development contribute to this

challenge? The following principles may provide some
guidance.

1. We need to develop a clear understanding of radical
   Christian discipleship today. We can build on the
   foundation begun by the generations who took Anabaptism seriously, especially at times when the
   world seemed to be falling apart.

2. If we want to rise above current conflicts and divisions, we will need to move beyond the neat distinc-
   tions between the church and the rest of the world.
   We will need to engage in relationships—individually and institutionally—that are built on values of mutuality, humility, people-centeredness, peace, and
   justice. An ethic of conversion that focuses on one-
   way change in a highly polarized world only contributes to the problem. At a practical level we need
   to genuinely relate inter-religiously, as well as across
   other divides.

3. We will take seriously the power of institutions like
   the church, multilateral organizations like the World
   Bank, governments, nongovernmental organizations,
   and academia to neutralize prophetic voices. Therefore we will refuse to be trapped into assuming that
   as a host of separate individuals, we can influence
   these entities over the long-term. Instead we will
   link ourselves to a community of radical discipleship
   that has a vision and that practices accountability
   with energy. If we accept employment in one of the
   kinds of institutions named above, we will seek to
   find a community that will anchor us.

   Typically we do the reverse because we view the
   matter of community as secondary. The Anabaptist
   ethic suggests that it is the primary and first decision.

4. Addressing public policy issues by participating in social movements is a legitimate activity. However, in these activities also, we must avoid functioning as individuals for the same reasons as we note in Number 3 above. Social movements are particularly prone to conversion ideologies with many of the same pitfalls that the church tends to get caught in.

5. As individual church members we should support and encourage our denominations and respective congregations to go about their mission with greater mutuality and honesty, as highlighted in our description of the Mennonite Center models above (page 313).

6. Whether in development or in any other professional endeavor, we should work for the common good. This calls for a framework that addresses global and local issues and that makes relationships central. As individuals we must foster good personal relationships. At the institutional level we need to form organizational partnerships and then maintain them based on the core values highlighted in the Anabaptist ethic of development.

7. We must recognize that the Anabaptist ethic of development and Anabaptism itself are social constructions of reality. In other words, they were developed by persons much like us who were committed to a particular set of values in a specific place and time. As such, they provide an excellent point from which we can analyze and reflect on our role and imagine our contribution to the global challenge before us. We ought to constantly interact with our history and tradition, an inspiring and transforming process to be sure. Further, we ought to permit that action to be our source of strength. Of course we

must resist the imperial impulse to generalize Anabaptism to the rest of the world by using the very
structures from which we want to free ourselves.

Our hope is that this book will serve as a platform
for serious conversation on such issues. May it not
be yet another book full of "truth" and "certitude"
that views deviations from it with skepticism.

Power: Acknowledging, Using, and Misusing It

One of the inescapable, but perhaps most subtle and
least acknowledged, tensions faced by all development
practitioners is that of power—its negative and positive
uses, and the difficulty of reconciling power with the servant perspective which practitioners claim to value. Power, characterized as the ability to influence other people
or events, is most often associated with large development organizations. But power flows from whoever has
access to or control over resources, including development practitioners in all types of development organizations.

What are these major forms and sources of power? Six
are of particular relevance to development practitioners,
the last of which is not usually found in the mainstream
literature.[169]

1. *Financial power.* This is generally one of the most significant sources of power since development work
   brings money with it, and money is the resource
   typically most desired. In fact, with few exceptions,
   we may say that the less money, in cash or in kind,
   associated with a development initiative, the less interest there is in the initiative from host countries or

host country nationals. A $100 million program carries more power than a $25,000 program.

2. *Organizational power.* This is held not only by the organization itself, but it extends as well to the "culture" of the organization. Stating that you work for MCC or the World Bank carries weight far beyond the stature which you carry as a single individual. In light of the tendency for people unconsciously to become like those they associate with (regression to the mean), an organization's culture is particularly influential in its individual staff members' self-understanding and use of power.

3. *Position power.* Sometimes called "legitimate power," position power is derived from a person's position within an organization. The head of an organization has more power than a janitor or receptionist.

4. *Expert power.* This involves having skills or knowledge that others don't have. It may be a farming method that can double food output with no additional risk to the farmer or the ability to use sophisticated computer spreadsheets to estimate returns on alternative development investment projects.

5. *Referent, or personal, power.* This comes from within a person and typically is associated with characteristics or qualities such as appearance, gender, personality, or interpersonal skills. Charismatic leaders are examples of this type of power.

6. *Values-based power.* Not commonly found in mainstream literature, values-based power derives from the strength of ideas.[170] The nonviolence taught and practiced by Jesus, Gandhi, and Martin Luther King Jr., or the enormous moral authority of Nelson Mandela, are examples, as is the "service" orientation common among the development practitioner cases

in Part II. Negative values, such as racism or sexism, are also value-based and can carry significant power.

In general, the more of these resources one possesses, along with the ability to withhold or share them, the greater the amount of power one holds. This power can be used in negative ways by influencing (or even coercing) recipients to act in ways the holder of power desires, and not necessarily in a way recipients wish or feel is best for them. Power can be used in positive ways that enhance life and promote the common good. When its resources are equally distributed, power and its coercive aspects are dramatically diminished, and the relationships that are involved can approximate mutuality.

Acknowledging the presence of power—and understanding it and being able to use it in positive ways—has been particularly difficult for those raised in the Anabaptist, or similar faith, traditions. That happens because of the service orientation that has been such a dominant part of these traditions. Jesus' life and teachings are the model: going the second mile, giving one's coat, even laying down one's life for others. "Whosoever of you wants to be great must be your servant, and whoever wants to be first must be willing to be the slave of all. For even the Son of man did not come to be served, but to serve, and to give his life to set many others free" (Mark 10:44-45, Phillips). This motif is clearly present in the practitioners' cases in Part II and is a type of referent power.

Power is a profound force when almost any type of service to others is contemplated or enacted. That is because, in any human situation where service to others is expressed, the person being served and the person doing the serving are unequal in the possession of resources. The one who possesses the greater resources is in the giving position, while the other is in the recipient role.

The action of serving involves passing resources (power) to recipients who lack them. It tends to be essentially a one-way transaction. The consequences of this imbalance of power are not difficult to imagine. First, the recipients of service can very easily suffer from diminishment of self-esteem and self-worth, especially if they are not able to reciprocate with an act of similar value.[171] Self-worth is often not fully enhanced by simply receiving. Psychologically, persons must feel that it is right and legitimate for them to receive a gift, and that decision can be made only by the recipients themselves. Beyond that, recipients must feel that they have the ultimate right to decide whether the gift is appropriate for their particular situation and worthy of acceptance.

Practitioners with a service orientation face other temptations related to the misuse and abuse of power.[172] The desire to do good is not always a pure and unadulterated motive to "serve in the name of Christ." Individual development workers can be motivated by personal ambition to learn the techniques and requisites of a profession in order to move up the ladder in the employing organization. They may want to enhance their prestige with associates and peers, or to show off their expertise and knowledge. Development practitioners may want to show the recipient person or group the superiority of the values and culture of the practitioners' home country or area, thereby being unconsciously chauvinist about their country, religion, or development position. Paradoxically, the concept of service itself implies an imbalance in resources; hence, power. Service-oriented development workers oblivious to these issues can cause a great deal of power abuse.

If we aim to acknowledge the power we hold and to understand it as fully as possible, how can we use it more appropriately? Don Kraybill, in his book *The Upside-Down*

Kingdom, states that three factors undergirded Jesus' use of power.[173]

- Influence, not control, was his primary mode. His words and acts create a crisis and invite us to make a choice, a voluntary choice.
- His use of power focused on the needs of others. He mobilized resources to serve the needs of the hurting and the stigmatized.
- Jesus didn't use power for self-gain or glory. He willingly suspended his own rights and served at the bottom of the ladder. Defying social custom, he redefined rights and expectations.

Is there a redemptive side to the Anabaptist heritage which can provide guidelines and principles for the positive use of power and which is consistent with the teachings of Jesus? We propose that there is, and that many of these principles are embodied in the contents of the development ethic as presented in Chapter 8, particularly Exhibit 5. We highlight four in particular.

The first principle is *transparency.* It is essential to be clear and forthright about what your ultimate goals are as a development specialist, about who your "client" is, and about where your interests and loyalties lie. Conventional wisdom considers the client to be the funding agency, the institution paying you to do the work. If you work for a private organization which is carrying out a development project with USAID funds, your client is USAID. On occasion, a private organization with USAID funds may have the government, the ministry, or the community where the project is located as a client. Less often, but more common for organizations with nongovernmental sources of funding such as MCC, the client is considered to be the "target" group; for example, the poorest

20 percent of the population in a particular geographic location. Such NGOs are also accountable to the thousands of individuals who contribute money to them, as well as to the governments of countries that invite them or give permission for them to work within their jurisdictions.

The Anabaptist development ethic suggests an alternative—that one's ultimate goal is really what should be identified as "the client," and that that goal is to work to realize a more peaceful, just, and sustainable world, where people and communities are valued and empowered and where "life conditions" are enhanced.

Even if your national and international partners do not fully subscribe to your view of who your client is, they will know what your frame of reference is and, perhaps more importantly, what it is not—such as the strategic interest of the U.S. government. The ability to hold in balance, and be accountable to, the interests of the various actors (clients) present in any development initiative is of critical importance.

A second principle for the positive use of power, inspired by the development ethic, is *empowerment*. In the development context, empowerment can take the form of sharing power, of capacity building, or of institution building. Jointly making budgets, allocating discretionary resources, hiring and firing employees, setting priorities, and making work plans are all ways to share power. Developing and training people so that you work yourself out of a job, because the skills for which you were hired are now present in the host-country nationals, is an example of capacity building. Building a sustainable microfinance organization that is initially staffed with expatriate development specialists, obtaining loan capital funds, and training national staff to eventually lead and manage the organization, is an example of empowerment through institution building.

Related to empowerment is the *decentralization of decision-making,* the third principle. To establish organizational structures and systems in which people have a voice in decisions that affect their work and lives is a positive use of power. Flattened organizational structures lend themselves more to empowerment and decentralized decision-making than do more rigid and hierarchical structures. Giving people responsibility without authority, as often happens in decentralization schemes, is a non-starter, creating only frustration and disillusionment. At the same time, decentralized decision-making does not mean involving everybody in every decision. That is also a recipe for disaster. Finding appropriate balances is critical and is often related to the type of leadership practiced, which takes us to a fourth critical factor in the positive use of power.

Servant-leadership, the fourth principle, is the most appropriate style of leadership for using power positively. Servant-leaders acknowledge and understand the various sources and types of power, and they are able to use their power as both leaders and servants. Servant-leadership is particularly appropriate for development specialists because they are in a country other than their own as a guest and at the invitation of some formal organization in that country; at the same time, they bring desired resources that otherwise may not be available.[174]

The servant-leadership approach challenges mainstream notions of "command and control" types of leadership where decision-making is centralized and information closely guarded. Even so, firm and decisive leadership is absolutely essential. But it can be exercised in ways that focus on building a shared vision, having a systemic perspective, learning from mistakes, questioning assumptions, encouraging creativity, promoting trust, developing people, being held accountable, promoting work as a calling, and embracing humility.[175] Unlike mainstream business whose primary goal is typically to maximize profits or shareholder value, servant-leaders attempt to maximize *stakeholder* value. The stakeholders for the development specialist are numerous, and the effective servant-leader is able to hold these stakeholders, these clients, in balance, so that the broader goals are moved forward.

The Anabaptist development ethic (Exhibit 6) also provides a context, a value base, in which to use power positively. These are the values identified in the development ethic (and similar to Boulding's *integrative* form of power) and include: mutuality, service, humility, honesty, people-centeredness, integrity, and authenticity. For example, an attitude of humility, in the context of having power, does not go unnoticed by host-country colleagues and is highly valued by them. Being authentic and having integrity have enormously positive effects on building relationships and trust. An integral part of this value base is accountability—accountability to the kind of hermeneutic community described in previous sections of this chapter. Attempting to use power in positive ways as a single individual is not likely to have a major effect, although it can help to create positive relationships.

To summarize, what we propose with respect to the tensions which surround power is this: (a) that we first fully acknowledge that development specialists have power, rather than acting as though they do not; (b) that development specialists have a disproportionate share of power; (c) that power is not only a negative force, but can be a positive force; (d) that the development ethic provides a set of principles for using power positively, with four of those principles being especially important (transparency as to where our interests and loyalties lie, empowerment, decentralized decision-making, and servant-leadership); and (e) that these principles be driven by a set of faith-inspired values that include mutuality, service, humility, honesty, people-centeredness, integrity, and authenticity.

If the work and spirit of the development specialist, whether working at the grassroots or public policy level, for a secular or religious, public or private organization, is informed by these values and principles, then power can become a servant for the good. If the organization subscribes to and generates a culture that promotes these principles, then power can indeed become a creative and redeeming element in service to others.

We argue further that these principles are not only relevant in a world of competition, self-interest, and hardball politics, they are essential ingredients and sources of hope in moving us toward a more peaceful, just, and sustainable world.

The Nature of Development, and Where Best to Situate Policy Formation Efforts

In the preceding section we discussed the dilemmas that surround the use and abuse of power. This section follows closely on that theme, though with a different focus. We will explore the tension between the more impersonal, large-scale development, frequently associated with powerful bilateral or multilateral organizations, and the more relational focus of smaller, nongovernmental organizations operating at the grassroots. What is the nature of "good" development? What kind of policy should we formulate that would make large-scale development more consistent with what we believe constitutes "good" development at the grassroots? We could describe the latter as "people-centered development" or "development as if people mattered."

The stories presented in Part II show that some practitioners judge the effectiveness of their work, and that of others, according to the values that undergird it, as well as the ways in which many people are affected by a given development effort. In other words, they want to make development better, using Goulet's terms, or more in accord with Anabaptist values as identified in this book, not just more far-reaching. They share the values that guide localized grassroots Anabaptist development efforts, but they also want to apply those values at a higher scale, typically associated with large institutions like governments or multilateral organizations.

Practitioners working to develop social policy at national or regional levels believe that people-centered, large-scale development can be accomplished best by working within those large organizations, rather than by standing outside of them critiquing their efforts. Others feel that the effectiveness of development programs needs to be judged according to the quality of relationships that affect all aspects of peoples' lives—their emotional, identity-related, physical, and economic needs— and that they should be less concerned with how far-reaching an effort is. Some participants question whether large-scale development can be relational. Is there, in fact, at the large-scale level a structural equivalent to the relational, or people-centeredness, of grassroots development?

To what degree should development policy address the character and the nature of the development that it promotes? Where should such development policy be formulated? Is it possible for development to be carried out on a large scale so that it captures what relational development achieves at the grassroots? Anabaptist-Mennonite development workers are struck by the relatively impersonal structural relationships at the medium and macro-levels, versus the seemingly more personal integral nature of development at the grassroots. Until we are able to articulate what types of structural relationships at the large-scale are the ethical equivalents of personal relationships at the grassroots, community-level practitioners will tend to judge large-scale efforts as morally weaker than relationally rich grassroots projects. Likewise, societal level practitioners will be inclined to continue to think of grassroots development efforts as rich but inefficient, because they do not reach a critical mass in society.

Ideally, policy should try to find a balance between maximizing the numbers of people positively affected by development programs and the degree of person-centeredness of those efforts. Grassroots practitioners want macro-level policy, and they want it to create conditions and structures that will alleviate a wider range of needs that poor people experience and to empower them to recognize and use resources they already have. The practitioners in our study did not oppose dramatically increasing the number of persons affected by development programs, but they seemed cautious about fully embracing large-scale efforts. Their concern was that the integral nature of development would be sacrificed in order to reach larger numbers.

Practitioners working at the societal level, on the other hand, expressed support for grassroots efforts. They ultimately believed that the most effective type of development affects large numbers of persons in preventive ways, as highlighted in the ambulance-driver analogy. Consequently, the need for curative measures is greatly reduced. The argument could be made that if practitioners really wanted to make a difference, they should work with large-scale efforts, typically sponsored by organizations like USAID, CIDA, and the World Bank. In our study, grassroots practitioners, some middle ground practitioners, and a few societal-level practitioners were skeptical about how much an individual could affect a large organization. They preferred to address large-scale policy issues through social movements or effective lobbying efforts. Some were clearly concerned about what happens to the voices on the inside. Most practitioners would underscore that all types of efforts are needed to affect the formulation of large-scale policy.

We should be clear that helping to implement large-scale development projects is not the same as formulating policy. Practitioners often do not distinguish between policy that affects project implementation and macro policy that shapes the whole development enterprise. For example, a person working to formulate policy to guide a large-scale public health development project may be able to shape the project to make it more participatory, which would enable the poor to empower themselves to a greater degree. Such action is consistent with the development ethic. Nevertheless, that individual will find it very difficult to change the macro policy of the World Bank that calls for all development work to contribute ultimately to enhance international trade, or, if sponsored by USAID, that development further the interests of the United States.

Thus it may be fairer to judge the effectiveness of one's policy-formulation efforts based upon the ability to address policy concerns at the level *above* the one in which one works. In that sense, we all fell short since, with the exception of Wayne Nafziger (paper available from the EMU Library), no one openly addressed the ends ques-

tion of the entire development enterprise.[176] This issue
needs more conversation, especially if we take seriously
Anabaptist values related to power and efforts to maximize one's interests personally or collectively at the expense of others.

Based on her grassroots work in Latin America, Susan
Classen notes the need to risk "standing against the forces
of evil" as the development challenge. In the Latin American context, that means standing against development efforts whose ultimate purpose (not necessarily a given project's specific goals) is to further the interests of a particular nation, or block of nations, often at the expense of
others. Economic and cultural globalization would be a
case in point. While not ignoring the debate about the validity of the claim, we note that many sources, including
OXFAM, assert that under the current trade regulations,
the process itself widens the gap between rich and poor,
both at the global level as well as within countries themselves. But with fair-trade rules, trade is a powerful development tool.[177]

The debate about the nature of development—relationally rich at the personal level, or impersonal but structured to foster just patterns of interaction among large
numbers of people—and the debate about the nature of
policy leads to the question of where individuals should
situate themselves in order to affect development policy.
Practitioners at all levels agree that the best way to affect
project-specific policy in large-scale projects is to work
for the implementing or sponsoring institution, whether
USAID, CIDA, the World Bank, a large university, or
NGO subcontractor. However, it was grassroots and middle ground practitioners who addressed macropolicy undergirding the development enterprise. They raised
prophetic concerns about the foundational policy issues

related to development. The societal-level practitioners may have shared those concerns, but in their presentations they limited themselves primarily to large-scale, project-level policy concerns.

This observation should not lead us to conclude that common ground is impossible among practitioners working at the different levels. We noted earlier that participants in the development conference held at EMU agreed that it was important to arrange a meeting with the World Bank president to address Bank policy and its effect on the poor throughout the world. However, reports from the meeting indicate that the discussions did not go beyond macro project-level policy issues, important as they may be.

Susan Classen stated that socially relevant living, based on an Anabaptist ethic for living, will "result in development work that both nourishes good and denounces evil." This calls for a radically different understanding of development from that currently espoused by the vast majority of private, governmental, or multilateral organizations involved in the enterprise, irrespective of the level at which they are involved. Such a position requires that we ask questions about how to faithfully address the most macropolicy aspects of development, including the underlying assumptions driving the enterprise and the economic and political ends it pursues. This will be difficult as long as we do not have a clear vision about how values expressed in relationships at the grassroots can be expressed structurally at the societal level.

Afterward: An Invitation to Come Together with a Faithful and Prophetic Development Ethic

One of the primary purposes of this book is to hear the stories of Anabaptists/Mennonites who have done international development work in a variety of agencies, from those with a grassroots orientation to those in large development organizations with a macro-oriented public policy focus. We listened to these stories to see if there was a set of values held in common by the practitioners which informed why and how they did development work, regardless of their organizational affiliation. From that we attempted to articulate an Anabaptist ethic of development and to analyze how this compared with classical Anabaptist ethics. Finally, while still reflecting on the practitioners' experiences, we explored some of the major tensions, dilemmas, and opportunities experienced by Anabaptists doing development work.

What have we learned? While we have found diversity, we have also discovered considerable common ground— common ground from which an ethic of development could be articulated. Although it would be presumptuous to suggest that all practitioners would agree with all the elements of this development ethic, we believe that the development ethic remains true to the spirit of the practitioners and their stories.

The ultimate goals, or ends, of "global peace/*salaam/ shalom*, justice, sustainability, and an enriched quality of life" are promoted by means such as mutuality, praxis, servant-leadership, decentralized and participatory power structures and systems, "everyone a teacher and everyone a learner" systems-orientations, and listening, by practitioners who largely see development work as a sacred vocation. In turn, these ends and means are rooted in values such as service, humility, integrity, peace and justice, and people-centeredness.

We also found, in examining what we articulated as classical Anabaptist/Mennonite ethics, that there is considerable congruence between the practitioner-derived development ethic and Anabaptist/Mennonite ethics. Although this should not be surprising, since all the practitioners in our study have Anabaptist/Mennonite roots, it does indicate that the ethics-oriented theology of the Anabaptist tradition has been influential in shaping "life ethics" of those from that tradition.

We do not claim, of course, that this development ethic is unique to those of the Anabaptist tradition. Nor do we claim that there are not other development ethics which promote the common good and move toward the goals of the development ethic. However, we do believe

that, as we stated in the Preface, the Anabaptist development story has integrity and staying power and is worth
offering as part of the larger development conversation.

We have tried to make the case that all of the different
levels and types of development work described in this
book are important and represent a part in a seamless
web. Becoming tangled in easy but false dichotomies is
not helpful. All parts of the continuum require equal reflection and care.[178] We have also argued that since the
largest share of Anabaptist/Mennonite development resources have been at the grassroots level, balance would
call for more resources invested at the global/prevention
side of the continuum, but in such a way that the ethic of
development articulated in this book remains central.

The challenges and tensions of being both prophetic
and effective are not to be minimized. We have examined
some of these challenges; perhaps naively, we see them
as opportunities. At the same time, some questions have
been asked that have been inadequately addressed. "Is
there room in a book of this kind for a hard-hitting critique of the Western model of life which in so many ways
informs and undergirds very much of what passes for development?"[179] Further, testing the practitioner-derived
development ethic against Anabaptist theology, or any
other theology, has its own set of limitations, as illustrated in the following comment by Harold Miller, a long-
time development worker in East Africa:

> I do believe that it is important to "theologize" about
> our development engagements. But I think our de-
> velopment reflection must be informed by an en-
> counter between the host and the donor/foreign the-
> ology. . . . [I]t is not sufficient to test our overseas de-
> velopment doings solely against our own theological
> backdrop. Development encounters like all other

cross-cultural encounters move and shake the foundations of all who are engaged directly and indirectly with the enterprise. [One] should at the very least acknowledge the existence of a vast body of theological reflection throughout the so-called Third World which has been triggered into existence precisely in an effort to understand what has been happening to their cultures and their metaphysics, generally under the development assault from the industrialized world. . . . A theology of development needs to be done "in situ" [since] most of the so-called Third World can only be understood in the first instance in religious or spiritual terms. . . . Any helpful entry into those societies by the development worker must therefore be informed, firstly, by religious or spiritual categories and only secondarily by economic or bureaucratic/institutional or development considerations.[180]

Thus, an important question to consider further is the extent to which our development ethic has been shaped by the encounter between the development practitioners and the host-country partners. Values held in high esteem by the conference's participants, such as mutuality, service, and people-centeredness, plus the fact that all the practitioners began at the grassroots with the people, suggest that this ought to have taken place. The absence of stories from host-country partners suggests our study's inadequacy. What remains to be done is to test our proposed development ethic not only with development workers from rich countries but also, and more importantly, with the hosts—whether in poor areas in rich countries or in poor countries.

The Anabaptist ethic is not embodied simply in individuals, but it is resident in a community. By relying on the

stories of individual practitioners we skewed the focus of
our discussion in this book toward the individual's experience and reflection. When practitioners voiced concern
about being co-opted or about whether they had acted
faithfully, they did so in relation to their respective individual cases within a given organizational or community
context. Finding a way to express an ethic of development
for individuals may be essential to better understanding
discipleship in the twenty-first century. However, future
work in this area should also address the issue of faithfulness as a group characteristic, and its relationship to individual behavior and values. For example, is an Anabaptist
ethic applied at the individual level within any given social
group (a community, an organization) still an Anabaptist
ethic, or must it be embodied within a larger social context
in order to fulfill the Anabaptist understanding of faithfulness? Is faithfulness an individual quality?

Does an Anabaptist ethic require that we examine the
character of the organizations of which we become an integral part? This dilemma surfaces at various places
throughout the book, most notably in the discussion of
the "two-kingdom" perspective and again with the question of power. There is clearly more work to be done in
this area.

We end, then, by asking if the ethic of development
elicited from the experiences of Anabaptist/Mennonite
development practitioners is one that others can claim,
embody, and further shape. Who will find it to be of value as they do development work and reflect on development work? Can it, in fact, serve as the basis for promoting people-centered and mutually transforming development from the grassroots to the global level? Or is it an
ethic that has the appearance of rootedness and integrity,
but ultimately is not so relevant in the real world?

Appendix:
A Brief Sketch of the Anabaptist-Mennonite Movement

The Anabaptist-Mennonite movement emerged during the massive socio-religious turmoil at the time of the sixteenth-century Protestant Reformation. A handful of young adherents to Huldrich Zwingli's attempt to reform Roman Catholicism's abuse of the sacraments and church order parted company with him in 1525 because he (Zwingli) wanted the Swiss state to support his "reformation," whereas the more radical ones proposed: 1) a total separation of the church from state control, including rejection of military service and killing, so that the state would have no authority in religious matters; 2) a personal conversion experience with baptism based upon an adult confession of faith (hence the term "Anabaptist," meaning "re-baptizers"); 3) democratic and congregational church polity, including rejection of the sacramental/

priestly authority structure; 4) and a commitment to follow literally the teachings of Jesus, expressed in daily discipleship within a caring faith community. Contrary to conventional perceptions, these radicals accepted the basic and orthodox theology of both Roman Catholic and Reformed traditions.

This movement spread from Switzerland through Germany to Holland, where a Catholic priest named Menno Simons converted in 1536. He became a leader of the movement, and it was after him that "Mennonites" were nicknamed. The Anabaptist "rebellion" aroused opposition and persecution almost immediately. Over a 150-year period, over 4,000 were martyred for their faith. It is generally agreed that the basic motivation for the brutal persecution was the threat the Anabaptists posed to the authority of the state, as well as to the authority of both Roman Catholicism and the newly emerging Lutheran and Calvinist hierarchies. The struggle centered basically on where the power and authority to decide religious belief and behavior resided—in the state, the church hierarchy, or the "Believers Church."

The struggle to preserve their faith and community life caused the Anabaptists to develop isolated enclaves. They became known as the "quiet in the land," minding their own business and eventually achieving grudging toleration because of their industriousness and sober lives. Experiencing continued rejection, largely because of their refusal to serve the state in military service, the Anabaptists formed settlements where they could find religious freedom, including exemption from military service, in the backwoods of Switzerland, Bohemia, Germany, and Holland. Harassment continued, so some migrated to West Prussia (1539), others to America (1683), and still others to Russia (1789), where they were promised freedom to live their lives in peace. From these settlements, daughter colonies spread to Canada, Mexico, Paraguay, and Siberian Russia. In the meantime, missionary work begun in 1851 resulted in the establishing of Mennonite communities in Asia, Africa, South America, and, in recent decades, in almost all parts of the globe.

Mennonites were tolerated in many places because they were innovative agriculturalists. Consequently, Mennonite culture was strongly rural/agrarian for the first several centuries, but since about 1940, many Mennonites (in North America) have become urbanized, professionalized, and industrialized. Mennonite educational institutions participated markedly in this evolution. Mennonites today are involved in numerous professions, especially education, health and medicine, social welfare, law, and even politics, as well as in business and industry, including sizable enterprises in a variety of sectors, among them high technology.

Mennonites are recognized worldwide for their ethical traditions, especially mutual aid expressed in financial, social, and material assistance, illustrated by the "barn raising" practice. Mutual insurance and burial aid organizations, credit unions, disaster relief, and international voluntary relief and service organizations are other examples. Beginning with World War I, Mennonites have served in volunteer capacities in work camps, relief services, and reconstruction under the Mennonite Central Committee during war and peace. Mennonite Economic Development Associates is the expression of the economic and business end of the mutual-aid dynamic in global development.

Mennonites, basically congregational in polity, have experienced many divisions. Earlier those divisions were based less on theological differences and more on outward expressions of faith, such as modes of baptism, allowed dress, leisure activities, lifestyles, education, and so on. More recently, however, fundamentalism and evangelicalism, partly theologically-based, have contributed to more of the divisions. There are today literally scores of Mennonite "denominations" and "fellowships" resulting from these differences. Mennonite Church USA in 2003 is the largest, with approximately 323,330 members. Other groups include the Mennonite Brethren, plus many smaller groups of Mennonites which have formed their own independent fellowships. This proliferation reflects the Anabaptist congregational understanding of the Christian faith.

There are about 451,000 Mennonites in North America (the Brethren in Christ, a more pietistic group, is considered a part of the Anabaptist movement). The world population of Anabaptists/Mennonites numbers around 1,3000,000 in 2003.

Endnotes

1 For a brief sketch of who the Anabaptists/Mennonites are, see the Appendix.

2 Denis Goulet, *The Cruel Choice: A New Concept in the Theory of Development* (New York: Atheneum, 1973), vii.

3 See, for example, the March 5, 2002 issue of *The Mennonite,* the official biweekly publication of Mennonite Church USA, which has several articles relating to the question "Anabaptist or Mennonite?" and from which information for this section is taken.

4 It is of some interest to note that the largest share of writing on the question, "What is development?", occurred in the 1960s and 1970s.

5 Irma Adelman and Cynthia Morris, *Economic Growth and Social Equity in Developing Countries* (Stanford, CA: Stanford University Press, 1973), 189.

6 Dudley Seers. "The Meaning of Development" (Paper presented at the Eleventh World Conference of the Society for International Development, New Delhi, 1969), 3.

7 Denis Goulet, 85-95.

8 Michael Todaro and Stephen C. Smith, *Economic Development,* 8th edition (New York: Addison-Wesley, 2003), 22.

9 Dwight H. Perkins, Steven Radelet, Donald R. Snodgrass, Malcolm Gillis, and Michael Roemer, *Economics of Development,* 5th edition (New York: W.W. Norton, 2001), 10.

10 It has been argued that perhaps the reason economic growth (or income per person) became dominant in defining development is because: (a) it is easily measured, and (b) it is typically a necessary but not sufficient condition for improved health, education, nutrition, etc.

11 Adapted from Vernon E. Jantzi, "Helping Developing Nations: Socio-Political Paradigms of Development," Charles De Santo, Zondra G. Lindblade, and Margaret M. Poloma, eds., *Christian Perspectives on Social Problems* (Indianapolis: Wesley Press, 1992).

12 Comparative advantage is the ability of a country to produce a specific good at a lower opportunity cost (the highest valued alternative that is given up) than its trading partners. See any introductory economics text such as Bradley R. Schiller, *The Economy Today* (New York, New York: McGraw-Hill, 2003).

13 Steven Pearlstein and Paul Blustein, *The Washington Post,* June 23, 1997, A12.

14 James H. Weaver and Kenneth Jameson, *Economic Development: Competing Paradigms* (Lanham, MD.: University Press of America, 1989).

15 David Korten, *Getting to the 21st Century* (New Haven, CT: Kumarian Press, 1997).

16 This section is adapted from Terrence Jantzi's unpublished Ph.D. dissertation, "Local Program Theories and Social Capital: A Case Study of a Non-Governmental Organization in Eastern Bolivia," Ithaca, NY: Cornell University, 2000; see also David Korten, "Third Generation

NGO Strategies: A Key to People-centered Development," *World Development*, Vol. 15 (1987): Supplement, 145-197.

17 Derald W. Sue and others. *Counseling the Culturally Different* (New York: John Wiley and Sons, 1981), as described in David Augsburger, *Pastoral Counseling Across Cultures* (Philadelphia: Westminster Press, 1986), 79-110.

18 Jean Masamba Ma Mpolo, "African Symbols and Stories in Pastoral Care," *Journal of Pastoral Care,* 39(4): 314-326, as quoted in David Augsburger, Ibid., p. 79.

19 Terrence Jantzi, Ibid. See also Robert Putnam, *Bowling Alone: The collapse and revival of American community* (New York: Touchstone, 2000).

20 "Development Work," *Mennonite Encyclopedia*. Vol. V, 230.

21 "Mennonite Missions in India," *Mennonite Encyclopedia. Vol. III, 22.*

22 For a history of Mennonite mission work, see Wilbert Shenk, "Growth through Missions," in Paul N. Kraybill, ed., *Mennonite World Handbook* (Lombard, IL: Mennonite World Conference, 1978); also Wilbert Shenk, "Mission Boards," *Mennonite Encyclopedia. Vol. V,* 592-594, and S.F. Pannabecker, "Foreign Mennonite Missions," *Mennonite Encyclopedia. Vol. IV,* 712-717.

23 Edmund G. Kaufman, *Mennonite Missionary Interest* (Berne, IN: The Mennonite Book Concern, 1931).

24 John A. Lapp, *The Mennonite Church in India, 1897-1962* (Scottdale: Herald Press, 1972), 101.

25 Ibid., 101.

26 Kaufman, 387. "Since the beginning of the Mission various attempts have been made at teaching such courses as carpentry, cabinet making, gardening, sewing, rope making, weaving, tailoring and blacksmithing. About the year 1906 a small carpenter shop was opened for the sake of the orphan boys, which by 1917 had grown into the Mennonite Mission carpentry school entirely supported by the government."

27 Lapp, 132.

28 Ibid., 101.

29 Kaufman, 383.

30 Lapp, 112.

31 Ibid., 139.

32 Ibid., 139.

33 The emergency relief work of Mennonite Central Committee and the work of the mission programs were ways in which Mennonites engaged in development work. This will be discussed extensively in the next section.

34 There are almost always exceptions. James Juhnke describes the case of Henry R. Voth, who "attended the [Sioux] Ghost Dance. Sitting Bull [in return] took time at the dance to admonish his people to attend the missionaries' meetings and learn the Bible." Voth's respect for the Sioux culture caused him to say, "It may become the sad duty of our mission to sing the funeral songs of almost the last Arapahoes." *Vision, Doctrine, War* (Scottdale: Herald Press,1989), 138.

35 Ibid., 142.

36 Robert S. Kreider and Rachel W. Goosen, *Hungry, Thirsty, A Stranger: The MCC Experience* (Scottdale: Herald Press, 1988), 20.

37 Ibid.

38 Ibid., 11-17.

39 *Mennonite Encyclopedia.* Vol. V, 228-231.

40 Barry Lessor, interviewed by Vernon Jantzi on October 13, 2000, in Waldheim, Saskatchewan for the

MCC Africa Listening Project, indicated that in 1970 he was part of the last group of Pax men in Africa. For a fuller account of the PAX efforts, see Calvin Redekop, *The PAX Story* (Telford, PA: Pandora Press, 2001).

41 Timothy C. Lind, *MCC Africa Program: Historical Background.* MCC Occasional Paper, No. 10 (Akron, PA: Mennonite Central Committee, 1989).

42 Stoesz also initiated a "Development Series" published by Mennonite Central Committee which documented the experiences and reflections of MCC fieldworkers.

43 *Mennonite Encyclopedia. Vol. V,* 228-231.

44 Ted Koontz, "Commitments and Complications in Doing Good," in Robert S. Kreider and Ronald J.R. Mathies, eds., *Unity Amidst Diversity* (Akron, PA: Mennonite Central Committee, Akron, 1996), 91-108.

45 M. Neufeld, "Critical Theory and Christian Service: Knowledge and Action in Situations of Social Conflict," *Conrad Grebel Review* (Fall, 1988), 249.

46 Robert Kreider, "The Multiple Visions of MCC's 75 Years," *Unity Amidst Diversity* (Akron, PA: Mennonite Central Committee, 1996), 1-10.

47 Based on 115 interviews in Canada from October 3-November 5, 2000 as part of the MCC Africa Listening Project, which also included interviews in Africa and the United Studies to provide data for re-visioning MCC's involvement in Africa during the first decade of the new millennium.

48 Ronald J. Mathies, "Service as Transformation: MCC as Educational Institution," in *Unity Amidst Diversity* (Akron, PA: Mennonite Central

Committee, 1996), 69-81.

49 Joseph Winfield Fretz, *Immigrant Group Settlement in Paraguay* (North Newton, KS: Bethel College, 1963), 92, passim.

50 J. Winfield Fretz, *The MEDA Experiment. Twenty-five Years of Economic Development*(Waterloo: Conrad Press, 1978), 14.

51 Ibid., 15.

52 The list includes Orie O. Miller, shoe manufacturer and executive secretary of MCC; Erie J. Sauder, president of Sauder Woodworking Company; Edward Snyder, potato grower and processor; Ivan Miller, potato grower; Howard Yoder, greenhouse operator; C.A. DeFehr, merchandiser and manufacturer; Ed. J. Peter and Henry Martens, fruit and vegetable growers and packers.

53 Ibid., 18.

54 Ibid, 19.

55 For an expanded description of this history, see Calvin Redekop, *Strangers Become Neighbors: Mennonite and Indigenous Relations in the Paraguayan Chaco* (Scottdale: Herald Press, 1980).

56 Ibid., chapters 9 and 10 for an analysis of the issues involved in a very complex development program.

57 Fretz, 1978, 97.

58 *MEDA Annual Report,* 2003.

59 "Ethics," *Mennonite Encyclopedia. Vol. IV,* 1079.

60 *The Marketplace,* July/August, 1992, 10-12.

61 *The Marketplace,* May/June, 1992, 4-7.

62 "Development Work," *Mennonite Encyclopedia. Vol. V,* 230. See also Henry Rempel, *A High Price for Abundant Living: The Story of Capitalism* (Scottdale, PA: Herald Press, 2003), chapters 11 and 12.

63 Letter in author's files.

64 Letter in author's files.

65 Letter in author's files.

66 Letter in author's files.

67 Ibid., 2.

68 This is the only specific statement regarding the goal and nature of development in the document.

69 This is not to imply in any way that the program has not been successful and effective. There are many success stories in the history of MEDA's work, but the propositions made by Rempel that there should be "changes in life, beliefs and attitudes" have not been extensively debated.

70 See, for example, "Missions" by Wilbert Shenk in *Mennonite Encyclopedia*. Vol. V, 590-592, which lists an extensive bibliography including a bibliography in *Mission Focus,* a Mennonite journal dedicated to the discussion of mission theology and practice.

71 Letter in author's files.

72 Ibid., 14-16. The documentation and analysis of this early period is sparse and begs analysis. See Calvin Redekop, "MEDA," in *Mennonite Encyclopedia*. Vol. V, 570-571. The "Mennonite Community movement" was a transitional development from the agricultural phase to the commercial. See "Mennonite Community Association," *Mennonite Encyclopedia*. Vol. III, 619. For a study of Mennonite entrepreneurship, see Calvin Redekop, et. al, *Mennonite Entrepreneurs* (Baltimore: The Johns Hopkins University Press), 100.

73 Fretz, *The Meda Experiment,* 108.

74 Ibid., 109.

75 *MEDA Annual Report, 1999,* 9.

76 For an analysis of this issue, see Calvin Redekop, Stephen Ainlay, and Robert Siemens, *Mennonite Entrepreneurs* (Baltimore: The Johns Hopkins University Press, 1995).

77 Letter in author's files.

78 Rempel, 230.

79 Letter in author's files.

80 Howard Thurman quoted in Gil Bailie, *Violence Unveiled: Humanity at the Crossroads* (New York: Crossroad Publishing Co. 1995), xv.

81 Wolfgang Sachs, "Archeology of the Idea of Development, *Envio,* September, 1997, 33-46.

82 Not his real name.

83 John Paul Lederach, *The Journey Toward Reconciliation* (Scottdale, PA: Herald Press, 1999); John Paul Lederach, *Building Peace: Sustainable Reconciliation in Divided Societies* (Washington, DC: United States Institute of Peace Press, 1997); John Paul Lederach, *Preparing for Peace: Conflict Transformation Across Cultures* (Syracuse, N.Y.: Syracuse University Press, 1995).

84 See K.R. Duba, Y.G. Kalacha, J. Rigano, F. Lesekali, M.A. Siekhow, F.N. ole Sakuda, J. Akeno, and S. Emweki, *Honey and Heifer, Grasses, Milk and Water: A Heritage of Diversity in Reconciliation* (Nairobi: Mennonite Central Committee, 1997); Robert Herr and Judy Zimmerman Herr, eds., *Transforming Violence: Linking Local and Global Peacemaking* (Scottdale, PA: Herald Press, 1998); D. Ibrahim and J. Jenner, "Breaking the Cycle of Violence in Wajir," in Robert Herr and Judy Zimmerman Herr, eds., *Transforming Violence: Linking Local and Global Peacemaking* (Scottdale, PA: Herald Press, 1998), 133-148.

85 Kathleen Norris, *Amazing Grace: A Vocabulary of Faith* (New York: Riverhead Books, 1998).

86 Since this paper was written, Allan has been appointed President

of MEDA.

87 United Nations Development Programme, *Human Development Report 1998* (New York: Oxford University Press, 1998).

88 Some anthropological literature indicates that two values that are universal are those against incest and murder within one's own group. See, for example, Clyde Kluckhohn, "Values and Value Orientations in the Theory of Action," Talcott Parsons, Edward Shills, et al., eds., *Toward a Theory of Action* (Cambridge, MA: Harvard University Press, 1951), 409-410.

89 Also know as "utilitarianism."

90 Sometimes called "intuitionism" (acting according to one's inner sense of what is right or wrong), which is sometimes linked to a "culturally relative" position ("when in Rome do as the Romans do").

91 Virtue theory is often seen as a fourth ethical system and considers an act to be good to the extent that it represents a positive character trait; for example, setting a good moral example for others to follow. See Dean Geuras and Charles Garofalo, *Practical Ethics in Public Administration* (Vienna, VA: Management Concepts, 2002).

92 The International Development Ethics Association is an organization active in promoting ethical considerations as being at the heart of development thought and practice through conferences, newsletters, and other forums.

93 Michael P. Todaro, *Economic Development* (Boston, MA: Addison-Wesley Publishers, 1999), 32.

94 Mennonite Central Committee Africa Listening Team, *Africa Revisioning: Walking Together into the 21st Century* (Akron, PA: Mennonite Central Committee, April 2001), and

Mennonite Central Committee-Bolivia Evaluation Team, MCC-Bolivia Evaluation Report (unpublished report by Mennonite Central Committee, September 2000).

95 *The Complete Writings of Menno Simons* (Scottdale, PA: Herald Press, 1956), 307.

96 E. F. Schumacher, *Small Is Beautiful: Economics as if People Mattered* (New York: Harper & Row, 1973).

97 The "servant leader" concept is explored further in the section on Power, pp. 316ff.

98 See Denis Goulet, *Development Ethics: A Guide to Theory and Practice* (London: Zed Books, 1995), 6-7.

99 Ronald J. Mathies, "Service as Transformation: MCC as Educational Institution," in *Unity Amidst Diversity* (Akron, PA: Mennonite Central Committee, 1996), 69-812.

100 Joseph Campbell, one of the world's foremost mythologists, has written extensively on the common themes present in the world's great religions. See, for example, *The Power of Myth* (New York: Doubleday, 1988).

101 Robert Friedman has proposed that Anabaptism promoted an "existential Christianity" which focused on action and reflection, that is, "praxis": "There existed no basic split between faith and life." *The Theology of Anabaptism* (Scottdale: Herald Press, 1973), 27.

102 Paul Tillich, *Systematic Theology* (Chicago: University of Chicago Press, 1951), 15.

103 C. Norman Kraus, *God Our Savior* (Scottdale, PA: Herald Press, 1991), 14.

104 James Leo Garrett, ed., *The Concept of the Believer's Church* (Scottdale, PA: Herald Press, 1969), 140-141.

105 Ibid., 316.

106 *Confession of Faith in a Mennonite Perspective* (Scottdale, PA: Herald Press, 1995).

107 Walter Klaassen, *Anabaptism: Neither Catholic nor Protestant* (revised edition) (Waterloo, Ontario, Canada: Conrad Press, 1981), 18-25.

108 Calvin Redekop, "The Community of Scholars and the Essence of Anabaptism," *Mennonite Quarterly Review,* 67:4 (October 1993), 438-439.

109 See "Anabaptism" by Walter Klaassen, *Mennonite Encyclopedia.* Vol.V, 23-26.

110 "Ethics, " *Mennonite Encyclopedia.* Vol. IV, 1081.

111 James C. Juhnke, *A People of Two Kingdoms: The Political Acculturation of Kansas Mennonites* (Newton, KS: Faith and Life Press, 1975), 10.

112 Leo Driedger and Donald B. Kraybill, *Mennonite Peacemaking: From Quietism to Activism* (Scottdale, PA: Herald Press, 1994), 54.

113 Ibid., 54.

114 Ibid., 241.

115 Perry Bush, *Two Kingdoms, Two Loyalties: Mennonite Pacifism in Modern America* (Baltimore: The Johns Hopkins University Press, 1998), 6.

116 James Halteman, *The Clashing Worlds of Economics and Faith* (Scottdale, PA.: Herald Press, 1995), see especially chapters 4 and 13.

117 Guy F. Hershberger, *The Way of the Cross in Human Relations* (Scottdale, PA: Herald Press, 1958), 374.

118 Ranking second was "when communities are organized and act."

119 Merrill Ewert, "World View and Community Development," presentation at the conference on "An-abaptist/Mennonite Experiences in International Development, Eastern Mennonite University, Harrisonburg, VA, October 1-4, 1998.

120 J. Lawrence Burkholder, *The Problem of Social Responsibility from the Perspective of the Mennonite Church.* Unpublished Th.D. dissertation, Princeton Theological Seminary, as found in Dreidger and Kraybill, *Mennonite Peacemaking: From Quietism to Activism* (Scottdale, PA: Herald Press, 1994), 95.

121 Driedger and Kraybill, *Mennonite Peacemaking: From Quietism to Activism* (Scottdale, PA: Herald Press, 1994), 153-154.

122 John Paul Lederach, *The Journey Toward Reconciliation* (Scottdale, PA: Herald Press, 1999), 92-94

123 Driedger and Kraybill, *Mennonite Peacemaking: From Quietism to Activism* (Scottdale, PA: Herald Press, 1994). See especially chapter 5 for an historical account.

124 Ibid., 107.

125 John D. Clark, *Worlds Apart: Civil Society and the Battle for Ethical Globalization* (Bloomfield, CT: Kumarian Press, 2003), 6.

126 *Rigged Rules and Double Standards: Trade, Globalisation and the Fight against Poverty* (London: OXFAM, 2002), 3.

127 Chris Gingrich, "The Impact of Globalization on Low-Income Coun-tries: What is the Evidence?" MCC Occasional Paper Number 31 (Akron, PA: Mennonite Central Committee, 2003).

128 *Rigged Rules and Double Standards: Trade, Globalisation and the Fight against Poverty* (London: OXFAM, 2002), 68.

129 Yildiz Atasoy, "Explaining Globalization," in Yildiz Atasoy and William K. Carroll, eds., *Global*

Shaping and Its Alternatives (Bloomfield, CT: Kumarian Press, 2003), 5.

130 Recounted by a participant in the "Reflecting on Peace Practice Feedback Workshop," Ghana, January 2002.

131 George Ritzer, *The McDonaldization of Society* (Thousand Oaks, CA: Pine Ridge Press, 2000).

132 Participants in the class, "Globalization and Conflict," at Eastern Mennonite University's Summer Peacebuilding Institute, Harrisonburg, VA, May 2002.

133 Donald Kraybill, *Our Star-Spangled Faith* (Scottdale, PA: Herald Press, 1976).

134 Samuel P. Huntington, *The Clash of Civilizations and the Remaking of the World Order* (New York: Touchstone, 1997), 125.

135 Francis Fukuyama, *The End of History and the Last Man* (New York: Avon Books, 1992), 328 ff.

136 Allison Brysk, *From Tribal Village to Global Village: Indian Rights and International Relations in Latin America* (Stanford, CA: Stanford University Press, 2000).

137 John D. Clark, "Ethical Globalization: The Dilemmas and Challenges of Internationalizing Civil Society," in Michael Edwards and John Gaventa, eds., *Global Citizen Action* (Boulder, CO: Lynne Rienner Publishers, 2001), 18.

138 John Paul Lederach, *The Journey Toward Reconciliation* (Scottdale, PA: Herald Press, 1999), 92-94.

139 Although the types and levels of action shown in Exhibit 10 appear to have clear boundaries, in reality they are not discrete at all; it is better to view them as continua.

140 Walter Wink, *Naming the Powers: The Language of Power in the New Testament* (Philadelphia: Fortress Press, 1984); *Unmasking the Powers: The Invisible Powers That Determine Human Existence* (Philadelphia: Fortress Press, 1986); and *Engaging the Powers: Discernment and Resistance in a World of Domination* (Philadelphia: Fortress Press, 1992).

141 John Driver letter in author's files dated 12 December 2002.

142 Ted Koontz, "Thinking Theologically about the War against Iraq," *The Mennonite Quarterly Review,* 77 (January, 2003), 93-108.

143 See Driedger and Kraybill, 1994, especially chapters 4, 5, and 6.

144 This important issue deserves a more thorough examination than is being given here. By way of comparison, the February 10, 2003 issue of *The Washington Post* reported that the ratio between executive salaries and the biggest U.S. companies and hourly wage-earners had increased from 40:1 in 1980 to 500:1 in 2003; that is, average executive salaries were 500 times greater than that of wage-earning labor in 2003.

John Isbister in his book *Capitalism and Justice: Envisioning Social and Economic Fairness* (Bloomfield, CT: Kumarian Press, 2001), especially chapter 3, provides a very readable discussion of distributing income equitably and in such a way that it does not distort efficient workings of the market. For a technical discussion of the subject, see Ray C. Fair, "The Optimal Distribution of Income," *The Quarterly Journal of Economics,* Vol. LXXXV, No. 4 (November, 1971).

145 As we write this, we are keenly aware of the human ability to rationalize in ways that justify choices and behavior that perhaps should not be justified. But read on to see

how this proposal is operationalized; the reader will need to assess the extent of rationalization present.

146 Ronald J. Sider, *Rich Christians in an Age of Hunger: Moving from Affluence to Generosity* (Dallas, TX: Word Publishing, 1997).

147 This is in reference to the biblical text of 2 Corinthians 8:13-14 where Paul states, "I do not mean that others should be eased and you burdened, but that as a matter of equality your abundance at the present time should supply their want . . . that there may be equality" (RSV).

148 Sider, op.cit., 194-196.

149 It is estimated that Mennonites give between 4 percent and 5 percent of their household income to the church and other charitable causes, with that percentage being on the decline (see J. Howard Kauffman and Leo Driedger, *The Mennonite Mosaic: Identity and Modernization* (Scottdale, PA: Herald Press, 1992) for details on Mennonite giving patterns, especially pages 113-114, 144-146, and 178-179. For U.S. Protestants and U.S. Catholics, giving as a percent of household income is estimated to be about 2 percent and 1.5 percent respectively. Lower income households give a greater percentage than do higher income households. The more "sectlike" the denomination (distinctiveness from the prevailing culture), the greater the percentage given. For more details see Dean R. Hoge, Charles Zech, Patrick McNamara, and Michael J. Donahue, *Money Matters: Personal Giving in American Churches* (Louisville, KY: Westminster John Knox Press, 1996).

150 James Halteman, 1995, especially chapters 5-7.

151 Ibid., 72.

152 Denis Goulet, *The Cruel Choice* (New York: Atheneum Publishers, 1971); Denis Goulet, *The Uncertain Promise: Value Conflicts in Technology Transfer* (Washington, D.C.: IDOC/North America, New York & Overseas Development Council, 1977); Denis Goulet, *Incentives for Development: The Key to Equity* (New York: New Horizons Press, 1989); Denis Goulet, *Development Ethics: A Guide to Theory and Practice* (New York: Apex Press, 1995).

153 Ibid., 1971.

154 Chinua Achebe, *Things Fall Apart* (New York: McDowell, Obolensky, 1959).

155 Manfred A. Max-Neef, *Human Scale Development: Conception, Application, and Further Reflections* (New York: The Apex Press, 1991).

156 Goulet, 1971, xiii.

157 Goulet, 1977, 17-31.

158 Philip McMichael, *Development and Social Change: A Global Perspective*, second edition (Thousand Oaks, CA: Pine Forge Press, 2000), 277-278.

159 David P. Ross and Peter J. Usher, *From the Roots Up: Economic Development as if Community Mattered* (Croton-on-Hudson, NY: The Bootstrap Press, 1986), 36.

160 Edited by Calvin Redekop (Baltimore: The Johns Hopkins University Press, 2000). For more writings on the environment by Anabaptists see Thomas N. Finger, *Evangelicals, Eschatology, and the Environment* (Wynnewood, PA: Evangelical Environmental Network, 1998).

161 (Scottdale, PA: Herald Press, 1995), 26.

162 McMichael, 2000, 302.

163 Wilbert R. Shenk, "Focused on Mission," *Our Faith* (Autumn

2001), 21.

164 Albert N. Keim, *Harold S. Bender: 1897-1962* (Scottdale, PA: Herald Press, 1998), 75.

165 Shenk, 21.

166 See John Driver's comments on this topic in Wilbert R. Shenk, ed., *The Transfiguration of Mission* (Scottdale, PA: Herald Press, 1993), 199-219.

167 See the series of booklets by the Mennonite Mission Network that discusses the integral mission of the church from this perspective.

168 For more information on this topic, see the wealth of writing by John Driver and other works published by the Anabaptist-oriented publishers in Latin America, such as SEMILLA and CLARA.

169 Mainstream literature continues to list the major forms and sources of power in organizations as being: legitimate (power based on position or mutual agreement), reward (power based on a person's ability to control or allocate rewards desired by another), coercive (power derived from the ability to apply sanctions), expert (power derived from specialized knowledge or skills), and referent (power based on some sort of interpersonal attraction). See J.R.P. French and B. Raven, "The Bases of Social Power," in D. Cartwright, ed., *Studies in Social Power* (Ann Arbor, MI: University of Michigan Press, 1959). For an extended analysis of power in the Anabaptist context, see Benjamin Redekop and Calvin Redekop, eds. *Power, Authority and the Anabaptist Tradition* (Baltimore: The Johns Hopkins University Press, 2001), especially chapter 9, "Power in the Anabaptist Community."

170 Values-based power is similar to what Boulding calls *integra-* *tive* power, which is based on relationships and values such as legitimacy, respect, affection, love, community, and identity. See Kenneth E. Boulding, *The Three Faces of Power* (Newbury Park, CA: Sage Publications, Inc., 1989).

171 For example, as a way of saying thank you for some personal help provided by a host-country colleague while working overseas, one of the authors of this book wanted to take him to a middle-class restaurant to share a meal and conversation. He objected and instead wanted to go to a lower-class restaurant because, as he said, he could not reciprocate in kind at the middle-class restaurant.

172 This includes both misuse and abuse of power. The former implies good intentions but lack of understanding of how power should be used, while the latter implies actions intentionally harmful to the other person.

173 Donald B. Kraybill, *The Upside-Down Kingdom* (Scottdale, PA: Herald Press, 1990), 252.

174 Robert Greenleaf, director of management research at AT&T for many years and rooted in Quaker spirituality, has reflected and written extensively on servant-leadership. His classic work is *Servant Leadership: A Journey into the Nature of Legitimate Power and Greatness* (New York: Paulist Press, 1977). See also Robert K. Greenleaf, L.C. Spears, and D.T. Fricks, eds., *On Becoming A Servant-Leader* (San Francisco: Jossey-Bass, 1996).

175 For more discussion see Ann McGee-Cooper and Gary Looper, *The Essentials of Servant-Leadership: Principles in Practice* (Innovations in Management Series, Pegasus Communications, 2001).

176 Paper presented at the conference, "Anabaptist/Mennonite Experiences in International Development," Eastern Mennonite University, Harrisonburg, VA, October 1-4, 1998.

177 *Rigged Rules and Double Standards: Trade, Globalization, and the Fight against Poverty* (Boston, MA: OXFAM, 2002). (See also www.maketradefair.com.

178 Personal communication from Harold Miller, January 30, 2002.

179 Ibid.

180 Ibid. See also Douglas Johnson and Cynthia Sampson, eds., *Religion, The Missing Dimension of Statecraft* (New York: Oxford University Press, 1994), who make a similar case that, as the title states, "religion is the missing dimension of statecraft."

Bibliography

Achebe, Chinua. *Things Fall Apart.* New York: McDowell, Obolensky, 1959.

"Anabaptist or Mennonite?" *The Mennonite*, March 5, 2002.

Adelman, Irma and Cynthia Morris. *Economic Growth and Social Equity in Developing Countries.* Stanford: Stanford University Press, 1973.

Atasoy, Yildiz. "Explaining Globalization" in Yildiz Atasoy and Willliam K. Carroll, eds. *Global Shaping and Its Alternatives.* Bloomfield, CT: Kumarian Press, 2003.

Augsburger, David. *Pastoral Counseling Across Cultures.* Philadelphia: Westminster Press, 1986.

Bailie, Gil. *Violence Unveiled: Humanity at the Crossroads.* New York: Crossroad, 1995.

Boulding, Kenneth. *The Three Faces of Power.* Newbury Park, CA: Sage Publications, 1989.

Brysk, Allison. *From Tribal Village to Global Village: Indian Rights and International Relations in Latin America.* Stanford, CA: Stanford University Press, 2000.

Burkholder, J. Lawrence. "Ethics." *Mennonite Encyclopedia.* Vol. IV.

_____. "The Problem of Social Responsibility in the Mennonite Church." Unpublished Ph.D dissertation, Princeton Theological Seminary, 1958.

Bush, Perry. *Two Kingdoms, Two Loyalties: Mennonite Pacifism in Modern America.* Baltimore: The Johns Hopkins University Press, 1998.

Campbell, Joseph. *The Power of Myth.* New York: Doubleday, 1988.

Clark, John D. "Ethical Globalization: The Dilemmas and Challenges of International Civil Society," in Michael Edwards and John Gavents, eds. *Global Citizen Action.* Boulder, CO: Lynne Rienner Publishers, 2001.

_____. *Worlds Apart: Civil Society and the Battle for Ethical Globalism.* Bloomfield, CT: Kumarian Press, 2003.

Confessions of Faith in a Mennonite Perspective. Scottdale, PA: Herald Press, 1995.

Driedger, Leo and Donald Kraybill. *Mennonite Peacemaking: From Quietism to Activism.* Scottdale, PA: Herald Press, 1994.

Duba, K.R. et. al. *Honey and Heifer, Grasses, Milk and Water: A Heritage of Diversity in Reconciliation.* Nairobi: Mennonite Central Committee, 1997.

Ewert, Merrill. "World View and Community Development." Paper presented at conference on "Anabaptist/Mennonite Experiences in International Development," Eastern Mennonite University, 1998.

Finger, Thomas. *Evangelicals, Eschatology and the Environment.* Wynnewood, PA: Evangelical Environmental Network, 1998.

French, J.R.P. and B. Raven, "The Bases of Social Power" in Dorwin Cartwright, ed. *Studies in Social Power.* Ann Arbor: University of Michigan Press, 1959.

Fretz, J. Winfield. *Immigrant Group Settlements in Paraguay*. Newton, KS: Bethel College, 1963.

_____. *The MEDA Experiment: Twenty-Five Years of Economic Development*. Waterloo, ON: Conrad Press, 1978.

Friedmann, Robert. *The Theology of Anabaptism*. Scottdale, PA: Herald Press, 1973.

Garrett, James Lee, ed. *The Concept of the Believer's Church*. Scottdale, PA: Herald Press, 1969.

Fair, Ray C. "The Optimal Distribution of Income." *The Quarterly Journal of Economics*, Vol. LXXXV, No. 4, November 1971.

Fukuyama, Francis. *The End of History and the Last Man*. New York: Avon Books, 1992.

Geuras, Dean and Charles Garafalo. *Practical Ethics in Public Administration*. Vienna, VA: Management Concepts, 2002.

Gingrich, Chris. "The Impact of Globalization on Low-Income Countries: What is the Evidence?" MCC Occasional Paper, No. 31. Akron, PA: Mennonite Central Committee, 2003.

Goulet, Dennis. *Development Ethics: A Guide to Theory and Practice*. New York: Apex Press, 1995.

_____. *The Uncertain Promise: Value Conflicts in Technology Transfer*. Washington, D.C.: IDOC/North America, New York and Overseas Development Council, 1977.

_____. *Incentives for Development: The Key to Equity*. New York: New Horizons Press, 1989.

_____. *Development Ethics: A Guide to Theory and Practice*. New York: Apex Press, 1995.

_____. *The Cruel Choice: A New Concept in the Theory of Development*. New York: Atheneum, 1973.

Greenleaf, Robert. *Servant Leadership: A Journey into the Nature of Legitimate Power and Greatness*. New York: Paulist Press, 1977.

Greenleaf, Robert, L.C. Spears and D.T. Fricks, eds., *On Becoming a Servant-Leader*. San Francisco: Jossey-Bass, 1996.

Halteman, James. *The Clashing Worlds of Economics and Faith*. Scottdale, PA: Herald Press, 1995.

Herr, Robert and Judy Zimmerman Herr, eds. *Transforming Violence: Linking Local and Global Peacemaking*. Scottdale, PA: Herald Press, 1998.

Hershberger, Guy F. *The Way of the Cross in Human Relations*. Scottdale, PA: Herald Press, 1958.

Hoge, Dean R., et. al. *Money Matters: Personal Giving in American Churches*. Louisville, KY: Westminster John Knox Press, 1996.

Huntington, Samuel P. *The Clash of Civilizations and the Remaking of the World Order*. New York: Touchstone, 1997.

Ibrahim, D., and Jan Jenner. "Breaking the Cycle of Violence in Wajir" in Herr, Robert and Judy Zimmerman Herr, eds. *Transforming Violence: Linking Local and Global Peacemaking*. Scottdale, PA: Herald Press, 1998.

Isbister, John. *Capitalism and Justice: Envisioning Social and*

Economic Fairness. Bloomfield, CT: Kumarian Press, 2001.

Jantzi, Terrence. "Local Program Theories and Social Capital: A Case Study of Non-Governmental Organization in Eastern Bolivia." Ph.D. thesis, Cornell University, 2000.

Jantzi, Vernon E. "Helping Developing Nations: Socio-Political Paradigms of Development" in De Santo, Charles, Zondra G. Lindblade and Margaret M. Poloma, eds. *Christian Perspectives on Social Problems.* Indianapolis: Wesley Press, 1992.

Johnson, Douglas and Cynthia Sampson, eds. *Religion; The Missing Dimension of Statecraft.* New York: Oxford University Press, 1994.

Juhnke, James. *Vision, Doctrine, War.* Scottdale, PA: Herald Press, 1989.

Kauffman, J. Howard and Leo Driedger. *Mennonite Mosaic: Identity and Modernization.* Scottdale, PA: Herald Press, 1992.

Kaufman, Edmund George. *Mennonite Missionary Interest.* Berne, IN: The Mennonite Book Concern, 1931.

Keim, Albert M. *Harold S. Bender, 1897-1962.* Scottdale, PA: Herald Press, 1998.

Klaassen, Walter. *Anabaptism: Neither Catholic nor Protestant.* Waterloo, ON: Conrad Press, 1981.

_____. "Anabaptism." *Mennonite Encyclopedia*, Vol. V, 23-26.

Kluckhohn, Clyde. "Values and Value Orientations in the Theory of Action" in Parsons, Talcott, Edward Shils, et. al. *Toward a General Theory of Action.* Cambridge, MA: Harvard University Press, 1951.

Koontz, Ted. "Thinking Theologically about the War in Iraq."

Mennonite Quarterly Review 77 (January, 2003): 93-108.

_____. "Commitments and Complications in Doing Good" in Kreider, Robert S. and Ronald J.R. Mathies, eds. *Unity Amidst Diversity.* Akron, PA: Mennonite Central Committee, 1996.

Korten, David. *Getting to the 21st Century.* New Haven: Kumarian Press, 1997.

_____. *When Corporations Rule the World.* Bloomfield, CT: Kumarian Press, 2001.

_____. "Third Generation NGO Strategies: A Key to People-Centered Development." *World Development* 15 (Supplement) (1987).

Kraus, C. Norman. *God Our Savior.* Scottdale, PA: Herald Press, 1991.

Kraybill, Donald. *Our Star-Spangled Faith.* Scottdale, PA: Herald Press, 1976.

_____. *The Upside-Down Kingdom.* Scottdale, PA: Herald Press, 1990.

Kreider, Robert S. and Rachel W. Goosen. *Hungry, Thirsty, a Stranger: The MCC Experience.* Scottdale, PA: Herald Press, 1988.

Kreider, Robert S. and Ronald J. R. Mathies. *Unity Amidst Diversity.* Akron, PA: Mennonite Central Committee, 1996.

Lapp, John A. "Mennonite Missions in India." *Mennonite Encyclopedia.* Vol. III.

_____. *The Mennonite Church in India, 1897-1962.* Scottdale, PA: Herald Press, 1972.

Lederach, John Paul. *The Journey Toward Reconciliation.* Scottdale: PA: Herald Press, 1999.

_____. *Building Peace:Sustainable Reconciliation in Divided Societies*. Washington, D.C.: United States Institute of Peace Press, 1997.

_____. *Preparing forPeace: Conflict Transformation Across Cultures*. Syracuse: Syracuse University Press, 1995.

Lind. Timothy C. *MCC Africa Program: Historical Background*. MCC Occasional Paper, No. 10. Akron, PA: Mennonite Central Committee, 1989.

Marketkplace, The. July/August, 1992.

Masamba Ma Mpolo, Jean. "African Symbols and Stories" in *Journal of Pastoral Care*, as quoted in Augsburger, David. *Pastoral Counseling Across Cultures*. Philadelphia: Westminster Press, 1986.

Mathies, Ronald J.R. "Service as Transformation: MCC as Educational Institution" in *Unity Amidst Diversity*. Akron, PA: Mennonite Central Committee, 1996.

Max-Neef, Manfred. *Human Scale Development: Conception, Application, and Further Reflections*. New York: The Apex Press, 1991.

McGee-Cooper, Ann and Gary Looper. *The Essentials of Servant Leadership: Principles in Practice*. Williston, VT: Pegasus Communications, 2001.

McMichael, Philip. *Development and Social Change: A Global Perspective*, 2nd ed. Thousand Oaks, CA: Pine Oaks, 2000.

Nafziger, Wayne. Unpublished paper presented at conference on " Anabaptist/Mennonite Experiences in International Development," at Eastern Mennonite University, 1998.

Neufeld, Mark. "Critical Theory and Christian Service: Knowledge and Action in Situations of Social Conflict." *Conrad Grebel Review*, Fall (1988).

Norris, Kathleen. *Amazing Grace: A Vocabulary of Faith*. New York: Riverhead Books, 1998.

OXFAM. *Rigged Rules and Double Standards: Trade, Globalization and the Fight Against Poverty*. London: OXFAM, 2002.

Pannabecker, S.F. "Foreign Mennonite Missions." *Mennonite Encyclopedia*. Vol. IV.

Perkins, Dwight H., Steven Radelet, Donald R. Snodgrass, Malcolm Gillis, and Michael Roemer. *Economics of Development*. New York: W.W. Norton, 2001.

Redekop, Benjamin and Calvin Redekop, eds. *Power, Authority and the Anabaptist Tradition*. Baltimore: The Johns Hopkins University Press, 2001.

Redekop, Calvin. *Strangers Become Neighbors: Mennonite and Indigenous Relations in the Paraguayan Chaco*. Scottdale, PA: Herald Press, 1980.

_____. "MEDA." *Mennonite Encyclopedia*. Vol. V.

_____. " The Community of Scholars and the Essence of Anabaptism." *Mennonite Quarterly Review* 67, Fall (1993): 438-439.

_____. ed. *Creation and Environment: An Anabaptist Perspective on a Sustainable World*. Baltimore: The Johns Hopkins University Press, 2000.

Redekop, Calvin, Stephen Ainlay, and Robert Siemens. *Mennonite Entrepreneurs*. Baltimore: The Johns Hopkins University Press, 1995.

Rempel, Henry. *A High Price for Abundant Living: The Story of Capitalism*. Scottdale, PA: Herald Press. 2003.

Rempel. Henry. "Development Work." *Mennonite Encyclopedia.* Vol. III.

Ritzer, George. *The McDonaldization of Society.* Thousand Oaks, CA: Pine Ridge Press, 2000.

Ross, David P. and Peter J. Usher. *From the Roots Up: Economic Development As If Community Mattered.* New York: The Bootstrap Press, 1986.

Sachs, Wolfgang. "Archaeology of the Idea of Development." *Envio,* Fall (1997).

Schumacher, E.F. *Small Is Beautiful: Economics As If People Mattered.* New York: Harper and Row, 1973.

Seers, Dudley. "The Meaning of Development." Eleventh World Conference of the Society for International Development, 1969.

Shenk, Wilbert. *The Transfiguration of Mission.* Scottdale, PA: Herald Press, 1993.

_____. "Focused on Mission." *Our Faith,* Autumn (2001): 21.

_____. "Growth through Missions" in Kraybill, Paul N., ed. *Mennonite World Handbook.* Lombard, IL: Mennonite World Conference, 1978.

_____."Mission Boards." *Mennonite Encyclopedia,* Vol. V.

Sider, Ronald. *Rich Christians in an Age of Hunger: Moving from Affluence to Generosity.* Dallas: Word Publishing, 1997.

Simons, Menno. *The Complete Writings of Menno Simons.* Scottdale, PA: Herald Press, 1956.

Stoesz, Edgar. *Beyond Good Intentions.* Akron, PA: Mennonite Central Committee, 1972.

_____. *Thoughts on Development.* MCC Occasional Paper. Akron, PA: Mennonite Central Committee, 1977.

Sue, Derald W. et. al. *Counseling the Culturally Different.* New York: John Wiley and Sons, 1981.

United Nations Develoment Program. *Human Development Programme Report, 1998.* New York: Oxford University Press, 1998.

Tillich, Paul. *Systematic Theology.* Chicago: University of Chicago Press, 1951.

Todaro, Michael. *Economic Development.* New York: Addison-Wesley, 2000.

Weaver, James H. and Kenneth Jameson. *Economic Development: Competing Paradigms.* Lanham, MD: University Press of America, 1989.

MCC Africa Listening Team. *After Revisioning: Walking Together into the 21st Century.* Akron, PA: Mennonite Central Committee, 2000.

Wink, Walter. *Naming the Powers: The Language of Power in the New Testament.* Philadelphia: Fortress Press, 1983.

_____. *Engaging the Powers: Discernment and Resistance in a World of Domination.* Philadelphia: Fortress Press, 1992.

_____. *Unmasking the Powers: The Invisible Powers that Determine Human Existence.* Philadelphia: Fortress Press, 1986.

Index

About the Authors

Richard A. (Rick) Yoder combines teaching and research at Eastern Mennonite University (EMU) with international development work in low-income countries. He joined the EMU faculty in 1985 after working for five years in Bangladesh on a United Nations project and in Swaziland on a U.S. Agency for International Development project. He has also worked long-term in Kenya, Jordan, and Afghanistan. Yoder has consulted on short-term development projects in more than 15 countries with a variety of private-sector consulting firms, bilateral and multilateral development agencies, and NGOs.

At EMU he teaches economics, development, and management. He has published in the areas of health-sector reform, privatization, and quality of worklife in low-income countries. Rick has an interdisciplinary Ph.D. combining study in public policy, economic development, and public administration, as well as masters degrees in public health and in public and international affairs.

For fun, he runs marathons. He and his wife, Carolyn, have three young adult daughters.

Calvin Wall Redekop received his undergraduate training at Goshen (IN) College, graduating in 1949. He spent the next three years in post-World War II Europe promoting voluntary service and developing the PAX program for Mennonite Central Committee. The Greece PAX agricultural program, which he helped initiate, is probably the first international development work conducted by American Mennonites.

Upon his return to the U.S., he completed an M.A. in European History and Sociology at the University of Minnesota in 1954. In 1959 he received his Ph.D. in Sociology/Anthropology at the University of Chicago.

Redekop spent a sabbatical year from Goshen College in 1971-1972 evaluating Mennonite Central Committee's development program for the indigenous tribes of the Paraguayan Chaco. His conclusions were published in *Strangers Become Neighbors* (Scottdale: Herald Press, 1980).

Redekop has been active in Mennonite Economic Development Associates activities since 1969 and was the founding editor of *The Marketplace,* the official MEDA magazine.

He is married to Freda Pellman; they have three married sons.

Vernon E. Jantzi, professor of sociology and former director of the Conflict Transformation Program at Eastern Mennonite University, began international development work in 1964 in Costa Rica as a Mennonite Voluntary Service (VS) volunteer. He directed the VS program from 1965-67, and from 1968-70 headed up the adult literacy program of the Nicaraguan Protestant Churches.

Jantzi completed M.S. and Ph.D. studies in Sociology of Development at Cornell University in 1975. Subsequently he served as advisor to the Peruvian Ministry of Education for Spanish-Quechua bilingual education and to the Costa Rican land reform program. In the late '80s with the Central American Management Institute, he studied management problems of private development organizations in war zones.

He has collaborated with Mennonite peace organizations, JustaPaz in Colombia and Redpaz in Central America, since the mid 1990s, training for conflict transformation and development. Jantzi helped evaluate Mennonite Central Committee programs in Bolivia, Brazil, Haiti, and Zambia and currently serves on the boards of MCC and Ten Thousand Villages.

He is married to Dorothy Leaman who shared and helped shape their 30 years of development experience. They have two adult children.

If you would like to order multiple copies of this book for yourself, for a class, or for a group you are a part of, call 800/762-7171 or email customer service at custserv@goodbks.com and request the "Group Discount Order Form" for *Development to a Different Drummer.*